ENCYCLOPAEDIA OF WORLD TRIBES

ENCYCLOPAEDIA OF WORLD TRIBES

S. K. PANIGRAHI

CYBER TECH PUBLICATIONS
4264/3, Ansari Road, Daryaganj, New Delhi-110002 (India)
Ph.: 011-23244078, 011-43559448 Fax: 011-23280028
E-Mail: cyberpublicationsdelhi@yahoo.com
Website: www.cybertechpublications.com

ENCYCLOPAEDIA OF WORLD TRIBES

S. K. PANIGRAHI

First Edition 2011

Published by :

G.S. Rawat for Cyber Tech Publications
4264/3, Ansari Road, Daryaganj, New Delhi-110002 (India)
Ph.: 011-23244078, 011-43559448 Fax: 011-23280028
E-Mail: cyberpublicationsdelhi@yahoo.com
Website: www.cybertechpublications.com

CONTENTS

Preface

During the Ninth Century BC, Egypt became dominated by foreign rulers including the Libyans and Assyrians and again looked for help from her southern Black neighbor. The Nubian emperor Piankhy conquered all of Egypt and became the first ruler of the 25th Egyptian dynasty. He sponsored a cultural revival in Egypt and resurrected the linguistic and artistic style of the old and middle Egyptian kingdoms. He refurbished all the Egyptian temples and monuments and had many new pyramids and other buildings erected.

It was during this 25th Egyptian dynasty, between 800 BC and 654 BC, called the "Nubian Renaissance," that Africans were also responsible for tremendously influencing the first American civilization called the Olmec civilization. Speculation as to a possible African element in the first major American civilization began in 1858 AD, when the first of many colossal stone heads were discovered by Mexican peasants. These colossal heads were over eight feet in height and weighed over 10 tons each. The colossal heads were carbon dated to 800 BC and all have typical Nubian features including full lips, fleshy noses, and Africoid facial contours. The ancient Egyptian harbor at Tanis is the only other place in the world with colossal heads of Nubian Blacks.

Dr. Ivan Van Sertima studied extensively the Egypto-Nubian presence in ancient Mexico and found tremendous technological and cultural contributions made to the Olmec civilization by Nubians.

These technological advancements included the art of mummification, the art of pyramid building, and the skills needed to transport massive blocks of stone for long distances. Buildings required great mathematical precision in the laying, reveling, and fitting of the stone, and this was done for the first time in ancient

America with Nubian instructors. Dr. Barry Fell of Harvard says the Egypto-Nubian hieroglyphic writing system has been found as far north as eastern Canada, among the Micmac tribe after spreading from its Olmec center. Bronze technology was also given to the Olmecs in addition to the Egyptian calendar.

Cultural traits adopted by the Olmecs from the Egypto-Nubians included the use of the color purple, the artificial beard, and the double crown headdress for signifying royalty. Professor Wiercinski, a Polish skull and skeletal expert, says that 13.5% of the bones found in one Olmec cemetery were African and that many were dressed in a royal or priest fashion and were lying side by side with a native American female.

—*Author*

1

Hatshepsut

Hatshepsut of ancient Egypt is considered the greatest female ruler of all time. This black empress is the first woman in recorded history to challenge and destroy the theory of male supremacy. After fighting her way to power, she held the throne of the world's mightiest empire at that time for 34 years. Since her father Thutmose I had conquered most of the known world, Hatshepsut was not faced with an external enemy. Her greatest nemeses were the priests of the God Amen who were determined not to end more than 3000 years of masculine tradition.

When the priests demanded that she step aside and allow her brother Thutmose II to rule as pharaoh, Hatshepsut tried to discredit her half brother by announcing that Thutmose II was the son of Mutnefert, a concubine, and therefore royal blood was only passed through to her.

She knew that all black African societies, including Egypt, were matrilineal, which means that inheritance, including the power of the throne, was passed through the female line. Hatshepsut could easily trace her female ancestry to her jet-black Ethiopian grandmother, Nefertari-Aahmes, but faced with the alternatives of possible civil war or compromise, she agreed to marry Thutmose II.

By all accounts, however, Thutmose II was an overweight, sickly, weakling and allowed Hatshepsut to run the affairs of the monarchy unopposed during their 13 years of marriage (1492-1479 BC). Upon the death of Thutmose II, Hatshepsut startled the nation by boldly announcing that she was a man. She donned a fake beard, male clothes, and changed her name from Hatshepsitu to Hatshepsut, its male equivalent. This would be similar to changing one's female name from Demetria to the male version of Demetrius. Hatshepsut crushed all further opposition by also announcing that she was not the daughter of Thutmose I, but the virgin birth son of God Amen and her mother Ahmose. She declared that the great God Amen appeared to her mother "in a flood of light and perfume" and by "Immaculate Conception" this union produced a baby boy. For those in doubt, she had the entire bedroom scene painted on the walls of her temple in intimate detail. Thereafter, her sculptured portraits depicted her with a beard and male features. She also demanded that her title be changed to "King/Pharaoh of the North and South; the Horus of Gold; Conqueror of All Lands; the Mighty One."

These changes must have come as quite a shock to the priests who had witnessed her giving birth to two daughters, Nefrure and Merytra-Hatshepset, while married to Thutmose II. Several priests also joked that the one title she could not add was "Mighty Bull of Maat" which implies male fertility.

Hatshepsut became firmly established as King/Pharaoh for the next 21 years (1479-1458 BC), and her popularity increased tremendously as did the prosperity of Egypt.

She was such a shrewd administrator, sending ambassadors to all her conquered lands, that gold tributes became so plentiful they no longer were weighed but measured in bushel baskets. J.A. Rogers wrote: "She began to publicize herself in the most sensational manner of that time, that is, by the building of temples, pyramids, and obelisks, the size and grandeur of which had never been seen before and regarded by the popular mind as a gauge of the ruler's power."

To further demonstrate her triumph over the priests of Amen, Hatshepsut commissioned her black architect boyfriend, Senmut, to build a structure that would overshadow the colossal temple of Amen-Ra (Karnak), which was the stronghold of her opponents. Under Senmet's genius was created a magnificent temple, called Deir el Bahari, out of the sheer rock cliff that looks down on the temple of Amen-Ra.

It sits high in the cliffs with a frontage of 800 feet and a series of courtyards and colonnades decorated with reliefs, shrines, inscriptions, innumerable statues, wonderful terraces, and paradisiacal gardens. Deir el Bahari is still considered one of the world's most remarkable architectural specimens and the embodiment of Senmut's multi-faceted genius. Hatshepsut lined the walkway to her temple with sandstone sphinxes of herself. Sphinx monuments were previously reserved only for the male as "Loving Horus".

As a final blow to her detractors, Hatshepsut ordered the creation of two of the largest most beautiful rose granite obelisks the world had ever seen and presented them as gifts to the temple of Amen-Ra.

Hatshepsut astutely ordered the obelisks taller than the temple so that the roof had to be removed to accommodate her gifts, despite the fact that this temple was one of the most colossal structures made by man. Hatshepsut made the obelisks even more conspicuous and overshadowing of the temple by encasing their tops with a precious gold-silver mixture. This made the obelisks so brilliant in sunlight that whenever a visitor looked out on the city, the most dazzling sight was no longer the temple of Amen-Ra but her obelisks.

By riding into battle with her troops, Hatshepsut was the forerunner to all the great African warrior queens from the Candaces of Ethiopia to Queen Nzinga of Angola. Although there were no major wars during her reign, there were revolts. One ancient scribe recounted Hatshepsut's military accomplishments during a Nubian revolt on a wall in Senmut's tomb: "I followed the 'Living Horus' (Hatshepsut) of upper and lower Egypt-may HE live forever! I saw when HE overthrew the Nubian Bowman, and when their chiefs were brought to HIM as living captives. I saw when HE razed Nubia, I being in HIS majesty's following..." Denoting Hatshepsut with masculine pronouns was demanded by her and was also a method used to exalt her position as "Living Horus".

Despite the fact that she often dressed as a male, she never lost touch with her feminine side. Scribes wrote that she was "lovely to look at; graceful in her movements, and fragrant as a flower." Hatshepsut wrote of herself: "My fragrance is like a divine breath; my scent reaches as far as the land of Punt; my skin is that of pure gold...I have no equal among the gods who were since the world was."

Hatshepsut's rule was one of the most prosperous times ever for the people of Egypt who had abundant work, shelter, and food. Memories of Hatshepsut persisted for many centuries after her reign and stories were passed down from generation to generation about her wonderful deeds, brave nature, beauty, and ingenuity until she reached godlike stature. Hatshepsut, a great black leader of Africa's Golden Age, has been called "the first great woman in history" but in actuality may be "history's greatest woman".

2

Black Egyptians

The ancient Egyptians produced one of the highest forms of civilization ever known. They were outstanding in the fields of mathematics, astronomy and astrology, medicine, religion, philosophy, architecture, engineering, art, government, science, mining and virtually all other fields involving the elements of civilization.

In mathematics, the ancient Egyptians gave us not only arithmetic, but algebra, geometry, trigonometry, and also calculus. Higher math was needed for building temples and pyramids. The Egyptian Great Pyramid is among the 7 Wonders of the World, and even today we could not reproduce this structure. Egyptian medical textbooks have been found which are over 5,000 years old and many of their methods of diagnosis and treatment are still used today.

Gerald Massey states that the religious records of virtually all religions including the Christian Bible, are traceable and in many cases, direct copies of the religious records of ancient Egypt. J.A. Rogers says, "every Christian priest from Moses through Jesus was taught in the Egyptian mysteries system". Acts 7:22 in the Bible confirms that Moses was learned in the wisdom of the Egyptians. Every Greek philosopher and writer from Homer to Pythagoras and Aristotle are known to have studied in ancient Egypt. The Egyptians were also the first to produce paper and had over 700,000 books in their libraries when invaded by Alexander.

Given the outstanding accomplishments of the ancient Egyptians, it is understandable why every society on Earth has claimed the ancient Egyptians as their ancestors including: Arabs,

Europeans, and Asians. However, the current Egyptian is as different from the ancient Egyptian as the current American is from the ancient American. Cheikh Anta Diop, a Senegalese professor and scientist, claims that the original ancient Egyptian civilization was built by Black Africans long before Egypt was invaded by Assyrians, Libyans, Persians, Greeks, Romans, and Arabs.

A Cairo symposium was held on February 3, 1974 by the United Nations Economic Social and Cultural Organization called (UNESCO) on the ethnicity of the ancient Egyptians. Diop convinced everyone in attendance that the ancient Egyptians were Black Africans based on his seven-(7) point presentation.

First of all, he developed a melanin dosage test and demonstrated that ancient Egyptian mummies had heavy doses of melanin in their skin, which was non-existent in White skinned races.

Second, he proved that ancient Egyptians had group B type blood, common among Africans, and not group A type blood, characteristic of the White race.

Third, he gave osteological measurements of the skull and long bones and demonstrated typical Negroid facial and bodily proportions among the Egyptians.

Fourth, Diop produced records from ancient Greek and Latin writers, who were contemporary with the ancient Egyptians, including Herodotus, Aristotle, Lucian and Diodorus. These writers all claimed that the ancient Egyptians, Ethiopians, and Colchidians all had Black skin, thick lips, kinky hair, and thin legs.

Fifth, Diop showed artwork by ancient Egyptians who drew themselves with Black skin and wooly hair. They even named their country Kemit, which means Black and called themselves Kemites.

Sixth, ancient Egyptian gods were all portrayed as jet-black in color and this in as much as most nations draw their deities in their own image.

Seventh, circumcision is of African origin beginning before 4000 BC in Ethiopia and Egypt. Circumcision was not practiced in the rest of the world unless they were taught by the Egyptians.

Finally, there is a strong linguistic kinship or affinity between the ancient Egyptian language and the languages of Africa, especially the West African language of Wolof. These languages have many words, which are the same in sound and meaning.

Cheikh Anta Diop was successful in convincing everyone at the 1974 UNESCO Symposium that the ancient Egyptians were Black Africans, and yet western society continues to portray them as White. The epitome of unconscionable cultural thievery is the Pyramid shaped Luxor hotel in Las Vegas, which displays White Egyptian figures inside, and a Sphinx outside with blue eyes and a European nose.

3

Ancient Nubian Blacks in America

Nubians played a major role in Egyptian civilization, both at its beginning and near its end. Nubia is an ancient Black country now located within southern Egypt and northern Sudan. Dr. Bruce Williams from the University of Chicago published in 1979, after extensive archaeological investigation, that a great Black Nubian dynasty preceded the 1st Egyptian dynasty by several hundred years and introduced all of the principles of civilization, which were later brought to fruition by the ancient Egyptians. Evidence of an advanced political organization with Pharaohs, an advanced writing system with hieroglyph, and an advanced religious concept with Horus and Osiris were all found to precede the first Egyptian dynasty.

During the Ninth Century BC, Egypt became dominated by foreign rulers including the Libyans and Assyrians and again looked for help from her southern Black neighbor. The Nubian emperor Piankhy conquered all of Egypt and became the first ruler of the 25th Egyptian dynasty. He sponsored a cultural revival in Egypt and resurrected the linguistic and artistic style of the old and middle Egyptian kingdoms. He refurbished all the Egyptian temples and monuments and had many new pyramids and other buildings erected.

It was during this 25th Egyptian dynasty, between 800 BC and 654 BC, called the "Nubian Renaissance," that Africans were also responsible for tremendously influencing the first American civilization called the Olmec civilization. Speculation as to a possible African element in the first major American civilization began in 1858 AD, when the first of many colossal stone heads were discovered by Mexican peasants. These colossal heads were over eight feet in height and weighed over 10 tons each. The colossal heads were carbon dated to 800 BC and all have typical Nubian features including full lips, fleshy noses, and Africoid facial contours. The ancient Egyptian harbor at Tanis is the only other place in the world with colossal heads of Nubian Blacks.

Dr. Ivan Van Sertima studied extensively the Egypto-Nubian presence in ancient Mexico and found tremendous technological and cultural contributions made to the Olmec civilization by Nubians.

These technological advancements included the art of mummification, the art of pyramid building, and the skills needed to transport massive blocks of stone for long distances. Buildings required great mathematical precision in the laying, reveling, and fitting of the stone, and this was done for the first time in ancient America with Nubian instructors. Dr. Barry Fell of Harvard says the Egypto-Nubian hieroglyphic writing system has been found as far north as eastern Canada, among the Micmac tribe after spreading from its Olmec center. Bronze technology was also given to the Olmecs in addition to the Egyptian calendar.

Cultural traits adopted by the Olmecs from the Egypto-Nubians included the use of the color purple, the artificial beard, and the double crown headdress for signifying royalty. Professor Wiercinski, a Polish skull and skeletal expert, says that 13.5% of the bones found in one Olmec cemetery were African and that many were dressed in a royal or priest fashion and were lying side by side with a native American female.

During the Nubian renaissance, long before Christopher Columbus and even before Jesus Christ, Blacks were masters of the old world of Egypt and the new world of America. Dr. Van Sertima says that this fact in itself opens a new historical window from which to view the history of America and of the entire Black race.

4

Black Multi-geniuses

World history has produced many men who have been described as geniuses but very few have ever been described as multi-genius. European historians have used the term multi-genius to describe such men as Aristotle and Leonardo de Vinci. However, these historians have never described a Black person as a multi-genius despite the fact that there have been just as many Black multi-geniuses as there are White. In fact, the world's first and greatest multi-genius in recorded history is a small Black Egyptian named Imhotep. Others include Benjamin Banneker and Cheikh Anta Diop.

Cheikh Anta Diop was born in 1923 in Western Senegal. He completed his bachelor's degree in Senegal and his doctorate degree in Paris. Diop began as an extremely promising physicist who did experiments in the world famous laboratory of Marie Curie (who earlier had won the Nobel Prize for the discovery of radiation). At a time when only a handful of people in the world understood Einstein's relativity theory, Diop translated the theory into his native Senegalese language of Wolof.

In mid stream, Diop decided to change his Ph.D. dissertation to ancient Egyptian history and to use his scientific background to prove that ancient Egyptians were Black skinned indigenous Africans, who taught the Greeks what later became Western civilization. Diop wanted Black people around the world to be able to claim the ancient Egyptians with great pride as their ancestors.

Diop's Ph.D. dissertation was rejected three times until he developed a chemical process for testing melanin in the skin of

Egyptian mummies and proved that ancient Egyptians were a dark skinned race. He also became an expert in linguistics and proved that the Egyptian language was African and that it was genetically related to a family of African languages including is own native Wolof. In 1966, Diop built a radiocarbon laboratory in Senegal for carbon-14 dating to help prove that the human race first started in Africa.

Another Black genius was Benjamin Banneker, who was born near Baltimore, Maryland in 1732. At the age of 22, he looked at a pocket watch from England and constructed America's first large wooden clock in his front yard, which kept accurate time for over 20 years. White people traveled from 5 neighboring states to see this unusual clock built by a Black man.

The first scientific book ever written by an African American is believed to be the Astronomical Almanac first published by Banneker in 1791, which accurately predicted eclipses, high and low tides, positions of the planets, times for sunrise and sunset, and many other useful items. Banneker was also the most important member of a federal surveying team, which laid out plans for the construction of Washington, D.C.

The first and greatest of all multi-geniuses was Imhotep, who served the Egyptian Pharaoh Zoser around 2980 BC. His titles included: Chief Physician, Grand Vizier, Chief Architect, Head Priest, Chief Scribe, and Astronomer. Imhotep was the real "Father of Medicine", and his reputation as a healer was so great that he was worshiped as the "God of Medicine" by Persians, Greeks, and Romans over a period of 3000 years.

As Grand Vizier, Imhotep served as the King's supervisor of all departments of State including: the judiciary, the treasury, the Army and Navy, agriculture, and on all the king's construction projects. Imhotep's father was a distinguished architect who taught his son very well. Imhotep built the first and largest stone structure in recorded history called the Step Pyramid of Zakkarah. It was designed to become the tomb of Pharaoh Zoser and consisted of large blocks of limestone, which reached 195 feet high and 396 feet wide at the base.

As Chief Priest, Imhotep was responsible for reading religious text during burial ceremonies. Common people held the Chief

Priest in high esteem because they felt that he influenced the final destinies of dead spirits and also served as a mediator between the king and unseen powers of the universe.

Imhotep was such a great philosopher that much of his advice has been passed along for 5000 years, such as, "Eat, drink, and be merry for tomorrow we die." As an astronomer, Imhotep believed that heavenly bodies exerted a profound influence on the welfare of men, so he carefully charted the movements of the planets, the moon, the sun, the eclipses, and the stars.

Malcolm X once wrote that history is best prepared to reward all research. With just a little research, one could uncover the enormous contributions for the benefit and betterment of mankind made by our brilliant Black multi-geniuses.

5

Hannibal: African Military Genius

Hannibal Barca (247-183 BC) from the ancient city of Carthage (North Africa), is considered the greatest military genius of all time. The maneuvers and strategies this Black general used to defeat the larger Roman armies repeatedly over a period of 14 years while on Italian soil have been studied for centuries at military academies throughout the world. Moreover, it is believed that the German army successfully used several of Hannibal's strategies in World War I, including the "Schlieffen Plan" of envelopment that was based on Hannibal's famous battle at Cannae.

Ancient Carthage was a magnificent city founded on the Northern coast of Africa (near present day Tunisia) around 800 BC. This city was the undisputed leader in maritime trade and commerce throughout the Mediterranean Sea and most of the known world for over 400 years. During the third century before Christ, Rome became powerful enough to challenge its African rival, and eventually they fought three bloody wars called the Punic Wars. Hannibal's father was also a great general named Hamilcar Barca, who lost to Rome in the first Punic War that was fought for control of the Mediterranean Sea and trade with several neighboring island, especially Sicily.

After loosing the first Punic War (264-241 BC), Hamilcar Barca conquered most of Southern Spain (called Iberia by the Romans) in an attempt to replace or compensate for the trade and commerce lost to Rome. It is believed that Barcelona, Spain was named for the Barca family. Hannibal's father made his sons pledge undying hatred for Rome and eventual revenge for Carthaginian losses during the first Punic War. Hamilar also made certain his sons were trained in the finest African military tradition, and also had them tutored by superlative Greek scholars. Hannibal was the eldest and most brilliant of the sons and could speak five languages, including Greek and Latin, before age 20.

Upon the death of his father, Hannibal was appointed supreme commander of the Carthaginan military at the tender age of 25. After Rome continued to attack Carthaginan allies and suppress trade routes, Hannibal decided to organize the world's most diversified army and attack Rome. His 90,000 men included soldiers from several different North African tribes, in addition to swarthy Spaniards, and white Celts and Gauls. His multiracial army was also multilingual and required over a dozen interpreters for Hannibal's every word. Few military minds today would have given Hannibal much of a chance against a powerful homogeneous single race, single language Roman army fighting in defense of its own homeland.

Hannibal's other greatest challenge was getting his army into Italy since Rome controlled the waterways. His decision to march his massive army over the Alps had never been attempted before and is again a testimony to his great genius. For example, in crossing turbid river, such as the Rhone, Hannibal would build large flat rafts and cover them with dirt so as to trick the elephants on board. The larger elephants were forced to cross upstream, which provided a partial damming of the river, that allowed the smaller pack animals and horses to cross down stream.

On one occasion, large 1,000-ton boulders blocked Hannibal's only path, and his soldiers were afraid they would have to turn back. Hannibal drew upon the Greek science he had learned and ordered his men to cut down all the neighboring trees and place them under the boulders. Once the trees were set afire and the boulders became so hot they glowed, he then ordered his men to pour large amounts of vinegar on the stones, which caused the boulders to break up into smaller movable pieces.

Hannibal repeatedly provided ingenious solutions to apparently unsolvable problems that made this African appear god-like in the eyes of his soldiers. However, traveling over 1,000 miles and five months through the Pyrenees Mountains and the Alps was still very treacherous, and Hannibal lost half of his army through harsh weather exposure and battling with hostile tribes seeking plunder.

Once Hannibal reached Northern Italy, he attempted to enlarge his army by telling local inhabitants that he had come to liberate them from the oppressive Romans. He had the wisdom to form an alliance with several of the larger tribes by using his army to defeat their local enemies. Hannibal thoroughly interviewed all the local leaders and also sent out scouts to determine the best areas for battle and ambush. He would also thoroughly investigate the character of his opposing Roman generals to determine which generals were most likely to be short tempered, impetuous, and prone to mistakes. The Roman Republic elected two different generals every six months and allowed those generals to rotate leadership every other day. Hannibal only did battle when the general he considered less capable was in charge.

In his first battle against the Roman army (217 BC) at the Trebia River, Hannibal hid several thousand of his best soldiers and cavalry in the swampy river bed overnight. Once the Romans arched past the hidden troops, Hannibal's army was able to attack them from the front and rear and destroyed them easily. The Romans soon regrouped and sent a second army after the Carthaginians. Hannibal studied a local lake adjacent to a steep mountain cliff (Lake Trasimene) and chose this as his second battleground. He noted that the lake produced a heavy fog in the morning, which allowed his soldiers to hide in the cliffs and pounce upon the unsuspecting Roman army, which could not see his trips until it was too late.

After having two large armies slaughtered by Hannibal in ambush, the Roman Senate decided to canvas all of Southern Italy and to produce the largest army in their history, which would only fight Hannibal in open combat. Over 80,000 troops were recruited to fight against Hannibal who had less than 40,000 soldiers left in his multiracial army. Hannibal defeated the large Roman army in a strategy that was copied for centuries thereafter. Noting that the Romans fought only in rigid columns, he placed his poorest Gaullic soldiers in a large semicircle facing the Romans and his best African soldiers far to the left and right of this semicircle. As their rigid Roman columns beat back the semicircle of Gaullic infantry, which went from convex to concave, they failed to notice that Hannibal's best African soldiers were forming a vice on the left and right. Hannibal's crack Numidian cavalry fought their way to the rear of the Roman army, which was now surrounded. In this deadly Battle of Cannae, more than 70,000 Roman soldiers were killed within three hours, which in comparison was more than one third of all Americans killed during the first four years of World War II.

One of the greatest mysteries of all time is why Hannibal did not attack the city of Rome after destroying its entire army. Many of his officers were bitterly disappointed. Some historians suggest that Hannibal may have become compassionate after seeing 70,000 Romans dead on the battlefield. Perhaps he felt he could not penetrate the fortified walls without bettering rams and other wall storming equipment he did not have. Over the next 14 years, Hannibal conquered all of Southern Italy virtually unopposed since Roman armies were afraid to confront him. Hannibal divided his war spoils and booty between his troops and Carthage, which disposed both to hold him in high esteem/

After many years, a brilliant young Roman general named Publius Cornelius Scipio, who spent most of his life studying Hannibal's warfare techniques, convinced the Roman Senate that Hannibal would leave Italy if Rome attacked Carthage. Scipio was also able to turn almost all of Hannibal's North African allies against him including the powerful Numidians by making outlandish and unfulfilled promises of land and riches. Upon returning to Africa (202 BC), Hannibal could not defeat the combined alliance of Africans and Romans at the Battle of Zama, and Carthage was forced to surrender. Unable to escape, Hannibal subsequently chose poisoning over imprisonment.

One has to speculate what type of world we would have if Hannibal had destroyed the city of Rome after completely destroying her entire army. Perhaps the Black Africans of Carthage could have provided a "kinder and gentler" world than the Roman Empire did over the next 700 years.

6

Who are the Dogon?

An illiterate West African tribe known as the Dogon-who live in the Bandiagara Cliffs of Southeastern Mali-startled the scientific world in the 1950s when it was discovered that their priests have had extremely complex knowledge of astronomy for at least 700 years. They have known for centuries about the rings of Saturn, the moons of Jupiter, the spiral structure of the Milky Way Galaxy, and intricate details about the stars including their mass and orbits. Much of the complex astrological knowledge that the Dogon have had since the 13th century either can not be confirmed by modern scientists or was not discovered until the 20th century. Kenneth Brecher of the Massachusetts Institute of Technology was dumbfounded and stated bluntly: "The Dogon have no business knowing any of this." Robert Temple, an acclaimed member of the Royal Astronomical Society, speculates in his book The Sirius Mystery that "space-beings from the Sirius star-system must have brought this marvelous knowledge down to the Africans."

Two French Anthropologists, Marcel Griaule and Germaine Dieterlen, lived and worked with the Dogon from 1931 to 1956 and eventually became so loved and trusted that they were initiated into the tribe. After 16 years of stage by stage initiations, the Dogon called a conference and revealed to these Europeans their intimate secret knowledge of the solar system that was eventually recorded in a book entitled The Pale Fox. The Frenchmen were told that our solar system consists of a fixed star with planets rotating around this star and moons rotating around the planets. They said a force we describe as "gravity" was responsible for holding the planets and moons in place. The Dogon gave names and a complete description of the properties and behavior of the planets, moons, and fixed stars such as Polaris, Sirius, and the Pleiades. Mars, for example, was called "Yapunu toll" meaning "planet of menstruation" perhaps because of its red color. A calendar based on the six positions or phases of Venus determined when the Dogon would plant and harvest their food for best results. However, no aspect of Dogon knowledge has created more astonishment than their description of the properties of the star known as Sirius B (po tolo to the Dogon).

It is incomprehensible to modern scientists how the Dogon could know so much about Sirius B, an invisible star to the naked eye, located 51 trillion miles away. The Frenchmen were told that Sirius B is the sky's tiniest and yet heaviest star and has a 50 year elliptical orbit around Sirius A, the brightest star in the sky. The Dogon said that this dwarf star (Sirius B) is the most important star and the origin of all other stars and that it is composed of a metal heavier and brighter than iron. Although Sirius B is invisible to the naked eye, the Dogon have chosen a new astronomer-priest every 60 years when the orbits of Sirius B, Jupiter, and Saturn come into synchronization.

A ceremony called the "sigui" is held and a mask is carved to celebrate this 60-year event. Griaule and Dieterlen said they were shown a cave in Ibi, Mali that contained 12 sigui ceremonial masks, which would date the ceremonies back to the 13th century. The first Western report of Sirius B was not until 1862 by Alvan Clark who observed the companion star through his new telescope. The Dogon told of several other companion stars around Sirius A that were not confirmed by modern astrophysicists until 1979 with the "Einstein" orbiting observatory. The Dogon also have an annual "bado" celebration that honors the one year period in which Sirius B rotates on its own axis. Modern scientists still can not confirm this one-year rotation on its own axis.

Charles Finch in his book entitled The Star of Deep Beginnings says that the Dogon have never been proven wrong in any of their descriptions of the properties and behavior of Sirius B and that they are also probably correct in calling Sirius B the mother of all stars. Finch says that Sirius B is as old as the universe (12 billion years) and the closest star to our solar system. Moreover, he states "since all newborn stars (like our sun) are created from older stars, our solar system including Earth and everything in it may owe its very existence to Sirius B as the Dogon say."

The advanced scientific knowledge of the Dogon makes them the most astonishing and enigmatic people in all Africa. Hunter Adams III of the Argonne National Laboratory admits that in certain domains of astronomy and cosmology the Dogon have no historical peers. He says there is nothing remotely similar to the knowledge of the Dogon in the literature of the ancient Egyptians, Sumerians, Greeks, Chinese, on Medieval Arabs. It's truly a shame that entrenched Western racist attitudes towards African scientific knowledge can only attribute Dogon knowledge to the presence of space aliens. Unfortunately, most agree with Robert Temple of the Royal Astronomical Society of Great Britain that "space-beings from the Sirius star-system must have brought this marvelous knowledge down to the Africans."

GREAT AFRICAN CIVILIZATIONS

The conquering nations throughout history have always rewritten or destroyed the history of the conquered nations. Racism and the brutal and devastating effects of slavery only intensified the need to change African history. It was argued that Africans were pagans, savages, and heathens in need of salvation and that the best thing the slave traders did for Black people was to have dragged our ancestors to the Americas in chains, because we lacked the intellectual capacity to succeed. Nothing could be further from the truth! While the Moors were re-civilizing Europe, great empires were thriving in Western Africa and frequently traded with the Moors. These included the empires of Ghana, Mali, and Songhay, which prospered between 700 AD and 1600 AD.

The founders of Ghana were known as the Soninkes, and they are experts in making tools and weapons with iron. In fact, their iron weapons helped them to conquer the neighboring tribes and to form their empire. They are also said to have had an inexhaustible supply of gold. It was so plentiful that the emperor passed a law, which said that all gold in nugget form belonged to him and that the people could only use gold dust. It was said that without this precaution, gold would have become so plentiful that it would have lost its value. One gold nugget was so large that it was used as a hitching post for the ruler's favorite horse. Ghana was also famous as a trading center where locally produced metal tools, jewelry, leather, and cotton clothes were traded for imports from Moorish Spain and Morocco.

The Mali Empire began in 1230 AD with King Sundiata. He gained control of all the trade that had been monopolized by Ghana. In 1342, Mansa Musa made a pilgrimage to Mecca, which made the Mali Empire world famous. He took a caravan of 60,000 people to Mecca and gave away so much gold as presents that the gold market in the world was devalued for 12 years. When he was asked in Cairo how he became emperor, he said that his brother, Emperor Abubakari II took 2,000 ships in 1311 AD, sailed west, and never returned. Ivan Van Sertima in his book They Came Before Columbus, acknowledges Abubakari II as one of the discovers of America who preceded Columbus. The Mali Empire had a standing army of 100,000 men and is said to have included an area the size of Western Europe.

The Songhay Empire rose to supremacy approximately 1457 AD and eventually became as large as the United States of America. The Songhay Empire was also a prosperous trading center but became world famous as a center of advanced culture and higher education. Famous universities were established in the cities of Gao, Jenne, and Timbuktu, which employed thousands of teachers who offered courses that included astronomy, mathematics, medicine, hygiene, music, and many others. Jenne also had a medical school that was especially famous for training surgeons in difficult operations such as cataract surgery. Professor Ahmed Baba, who was chancellor of the University of Sankore in Timbuktu, was the author of more than 40 books and had a personal library of 1,600 volumes; which he said was small, compared to the library of his colleagues. During the slave trade, many of the slaves from the former Songhay Empire were highly educated and were credited with teaching Caribbean and American farmers successful agricultural techniques. They also invented various tools and equipment to lessen the burden of their daily work.

The Songhay Empire prospered until 1591 when it was finally conquered by Moorish invaders from North Africa.

7

The Moors

During the European Dark Ages, between the 7th and 14th century AD, the Moorish Empire in Spain became one of the world's finest civilizations. General Tarik and his Black Moorish army from Morocco, conquered Spain after a week long battle with King Roderick in 711 AD. (The word tariff and the Rock of Gibraltar were named after him). They found that Europe, with the assistance of the Catholic Church, had returned almost to complete barbarism. The population was 90% illiterate and had lost all of the civilizing principles that were passed on by the ancient Greeks and Romans.

The Moors reintroduced mathematics, medicine, agriculture, and the physical sciences. The clumsy Roman numerals were replaced by Arabic figures including the zero and the decimal point. As Dr. Van Sertima says, "You can't do higher mathematics with Roman numerals." The Moors introduced agriculture to Europe including cotton, rice, sugar cane, dates, ginger, lemons, and strawberries. They also taught them how to store grain for up to 100 years and built underground grain silos. They established a world famous silk industry in Spain. The Moorish achievement in hydraulic engineering was outstanding. They constructed an aqueduct, that conveyed water from the mountains to the city through lead pipes from the mountains to the city. They taught them how to mine for minerals on a large scale, including copper, gold, silver, tin, lead, and aluminum. Spain soon became the world center for high quality sword blades and shields. Spain was eventually manufacturing up to 12,000 blades and shields per year. Spanish craft and woolen became world famous. The Moorish craftsman also produced world class glass, pottery, vases, mosaics, and jewelry.

The Moors introduced to Europe paved, lighted streets with raised sidewalks for pedestrians, flanked by uninterrupted rows of buildings. Paved and lighted streets did not appear in London or Paris for hundreds of years. They constructed thousands of public markets and mills in each city. Cordova alone had 5,000 of each. They also introduced to Spain underwear and bathing with soap.

Their public baths numbered in the thousands when bathing in the rest of Europe was frowned upon as a diabolical custom to be avoided by all good Christians. Poor hygiene contributed to the plagues in the rest of Europe. Moorish monarchs dwelled in sumptuous palaces while the crowned heads of England, France, and Germany lived in barns, lacking windows, toilets, and chimneys, with only a hole in the roof as the exit for smoke. Human waste material was thrown in the streets since no bathrooms were present.

Education was made mandatory by the Moors, while 90% of Europe was illiterate, including the kings and queens. The Moors introduced public libraries to Europe with 600,000 books housed in Cordova alone.

They established 17 outstanding universities in Spain. Since Africa is a matriarchal society, women were also encouraged to devote themselves to serious study, and it was only in Spain that one could find female doctors, lawyers, and scientists.

Moorish schoolteachers knew that the world was round and taught geography from a globe. They produced expert maps with all sea and land routes accurately located with respect to latitude and longitude; while also introducing compasses to Europe.

They were such expert shipbuilders that they were able to use their geography expertise to import and export as far away as India and China. It was not by accident that a Moor named Pietro Olonzo Nino was the chief navigator for Christopher Columbus on the flagship Santa Maria. He is said to have argued with Columbus as to who really discovered America. One of the worst mistakes the Moors made was to introduce gunpowder technology from China into Europe, because their enemies adopted this weapon and used it to drive them out of Spain.

Europe then took the 700 years of civilization and education re-taught to them by the Moors and used this knowledge to attack Africa. While the Moors were re-civilizing Europe, great empires were thriving in Western Africa and frequently traded with the Moors. These included the empires of Ghana, Mali, and Songhay, which prospered between 700 AD and 1600 AD. Africa was not a dark continent awaiting European civilization. In fact, Black African Egyptians and Black African Moors are credited with civilizing Europe.

BLACK POPES

Black Roman Africans made significant contributions to the growth of Christianity and the development of the Roman Catholic faith. The three greatest scholars and founding theologians of Christianity were all Roman Africans including Tetulian, Cyperian, and St. Augustine. However, the greatest contribution was probably made by the three Black popes who were Pope Victor I, Pope Miltiades, and Pope Galasius I.

Pope Victor I was the 14th pope and served from 189 AD-199 AD. In 189 AD, the date of Easter was a matter of great controversy. In Asia, Easter was celebrated on the 14th day after the full moon, which meant that some Christians were celebrating lent while others were celebrating resurrection.

Pope Victor I declared that Easter would only be celebrated on Sunday and that he would excommunicate all of the Christians of Asia if they failed to abide by his ruling. Easter has been on Sunday ever since. Under the influence of the Black theologian Tetulian, the Black Pope Victor I also declared that Latin would replace Greek as the official language of the Roman church. Both Victor and Tetulian only wrote in Latin thereafter. Pope Victor I is now celebrated as a saint with a feast day of July 28th.

At the same time that Black Romans controlled the world religiously with Victor and Tetullian, the Black Romans gained control of the world politically and militarily in 193 AD, when the Black Roman African Septimius Severus became the Roman Emperor. He remembered his roots by making large donations to the urban poor and employing them in extensive building campaigns. The month of September was named after Septimius Severus who was seceded as emperor of the Roman Empire by his Black son Caracalla from 211 AD until 217 AD.

The second Black pope was Pope Miltiades who served from 311 AD until 314 AD as our 32nd pope. All Christians were persecuted when Miltiades took office until he obtained an edict of toleration signed by Emperor Galerius, which put an end to the great persecutions and allowed the Christians to come out of their catacombs. Pope Miltiades also convinced Emperor Maxentius to return all church buildings and possessions, which had been confiscated during the persecutions. It was also during the reign of Pope Miltiades that the Emperor Constantine was converted to Christianity after he saw the cross in a vision.

Constantine's army marched into Rome in 312 AD and overthrew the tyrant Maxentius. He subsequently made Christianity the official religion of the Roman Empire. Miltiades was made a saint with his feast celebrated on December 10. The Black Roman theologian St. Augustine called Pope Miltiades "an excellent pontiff, a true son of peace, and father of Christians."

The third Black pope was Galasius I, our 49th pope, who took office 492 AD (exactly 1,000 years before America was so-called "discovered"). He is described by his contemporaries as "famous all over the world for his learning and holiness." Galasius I was devoted to uplifting the poor and weak and commanded his bishops to donate 25% of their revenue to charity, stressing that "nothing is more becoming to the priestly office that the protection of the poor and the weak."

Pope Galasius I is also credited with ending the pagan ritual of Lupercalia in which young men would dress in skins and strike any woman they met with a whip, which was supposed to confer fertility and to chase away bad luck. He replaced Lupercalia with the "feast of the purification of the blessed virgin" now called "Candlemas". Galasius I is most famous for his firm letter to Emperor Anastasius about the need for independence of church and state. He told the emperor that the world is governed by two great powers: that of the popes and that of kings; but the authority of the popes is so much greater because on judgment day, popes will have to render an account to God for the soul of kings. As were the other two African popes, Galasius I was also made a saint and his feast day is held on November 21.

Contrary to the belief of those who call Christianity a white man's religion, Christianity was founded with the genius of three Black theologians, and further developed and propelled by devoted contributions from three Black Roman African popes.

8

African Medicine

Although Africans and people of African descent are seldom given credit in standard textbooks, African wisdom contributed greatly toward the development of modern medicine. For example, in Western Africa during the Songhay Empire, about 1457 AD, (when Europe was still in its "Dark Ages") the city of Jeanne had a medical school which employed 100's of teachers and was world famous for training surgeons in difficult operations such as cataract surgery. They also taught the pharmacological use of over 1,000 animal and plant products for the treatment of medical illnesses. Many of these same medicines in pill or liquid form are used today. For example, castor seeds, the source of castor oil, was used for constipation and castor oil is still used today. Kaolin was used for diarrhea and is still used today in kaopectate. Night blindness caused by Vitamin "A" deficiency was treated with Ox liver, which is rich in vitamin "A". Vitamin "C" deficiency was treated with onions, which have a high vitamin "C" content.

The antibiotic penicillin (produced by penicillium mold) and its therapeutic properties were well known by the ancient Egyptians who far exceeded the rest of the ancient world in medical knowledge. However, the presence of the antibiotic tetracycline appears only in the bones of farmers from northern Sudan about 1500 years ago. The ancient Sudanese farmers discovered that streptomyces molds can easily produce tetracycline on stored grain and purposefully used tetracycline to treat infection. There is no evidence that tetracycline antibictic has been used anywhere else in the world. Tetracycline was not rediscovered until the twentieth century.

More than 40% of modern pharmacological medicines are derived from traditional African medicinal herbs. For example, the Yoruba of Nigeria used the plant Rauwolfia vomitoria as a sedative or tranquilizer to calm agitated or psychotic patients. Modern medicine was able to isolate a substance called reserpine from this plant that was marketed for the same purpose. Reserpine was also discovered to profoundly lower blood pressure and consequently, became one of the antihypertensive medications. In America, in 1721 an African slave named Onesimus taught his master an age old African technique for smallpox inoculation in which a pustule from an infected person was ruptured with a thorn and then used to puncture the skin of a normal person. Subsequently, during a smallpox epidemic in the Boston, MA area, Dr. Boylston inoculated 241 healthy people by this African technique and only six caught smallpox. During the American Revolutionary War, General George Washington ordered his entire army inoculated against smallpox by this African method. In the 1790's, the British Dr. Edward Jenner only changed the African smallpox inoculation technique by using a less dangerous kind of smallpox germ.

Finally, as recently as 1880 AD in Europe, the mortality rate was almost 100% for mothers delivering their babies by caesarian section (that is, delivering babies through the abdomen). Consequently, the operation was only performed to save the life of the infant. Dr. R. W. Felkin, a missionary, shocked the European medical community when he published in the Edinburgh Medical Journal in 1884 that the Banyoro surgeons in Uganda performed caesarian sections routinely, without harmful effects to the mother or the infant. A group of European surgeons went to study in Uganda for six months before they could successfully learn the advanced surgical techniques demonstrated by the Africans. The Europeans were also taught sophisticated concepts of anesthesia and antisepsis. For example, they were taught to routinely wash the surgeon's hands and the mother's abdomen with alcohol prior to surgery to prevent infection. This antisepsis technique had not been practiced in Europe prior to this African visit. In summary, Africans have contributed greatly toward the development of modern medicine and deserve to be better acknowledged in our medical textbooks.

9

The Black Madonna

Isis was a Black African goddess of Nile Valley civilizations whose worship eventually diffused to most of the ancient world. Isis was worshipped by the Nubians well over 300 years before the first Egyptian dynasty. The Egyptians then gave the Isis religion to Greece, Rome, and Western Asia. Gerald Massey says that the religious records of all the world's religions including Hinduism, Buddhism, and Christianity are nothing more than copies of the religious records of the Black goddess Isis, her son Horus, and her husband Osiris. For example, Horus was the first child born from a virgin mother's Immaculate Conception, and he was said to have walked on water just as Jesus later did. The Black goddess Isis is also credited with resurrecting Osiris after he was murdered.

The first "Black Madonna and Child" statutes and portraits were of Isis and Horus, and these were taken throughout the world by the Roman Empire. When other religions became more popular, these statues were not destroyed, but simply had their names changed. In India, Isis and Horus became Maya and Buddha in Buddhism or Devaki and Krishna in Hinduism. The Chinese called Isis Kwa-yin, and the Japanese changed the name to Kwannon.

In his 1985 book entitled "The Cult of the Black Virgin", Ean Begg was able to identify over 450 images of a Black virgin and child in Europe with over 190 statutes in France alone. J.A. Rogers says that Paris was actually named for Isis because Para-isis means "Place of Isis." He also says that Note Dame means "Our Lady" and that the cathedral is nothing more than an enlargement of the original Isis temple.

Millions of pilgrims visit the Black Madonna shrines annually because they are believed to possess magical powers, although the statues are now called Mary and Jesus. It is believed that only the Black statues are magical and all pilgrimages stopped whenever the statues were painted white. The Black Madonnas have been credited with healing towns of plagues, bringing dead babies to life, making infertile women pregnant, and saving nations during wars. Many crutches have been left at the feet of the Black Madonnas, who presumably gave their owners the power to walk. One of the most devoted pilgrims of the Black Madonna shrine in Poland is the current Pope John Paul II. He prayed to her image while recovering from his gun shot wound. She is credited with thousands of documented miracles including saving Poland from Russia in 1769. In 1968 alone, the Black Madonna shrine in Poland received over 66,000 thank you letters for healing and other miracles. Pilgrims frequently leave gold watches and rings at the feet of the Black Madonnas in appreciation.

Church literature absolutely refuses to acknowledge any association of Black Madonnas with Africa. Church officials claim that the Madonnas are Black because of smoke from candles and from dirt and old age. Church officials would never admit that the ancient Egyptians, Greeks, and Romans made pilgrimages until 536 AD to the Isis temple at Philae, Egypt to seek the same miracles that current pilgrims seek from the Black Madonna shrines. Isis was recognized as a supreme miracle and magic worker and is also credited with teaching mankind the art of curing disease. Isis was able to restore life to the dead as she did with her husband Osiris and later with the infant Horus, who was brought back to life after he was killed by a scorpion's sting. Isis was the goddess of corn and grain, water and navigation, and even clothing. She was also called a divine granter of salvation for souls of mankind. The ancient Black Egyptians acknowledged Isis as the source of all their prosperity, including the Nile River.

Isis worship was so strong in Europe that Roman citizens ignored Emperors Augustus and Tuberous, who outlawed Isis worship and persecuted her priests. Emperor Caligulia finally bowed to public pressure and re-established the Isis worship. Emperor Justinian caused an unsuccessful armed insurrection in

536 AD, when he ordered all Isis temples permanently closed. Religion in general (and the cult of the Black Virgin Madonna in specific) is yet another example of the many elements of civilization and civilizing ideas which were brought from Africa into Europe.

CHRISTMAS PAGANISM

Ministers encourage their congregations every year in December to put Christ back into Christmas. The truth is, Christ never was in Christmas nor will he ever be. The "Christmas Spirit" is created each year by mass media, not to honor Christ, but to sell merchandise. Most merchants obtain more than 50% of their annual revenues at Christmas. Christians in the United States did not practice the heathen custom of exchanging gifts at Christmas until the 19th century, when the merchants revived this Roman custom in order to enrich their coffers.

Everything about the Christmas holiday is false, corrupt, idolatrous, and pagan. There isn't a shred of truth in Christmas. Mary did not look up to her white, blue eyed husband, Joseph, on December 25th and say "let's call our son's birthday Christmas and celebrate it with a decorated evergreen tree." First of all, the worldwide images of Mary, Joseph, and Jesus were not painted until 1505 AD by Michelangelo and represented his aunt, uncle, and first cousin.

Secondly, every priest knows that Jesus was not born on December 25th. December 25th, as the birth date of Jesus was not adopted until 325 AD at the Nicaean Council where 318 bishops voted on that as the date.

The Eastern Orthodox Church never agreed to this date and continued to celebrate January 6th. Before 325 AD, most Christians celebrated Christ's birthday on March 25th or September 29th. December 25th was chosen as Christ's birthday because it was the most universally recognized and celebrated holiday in the ancient world.

December 25th is the day after the winter solstice, or the first day in winter when the length of daylight begins to increase. Every nation recognized December 25th as the birthday of their sun god including: Mitra, Horus, Hercules, Bacchus, Kristna, Buddha, Adonis, Jupiter, Tammuz, and Saturn.

The Romans called this season "Saturnalia" and celebrated it by exchanging gifts, merriment, revelry, and drunkenness. The sun god Saturn was also the first Santa Claus, which explains why he was omnipresent, that is, could visit every house on Earth in one night; and could know everything about every child's behavior. Santa Claus subsequently became St. Nicholas, a 4th Century bishop of Asia Minor who became the Russian patron saint of children. The St. Nicholas festival was celebrated on December 6th until Queen Victoria moved the date to December 25th and made St. Nicholas the father of Christmas.

Santa Claus did not have a sleigh pulled by reindeer until 1822 when Clement Moore wrote the poem "'Twas the night before Christmas."

The custom of kissing under the mistletoe is believed to have originated with the Celtic midsummer eve ceremony when mistletoe was gathered. During that festival the men would kiss each other as a display of their homosexuality. The custom was later moved to December and broadened to include both men and women.

The Christmas tree was first decorated by Pagans with small globes or suns to represent the sun god Adonis, who obtained eternal life as an evergreen tree. Gifts were placed under the tree in his honor.

When the Roman Catholic Church could not persuade the public to give up these idolatrous practices, they simply adopted the pagan celebrations and renamed them. Oliver Cromwell and the Puritans had the English parliament ban Christmas from 1642-1662 calling it the "profane man's ranting day." The Pilgrims carried this prohibition to New England. In 1659 Massachusetts passed a law fining anyone caught celebrating Christmas. Public schools remained open on December 25th in Boston until 1870.

It is estimated that Black people spend over $50 billion during the Christmas season and support an economic power system that never worked in our best interest. African Americans would be better served if we abandoned the European pagan holiday of Christmas and used our $50 billion to feed, clothe, house, and educate our people toward a better quality of life.

CHRISTOPHER COLUMBUS

The original Haitians were called the Arawaks or Tainos. Christopher Columbus wrote in his log that the Arawaks were well built with good bodies and handsome features. He also reported that the Arawaks were remarkable for their hospitality and their belief in sharing. He said, "they offered to share with anyone and that when you ask for something they never say no." The Arawaks lived in village communes with a well-developed agriculture of corn, yams, and cassava. They had the ability to spin and weave, as well as being able to swim long distances. The Arawaks did not bear arms nor did they have prisons or prisoners. Columbus wrote that when the Santa Maria became shipwrecked, the Arawaks worked for hours to save the crew and cargo and that they were so honest that not one thing was missing. Arawak women were treated so well in early Haitian society that it startled the Spaniards. Columbus said that the Arawak men were of great intelligence because they could navigate all of their islands and give an amazingly precise account of everything.

The chief source, and on many matters the only source of information about what happened on the islands after Columbus arrived, was noted by a Catholic priest named Bartolome De Las Casas who lived during the time of Columbus. He transcribed Columbus's journal and wrote a multi-volume "History of the Indies." Las Casas says that Columbus returned to America on his second voyage with seventeen ships and with more than 1,200 heavily armed men with horses and attack dogs. Their aim was clearly to obtain as much gold and as many slaves as possible according to De Las Casas. Columbus went from island to island in the Caribbean, taking Arawaks as captives. He ordered everyone over the age of 14 to produce specific quantities of gold every three months, and if the Arawak could not produce this quota, Columbus then had his hands cut off; and left him to bleed to death.

If the Arawaks ever tried to escape, they were hunted down by the attack dogs and either hanged or burned alive. Within just two years, half of the three million Arawaks of Haiti died from murder, mutilation or suicide. Bishop De Las Casas reported that the Spaniards became so lazy that they refused to walk any distance;

and either rode the backs of the Arawaks or were carried on hammocks by Arawaks who ran them in relays.

In other cases, the Spaniards had the Arawaks carry large leaves for their shade and had others to fan them with goose wings. Women were used as sex slaves and their children were murdered and then thrown into the sea. The Spaniards were so cruel, they thought nothing of cutting off slices of human flesh from the Arawaks just to test the sharpness of their blades. Bishop De Las Casas wrote, "My eyes have seen these acts so foreign to human nature that now I tremble as I write.

Christopher Columbus started the Trans-Atlantic slave trade by taking 500 of the healthiest men back to Spain to sell into slavery, and the proceeds from the sale helped to pay for his third voyage. The massive slave trade moving in the other direction, across the Atlantic from Africa to the Americas, was also begun in Haiti and was started by the son of Christopher Columbus in 1505 A.D. On his third voyage to Haiti, Queen Isabelle's new Governor, Francisco De Bobadilla, had Christopher Columbus and his two brothers arrested and sent back to Spain in chains as prisoners for their crimes against the Arawaks.

Would Columbus Day still be celebrated if the real history of Christopher Columbus were told from the viewpoint of his victims?

10

Black Indians

Black Indians, like other African Americans, have been treated by the writers of history as invisible. Two parallel institutions joined to create Black Indians: the seizure and mistreatment of Indians and their lands, and the enslavement of Africans. Today just about every African-American family tree has an Indian branch. Europeans forcefully entered the African blood stream, but native Americans and Africans merged by choice, invitation and love. The two people discovered that they shared many vital views such as the importance of the family with children and the elderly being treasured. Africans and native Americans both cherished there own trustworthiness and saw promises and treaties as bonds never to be broken. Religion was a daily part of cultural life, not merely practiced on Sundays. Both Africans and Native Americans found they shared a belief in economic cooperation rather than competition and rivalry. Indians taught Africans techniques in fishing and hunting, and Africans taught Indians techniques in tropical agriculture and working in agricultural labor groups. Further, Africans had a virtual immunity to European diseases such as small pox which wiped out large communities of Native Americans.

The first recorded alliance in early America occurred on Christmas Day, 1522, when African and Indian slaves on a plantation owned by Christopher Columbus's son, rebelled and murdered their white masters. These Indian and African slaves escaped into the woods together and were never recaptured. Another successful alliance occurred around 1600 when runaway slaves and friendly Indians formed the Republic of Palmares in

Northeastern Brazil, which successfully fought the Dutch and Portuguese for almost one hundred years. The Republic of Palmares grew to have one half-mile long streets that were six feet wide and lined with hundreds of homes, churches, and shops. Its well-kept lands produced cereals and crops irrigated by African style streams. The Republic was ruled by a king named "Ganga-Zumba" which combined the African word for great with the Indian word for ruler.

The history of the Saramaka people of Surinam in South America started around 1685, when African and Native American slaves escaped and together formed a maroon society which fought with the Dutch for 80 years, until the Europeans abandoned their wars and sued for peace. Today the Saramakans total 20,000 people of mixed African-Indian ancestry.

By 1650, Mexico had a mixed African-Indian population of 100,000. Race mixing became so common in Mexico that the Spanish government passed laws prohibiting the two races from living together or marrying. In 1810, Vincente Guerrero of mixed African-Indian ancestry led the war for independence. In 1829, he became president of Mexico and immediately abolished slavery and the death sentence. He also began far reaching reforms including the construction of schools and libraries for the poor.

Escaped slaves became Spanish Florida's first settlers. They joined refugees from the Creek Nation and called themselves Seminoles, which means runaways. Intermixing became so common that they were soon called Black Seminoles. Africans taught the Indians rice cultivation and how to survive in the tropical terrain of Florida. Eventually the Black Seminoles had well-built homes and raised fine crops of corn, sweet potatoes, and vegetables. They even owned large herds of live stock. The Black Seminoles struck frequently against slave plantations and runaway slaves swelled their ranks. The U.S. government launched three massive war campaigns against the Seminole nation over a period of 40 years. The second war alone cost the U.S. government over $40 million and 1500 soldiers. The Seminoles eventually signed a peace treaty with President Polk, which was violated in 1849, when the U.S. Attorney General ruled that Black Seminoles were still slaves under U.S. law.

Black Indian societies were so common in every east coast state that by 1812, state legislatures began to remove the tax exemption status of Indian land by claiming that the tribes were no longer Indian. A Moravian missionary visited the Nanticoke nation on Maryland's eastern shore to compile a vocabulary of their language and found they were speaking pure African Mandingo.

After the Civil War, very few Blacks ever left their Indian nation because this was the only society that could guarantee that they would never be brutalized nor lynched. If Europeans had followed the wonderfully unique model of harmony, honesty, friendship, and loyalty exhibited by the African and Indian populations in North and South America, the "new world" could truly have been the land of the free, the home of the brave, and a place where "all men are created equal."

11

Lord Dunmore's Ethiopian Regiment

Few textbooks acknowledge the tremendous contribution made by Black soldiers during the Revolutionary War. An even lesser known fact is that Black slaves also fought for the British in an attempt to win their freedom. Many slaves in fact were deceived by the British into thinking that American slavery would end if the British army defeated the American Continental Army. The British actually imprinted the inscription "Liberty to Slaves" across the chest of each Black volunteer soldier.

In November 1775, John Murray, the Earl of Dunmore and British Governor of Virginia, decided that the Revolutionary War would no longer continue as the "White man's war." Both the American and British senior strategists had banned the use of Black soldiers, but Lord Dunmore saw the British as hopelessly outnumbered and was unwilling to overlook any potential support. He also hoped a slave insurrection would deprive the American army of much needed labor for building fortifications and disrupt the American economy since slave labor produced most of the cash crops. Lord Dunmore's proclamation declared "all indentured servants, Negroes, or others: FREE, that are able and willing to bear arms...to his Majesty's crown and dignity."

Dunmore's proclamation led Blacks to believe that the British were genuinely opposed to slavery. Since most American leaders such as George Washington and Thomas Jefferson were prominent slaveholders, many Blacks saw the British opportunity as their only chance for freedom and consequently joined the British in large numbers. J.A. Rogers states that "5,000 joined Dunmore at Norfolk; 25,000 fled from their masters in South Carolina and nearly seven-eighths of the slaves in Georgia." Nearly 2,000 slaves joined the British forces under General Cornwallis including numerous slaves from George Washington's plantation. Thomas Jefferson declared that Virginia alone lost 30,000 and others estimate that as many as 100,000 slaves found their way to the British lines. One half of Dunmore's troops that fought at Great Bridge on December 9, 1775 were runaway slaves.

Runaway slaves armed by the British are said to have terrorized the South. Many slaves overpowered their masters and handed their plantations over to the British. In the North, a strong garrison of Blacks known as the "Negro Fort," defeated their former masters in a battle in the Bronx, New York City. Other Blacks joined the British Navy as seamen and pilots and successfully stole American ships and attacked numerous coastal towns. During the sieges of Charleston and Savannah, thousands of Black laborers built fortifications, while others in Virginia constructed two dams. Blacks also served as guides, spies, and intelligence agents for invading British armies. Ex-slave Thomas Johnson claimed to have conducted the detachment which surprised Colonial Washington at Monks Corner. The British even created a Black cavalry troop in 1782. British General William Phillips commented: "These Negroes have undoubtedly been of the greatest use."

George Washington told Congress that "Dunmore's appeal made him the most formidable enemy America has; and his strength will increase like a snowball by rolling and faster if some expedient cannot be hit upon to convince the slaves and servants of the impotency of his designs." American slaveholders were still unwilling to arm their slaves until all other countermeasures were tried. Highway and river patrols were instituted to capture runaway slaves. Vigorous anti-British propaganda was circulated and Southern slaves were frequently hidden in mines to avoid British capture. Several Southern states even approved the death penalty for recaptured slaves, but nothing could stop the Black contributions to the British war effort. General Washington wrote Colonel Henry Lee on December 20, 1775: "We must use the Negroes or run the risk of loosing the war...success will depend on which side can arm the Negroes faster."

The Continental army finally agreed to accept African American volunteers (both slave and free) when the desertion rate of White soldiers began to reach enormous proportions. Washington complained: "The lack of patriotism is infinitely more to be dreaded than the whole of Great Britain assisted by Negro allies." Once freedom was promised, African Americans showed the real "Spirit of '76" and joined the Continental army in such massive numbers that General Schuyler wrote: "Is it consistent with the sons of freedom to trust their all to be defended by slaves?" On October 23, 1777, a British officer named Schlozer wrote: "The Negro can take the field instead of his master and therefore no regiment is to be seen in which there are not Negroes in abundance and among them are able-bodied, strong, and brave fellows." Sir Henry Clinton wrote Lord Germaine, British Minister of State: "It is safe to say that but for the aid of the Negro, independence would not have been won."

The American victory required the evacuation of all persons who had been loyal to the British. About 27,000 White Loyalists were relocated to Nova Scotia, Canada, but the majority of the Black Loyalists were betrayed by the British government which sold almost all of the former slaves back into slavery. Only the original 3,500 Black soldiers who became "Lord Dunmore's Ethiopian Regiment" were relocated to Nova Scotia. Although they were promised land and provisions, most Blacks received neither and became beggars or cheap laborers for White Loyalists who were given farms as large as 200 acres by the government with free provisions for three years. When a London based abolition group headed by John Clarkson offered the Black Loyalists a new home in Africa, over 1,200 sailed in 15 crowded ships for Sierra Leone on January 15, 1792 where they founded the capital city of Freetown. The Nova Scotians eventually embraced and intermarried with the African community and provided the core of what became the national culture, language, and early leadership of Sierra Leone. However, more than two centuries later, their descendents still identify themselves as Nova Scotians and the direct descendents of "Lord Dunmore's Ethiopian Regiment".

12

Christopher Columbus Vs Belgium King Leopold II

In trying to determine the worse human rights violator over the past 500 years, two candidates far and away exceed all others. Adolph Hitler was not even close because he is only credited with killing six million people and his reign of terror only lasted about six years. Over a period of 25 years, Belgium King Leopold II was able to reduce the population of the Congo from 20 million to 10 million. Twenty five years after Christopher Columbus entered Haiti, the Arawak population was reduced to zero, that is, total annihilation or genocide.

In describing the exploits of Columbus, Dominican priest Bartolome de Las Casas wrote: "My eyes have seen these acts so foreign to human nature that I tremble as I write." Famous American author Joseph Conrad called Leopold's Congo: "The vilest scramble for loot that ever disfigured the history of human conscience." Despite a death toll of holocaust dimensions, these men are not even mentioned in the standard litany of human horrors. Our children are given history books that describe Columbus as a heroic adventurer and an outstanding seaman. This heroic image is further perpetuated by Columbus Day celebrations and the fact that streets, schools, cities, and even countries have been named after him. King Leopold II enjoys an equally positive reputation. Belgium history describes him as a "philanthropic monarch who was much admired throughout Europe." He is praised for investing a large portion of his personal fortune in pubic works projects to benefit both Europe and Africa. The current image of these two men could not be further from the truth! Both left behind a heritage of racism, greed, hunger, exploitation, and genocide. Leopold matched Columbus so closely in atrocities that one has to wonder whether they represent the same man reincarnated.

Both Columbus and Leopold were great salesmen and great liars. To help finance his second voyage, Columbus told the Spanish Monarch that "there are many wide rivers of which the majority contain gold...there are many spices, and great mines of gold and other metals." Columbus was so convincing the Queen Isabella provided him with 17 ships and 1,200 men for his second voyage and promised him 10% of all the gold and precious metals he brought back. Leopold's opportunity for salesmanship and lying came at the Berlin Conference (November 1884-February 1885) where European countries met to decide how they would divide up Africa. Leopold begged for the Congo Basin and guaranteed the well being of the Congo's native population. Leopold told the American delegation that "Belgium deserves the opportunity to prove to the world that it also was an imperial people, capable of dominating and enlightening others." Since Leopold knew that the Belgium parliament and Belgium people had no interest in Africa, he essentially was arguing for a land mass 80 times the size of Belgium, which he would own personally.

Columbus and Leopold saw the profits from their new lands as virtually limitless if enough free labor were available. Both men immediately proceeded to institute slavery among the native population and set quotas for individual production. The favorite method of punishment by Columbus and Leopold for not meeting quotas was to cut off the hands.

Columbus ordered all persons 14 years old and older to collect a certain quantity of gold every three months. When they brought it, they were given copper tokens to hang around their necks. Arawaks found without copper tokens to hang around their necks had their hands cut off and bled to death. Leopold chose to set quotas for ivory and rubber for each village. When a village fell short of its quota, his soldiers brutally raided the village and cut off the victims' right hands. Sean Kelly wrote: "Hands became a sort of currency in that soldiers were paid their bonuses on the basis of how many right hands they collected."

Columbus and Leopold were exceptionally cruel to women and children. Both men allowed their soldiers to kidnap women as sex slaves, and they also held women and children as hostages to insure that the native men would not run away. Female hostages were usually poorly fed and large numbers died of starvation. Newborns also had a very high mortality rate because the mothers were too famished to provide nursing milk.

The Arawaks and Africans both fought back but were no match for the armor and swords of Columbus nor the guns and artillery of Leopold's soldiers. Rebelling natives were treated exceedingly cruel by both oppressors. Although both men used hanging, Columbus preferred burning victims alive if possible or feeding them to the attack dogs. Leopold's soldiers enjoyed summary executions followed by chopping off the victims' heads and placing the heads on poles around their gardens. Guillaume Van Kerckhoven, a Leopold officer, cheerfully bragged to a missionary that he paid his Black soldiers five brass rods per human head they brought him during the course of any military operation he conducted. He said it was to stimulate their prowess in the face of the enemy.

A single man in both cases dedicated his life to exposing the atrocities of Columbus and Leopold to the world. Bartolome de Las Casas, a Dominican priest, was initially a friend of Columbus and helped transcribe his journals. However, he soon became a vehement critic of Spanish cruelty and published a two-volume book detailing Spanish torture. He estimates that three million Arawaks died between 1495 and 1508. Edmund Dene Morel, a trusted employee of the Liverpool shipping line, dedicated his life to exposing the atrocities of King Leopold. He single-handedly put this subject on the world's front pages for more than a decade, which resulted in worldwide protest rallies. Morel mobilized everyone from Booker T. Washington to the Archbishop of Canterbury to join his cause. He even went to the White House insisting to President Theodore Roosevelt that the United States had a special responsibility to do something about the Congo since the U.S. helped Leopold at the Berlin Conference. Morel's unrelenting efforts resulted in Western powers forcing King Leopold to sell the Congo to Belgium in 1908.

Despite responsibility for death tolls of holocaust dimensions, neither Christopher Columbus nor King Leopold II was convicted or imprisoned for any crimes. Both men lived a full life and died exceptionally rich. Columbus spent his last years living in a mansion in Valladolid with an annual income of $60,000 from his Hispaniola sugar plantations (a fortune in the 1500s). Leopold died in 1909 with a personal fortune (produced by the Congo's ivory and rubber) of well over a billion dollars in today's currency.

In order to prevent the human atrocities of Columbus and Leopold from ever reoccurring, it might be prudent to adopt the current philosophy regarding Adolph Hitler; that is, constant reminders of the holocausts in newspapers, magazines, books, radio, television, and even holocaust museums followed by the statement: "Never Again."

13

Blacks and the Revolutionary War

African American participation was enormous during the events leading to American Independence, but these contributions are seldom mentioned in contemporary history books. For example, Crispus Attucks, a black man and probably an escaped slave, was the first person killed in Boston when tensions between British soldiers and an angry crowd resulted in the death of five people. March 5, 1770 was initially called the day of the Boston Massacre but the name was soon changed to Crispus Attucks Day. Crispus Attucks Day remained the chief American anniversary until independence was won and it was replaced by July 4. John Adams, our second president, called March 5, 1770 the most important event in American history. On October 13, 1888 a monument was erected on Boston Common called the Crispus Attucks Memorial.

British resentment increased dramatically after the Boston Massacre until things finally exploded on April 19, 1775, into the Revolutionary War. At least a dozen black militiamen were among those firing the "shots heard round the world" at Lexington on April 19. One of the first Americans to fall was a black minuteman named Prince Estabrook. The second major clash was fought at Bunker Hill on June 17, where two African Americans again became great heroes. Peter Salem became famous after he shot and killed Major Pitcairn, the British commander. Salem Poor so distinguished himself in this same battle that 13 officers including his commander, Colonel Brewer, recommended him for official recognition to the General Court of Massachusetts.

However, less than 6 months after Lexington and the Battle of Bunker Hill, a pattern of exclusion of blacks from the new nation's military units had begun to develop. Southern slave owners protested vehemently against the use of black people in the Revolutionary War including George Washington who himself was a slave owner. Finally, on October 8, 1775, Continental Army headquarters bowed to southern pressure and issued a decree excluding all African Americans from service in Continental units.

As the war dragged on and the number of white deserters became enormous, Washington complained that "the lack of patriotism is infinitely more to be dreaded than the whole British army." Washington changed his mind drastically after his defeat by the British at New York, when he was greatly outnumbered. He then partitioned the new government to welcome all able-bodied men into the Continental Army whether black or white, slave or free. Accordingly, on March 14, 1779, Alexander recommended that South Carolina and Georgia " take measures for raising 3,000 able-bodied Negroes who would receive no pay but would be emancipated at the end of the war." White slave masters of the North and South who didn't want to risk their lives or their sons' lives were allowed to send slaves to take their place. There were soon so many black soldiers that General Schuyler wrote "is it consistent with the sons of freedom to trust their ALL to be defended by slaves?" Nineteenth century American historian, Ben J. Lossing, wrote that "as the war went on, and the ranks of the army grew thinner, an increasing number of Negroes took the place of the whites, until it began to appear that Ethiopia as well as America was in arms." Baron Von Clausen stated that of the 20,000 men he saw with Washington in January, 1781, "5000 were Negroes."

It is indisputable that African Americans provided the balance of power that brought America independence. They distinguished themselves in every possible manner from combat soldier to support personnel who built virtually every fortification and new building from Vermont to South Carolina. Sir Henry Clinton wrote Lord Germaine, British minister of state, "it is safe to say that but for the aid of the Negro, independence would not have been won." All black regiments as well as individual soldiers who distinguished themselves were mentioned by the hundreds. Rhode Island, with a small population and two thirds of its territory occupied by the British, became the first colony to authorize the enlistment of all slave regiments. At the battle of Rhode Island, August 27, 1778, a regiment of 226 slaves repelled a force of 6,000 British who charged them three times in an attempt to dislodge them from a strategic valley. Dr. Harris wrote "they preserved our army from capture and helped gain our liberty." General Lafayette called this "the best action of the whole war."

A company of blacks from Boston called the "Bucks of America" rendered such valuable service that John Hancock gave them a special flag and honored them with a special affair at Boston. George Bancroft wrote of the Battle of Monmouth in New Jersey in 1778, "may history record that more than 700 Black men offered their lives for their country and fought side by side with whites." Commander Nathaniel Shaler thought so highly of the black soldiers who fought under him that he sent a letter to Governor Thompkins stating that "they ought to be registered in the book of fame and remembered as long as bravery is considered a virtue."

In general, the contributions of black Americans who had fought to bring freedom to America were not forgotten. Virtually all of the slaves who fought in the war received their freedom after the war. In fact, the institution of slavery did not even last throughout the war in most northern states. In 1777, Vermont became the first state to abolish slavery. Pennsylvania followed in 1780, and Massachusetts in 1783. Rhode Island freed its slaves in 1784. Even Virginia passed a law freeing all slaves who participated in the war. Unfortunately, the contributions of African Americans were soon forgotten in the South, where the vast majority of them lived, and the institution of slavery soon returned to business as usual.

14

African Warrior: Queen Nzinga

Nzinga (1582-1663) became queen of what is now called Angola in 1623 and dedicated her entire life to fighting the Portuguese to prevent the enslavement of her people. She proved to be a cunning rival to the Portuguese and became famous for her intelligence, bravery, and brilliant military strategies, which were imitated for centuries during struggles for independence throughout Africa.

In the 16th century, the Portuguese stake in the slave trade was threatened by England, France, and the Dutch. This caused the Portuguese to transfer their slave-trading activities southward to the Congo and to Southwest Africa. Their most stubborn opposition, as they entered the final phase of the conquest of Angola, came from a queen who became a legendary head of state and military leader with few peers in world history.

Nzinga was one of five children born to her powerful father, King (or ngola) Kiluanji of Ndongo-which the Portuguese called Angola after the word for king: ngola. The Mbundu tribe of King Kiluanji initially welcomed the Portuguese as trading partners. In fact, King Kiluanji became wealthy and powerful enough through Portuguese trading that he conquered all the surrounding territories.

Subsequently, disputes over these new territories created the rift that eventually ended the Portuguese alliance. King Kiluanji was such a great fighter that he was able to repel the early Portuguese invasions of the border territories. When Kiluanji died, his eldest son Mbandi declared himself king. Mbandi, however, he greatly feared the Portuguese guns and canons and when they advanced, he fled to an island on the Cuanza River and asked his sister Nzinga to negotiate a peace treaty with the Portuguese governor. The arrogant Portuguese had been appointing governors over Angola for over forty years without having control.

Nzinga's 1622 negotiating conference with the new governor, Joao Correa DeSouza, has become a legend in the history of Africa's confrontation with Europe. Despite the fact that her brother had surrendered everything to the Portuguese, Nzinga arrived as a royal negotiator rather than a humble conquered messenger. When the governor only provided one chair for himself, she summoned one of her women, who provided a royal carpet and then fell to her hands and knees to become a human seat. When Governor DeSouza entered, he found himself already out maneuvered. When the governor asked for the release of all Portuguese war prisoners, Nzinga smilingly agreed, provided all her Mbundu people who had been carried off to Brazil and elsewhere were brought back in exchange. This condition was eventually reduced to returning Portuguese prisoners in exchange for allowing her brother, King Mbandi, to remain ruler of an independent Ndongo kingdom and withdrawing the Portuguese army. Nzinga made it clear she would only negotiate a treaty on equal terms.

Probably as part of a private agreement intended to reinforce the treaty, Nzinga stayed in town and became baptized as "Anna" in the Christian faith. Such a move was more political than religious because Nzinga knew that even her father had opposed the mass conversion to Christianity of the Mbundu. She knew that the Jesuit priests ran the slave trade for the Portuguese. They sprinkled "Holy Water" while officiating at daily mass baptisms on the docks, where lines of captives shuffled into slave ships with such names as "Jesus" and "John the Baptist." Nzinga also knew that her status as a "Christian" ally of Portugal would entitle her people to favored status. She was even politically astute enough to allow herself the full Christian name of Dona Anna DeSouza in order to strengthen her links with the governor.

Shortly after negotiating with Nzinga, Governor DeSouza was replaced by a new governor after quarreling with the Jesuit priests. The new governor promptly broke all the treaty agreements. Nzinga demanded that her brother, King Mbandi, declare war on the

Portuguese. Unfortunately, cowardly King Mbandi had no such intentions and went to the Portuguese asking for protection against Nzinga and to re-enforce his authority over his own people. Nzinga, now determined to do away with this treacherous weakling, had him killed and then promptly declared war on the Portuguese herself. She initially trained an all female army which repeatedly defeated the Portuguese using guerilla style tactics. She then recruited neighboring tribes and also allied with the Dutch. The Dutch military attaché who accompanied her reported that the people loved Nzinga so much that everyone fell to their knees and kissed the ground as she approached. He believed that all were willing to die under her leadership. The Portuguese retreated to their strongholds and forts on the coast giving the Dutch threat as an excuse and not the threat of being annihilated by the queen's forces. Nzinga's main goal was always to end the enslavement of her people. She even sent word throughout Africa in 1624, that any slave who could make it to her territory was henceforth and forever free. This act alone should make Nzinga one of the greatest women in history because there was no other place on the continent of Africa that offered such freedom.

The Portuguese responded to this threat by calling in a massive force of men and artillery from their colony of Brazil. Nzinga's guerilla warfare tactics for resisting the well armed Portuguese soldiers have been much admired and even imitated successfully in this century. Since the Portuguese used large numbers of black soldiers, she became the first Black leader and most successful to carefully organize efforts to undermine and destroy the effective employment of Black soldiers by Whites. She instructed her soldiers to infiltrate the Portuguese by allowing themselves to become recruited by Portuguese agents. Once members of the Portuguese military, her soldiers would encourage rebellion and desertion by the Black troops which frequently resulted in whole companies of Portuguese soldiers joining Nzinga along with much needed guns and ammunition. This quiet and effective work of Nzinga's agents among the Black troops of Portugal is one of the most glorious, yet unsung, pages of African history. The Portuguese generals frequently complained that they never knew which black soldier was friend or foe.

When the massive Portuguese manpower and firepower began to gain the upper hand, she sent word throughout Angola that she had died in order to stop the Portuguese offensive. While pretending to have died in Angola, Nzinga moved east to the neighboring country of Matamba where she defeated the ruling queen and created a new land for herself, her people, and all escaped slaves. She consolidated her power in Matamba and then began sending out war parties from Matamba to attack any settlement or tribe that had aided the Portuguese. In 1629 the Portuguese stood shocked when Queen Nzinga "burst upon them from the grave" recapturing large segments of her own country. She was now queen of both Matamba and Ndongo and redoubled her efforts against slavery by dealing ruthlessly with any Black chief found participating in the slave trade.

Nzinga never stopped resisting the powerful Portuguese even as she approached her 80th birthday. She was called the "Black Terror" by the Portuguese and was clearly the greatest adversary and military strategist that ever confronted the armed forces of Portugal. Her tactics kept the Portuguese commanders in confusion and dismay and her constant aim was never less than the total destruction of the slave trade. The long guerilla campaign that led to Angola independence 300 years later was continuously inspired by the queen who never surrendered.

15

Slave Children of Thomas Jefferson

In the 1860 census in the South, there were 500,000 mulatto or mixed race slaves and 350,000 slave owners. Thus, every slave owner had on average produced more than one slave child. The slave children of former President Thomas Jefferson, and their direct descendants, are among the most carefully studied families in the history of America because of their outstanding achievements up to and including Chairman of the Board of DuPont Chemical Corporation.

Thomas Jefferson is considered the greatest and most brilliant statesman this country has ever produced. Moreover, among the founding fathers, he was the one who was the most vocal opponent of slavery and did the most to contribute to its abolition. He wrote the Declaration of Independence with a clause opposing slavery, which was taken out at the insistence of the other signers. He wrote the Northwest Ordinance in 1783, and included a clause that prohibited slavery in the new areas of Ohio, Indiana, and Illinois. Jefferson negotiated the Louisiana Purchase from France in 1803, and included a provision, which prohibited the introduction of slavery into these new areas. While president, Thomas Jefferson pushed through Congress a bill in 1808, which prohibited the importation of slaves and authorized the U.S. Navy to seize and confiscate ships containing slaves on the high seas. Thomas Jefferson was married to Martha Wayles, the daughter of John Wayles, for 10 years before she died in 1776. Upon the death of Martha Wayles and her father, Jefferson inherited 11,000 acres of land and 135 slaves. Sally Hemmings was one of the slaves inherited. She was also a daughter of John Wayles and an African slave, and thus his wife's half sister. Jefferson fell in love with this mulatto slave after she accompanied his daughter to France, where he was U.S. Ambassador in 1787. Their first son "Tom" was born in 1789. Sally Hemmings produced Beverly Hemmings in 1798, while Thomas Jefferson was Vice President, and three other children while Jefferson was President, including Harriet in 1801, Madison in 1805, and Eston in 1808.

Beverly and Harriet Hemmings were allowed to run away in 1822. Harriet married a White person and never acknowledged her parents. Beverly ended up in England where he also passed for White. His great-grandson, Edward Graham Jefferson, migrated back to the U.S. and became a naturalized American citizen. He subsequently became CEO of DuPont Chemical Corporation, retiring in 1986 and was a member of the Board at AT&T Corporation, Chemical Bank, and Seagram Corporation.

Sally Hemming's first son, Tom, eventually married Jemima, the slave daughter of a master named Drury Woodson, and changed his name to Tom Woodson. He became the distributor of an abolitionist newspaper and a leader in the Black community. Federal Judge Timothy Lewis in 1991, became the first prominent person to admit publicly that he was a descendant of Sally Hemmings and son, Tom Woodson. This was only after his Senate confirmation hearings. Most descendants were ashamed of their slave ancestry.

Frederick Madison Roberts, the grandson of Madison Hemmings, became the first Black man ever elected to the State Assembly of California. He also became a close friend of Earl Warren and helped found UCLA, that is, the University of California at Los Angeles. Sally Hemming's last born son, Eston, had a son named John Wayles Jefferson who founded the Continental Cotton Company, which was very successful.

Thomas Jefferson was the most vocal opponent against slavery and spent his entire life working for the abolition of slavery. He strongly believed that "all men are created equal" and that they could achieve equally if only given the opportunity. Jefferson would be proud to know that his slave children confirmed his theory about racial equality by their outstanding achievements.

16

Paul Cuffe

AMERICA'S RICHEST AFRICAN AMERICAN

Paul Cuffe (1759-1817) was the richest African American in the United States during the early 1800's, but never stopped championing the cause of better conditions for his people. At the age of 19, he sued the Massachusetts courts for the right to vote stating that taxation without representation should be illegal. He built on his own farm, New Bedford's only school for the children of "free Negroes" and personally sponsored their teachers. He authored the first document of its kind addressed to the New Jersey Legislature asking that body "to petition the Congress of the United States that every slave be freed and that every Colored man that so desired be allowed to leave America." By 1811, Paul Cuffe finally concluded that if the richest Black person in America was considered a second class citizen, then emigration back to Africa was the only answer for Black social, economic, and political self-determination. On December 12, 1815 Cuffe personally sponsored and transported nine families (38 people) back to Africa in what he hoped would be the first of many such voyages.

Paul Cuffe was one of ten children born to a slave father, Saiz Kufu (later, Cuffe) and an Indian mother. The father was freed by his Quaker master in 1745, and earned enough money working for ship owners to buy a 116-acre farm in Dartmouth, Mass. in 1766. Paul left the farming to his siblings and chose a maritime life and by age 14 was working full time on whaling ships. By age 18, he had become so thoroughly self-taught in mathematics, navigation, and other seafaring skills that he decided to built his own boat for self-employment. During the Revolutionary War, he made enough money smuggling goods pass British blockade patrol ships that he was able to purchase a shipyard and construct three small whaling boats between 1787 and 1795. During one season alone, Cuffe and his crew captured six whales and Cuffe proved his courage and commitment by asking his crew to lower him to the side of the boat where he personally harpooned two whales.

Paul Cuffe's early activity was fraught with danger as he purchased and delivered freight along the Atlantic seaboard. Pirates were a constant threat and on more than one occasion his ship was captured and all of his merchandise stolen, but he never stopped pursuing his dream. The Fugitive Slave Act was also a constant threat, especially since Cuffe exclusively staffed his businesses and ships with Blacks to demonstrate their equally and to reinforce their self-confidence and sense of racial pride. The Fugitive Slave Act legalized the seizure of any Black person suspected of escape from slavery by any White person. Since African Americans could not testify in court, "the Black accused would have to find and persuade a White person to appear at his trial and convince the authorities that the accused was free" or risk being resold into slavery. Moreover, Paul Cuffe was once arrested for several days and his boat seized during a delivery to Vienna, Maryland by Federal Collector of Customs, James Frazier. In 1796, Maryland had passed a law "requiring any 'suspicious' free Black to six months of servitude." Since a vessel owned and operated by Blacks was unprecedented, it was certainly "suspicious". Whites were also concerned about what this demonstration of Black achievement might have on otherwise obedient slaves. However, Cuffe had "impeccable mercantile credentials, proof of registry at Bedford, Massachusetts, and receipts from such reliable merchant houses as William Rotch and Sons."

As the Cuffe commercial enterprises continued to prosper, he expanded by purchasing a 200-acre farm, a gristmill, and by building ships large enough to enable him to purchase and deliver freight internationally. In 1800 Cuffe built the 162-ton "Hero" which sailed around Africa's Cape of Good Hope eight times while delivering merchandise from Portuguese East Africa to Europe. Paul Cuffe's largest ship was the 268-ton "Alpha" which

Cuffe and nine Black crewmembers sailed from Savannah, Georgia to Gothenburg, Sweden with a large cargo in 1806.

Despite the fact that Paul Cuffe was the richest Black man and largest Black employer in America, he was convinced that no amount of wealth would make a Black man socially acceptable in America and that Blacks would always be "resident aliens." He felt the only answer was to develop a strong Black African nation. Cuffe declared: "Blacks would be better off in Africa, where we could rise to be a people." When William Rotch told him of a British program to repatriate unwanted Blacks living in London to Sierra Leone, he immediately sailed to England for more information.

Cuffe hoped that a strong Black nation could trade with Great Britain and the United States and that educated "free Negroes" from America could provide the much needed technology. American technology was needed because a British law (1731) forbid any White person from teaching any Black person a trade, thus reducing London's "Black Poor" to unemployable beggars whom the government wanted sent to Africa.

While traveling to England and Sierra Leone, Paul Cuffe used an introductory letter from President Thomas Jefferson to help him gather data on manufacturing, operating costs, threatening colonial practices, and available trade opportunities. Cuffe found the residents of Sierra Leone very receptive to his prescription for reviving Black industry. They also hoped that a strong economic and social return of Africa to its past glory would help dissuade the slave trade. A large percentage of the population of Freetown were former American slaves who had fought with the British during the Revolutionary War and then were evacuated to Nova Scotia, Canada with the White British Loyalists. Both severe racism and severe climate encouraged the Black Nova Scotians to leave en-mass for Sierra Leone in November 1792. Paul Cuffe hired Aaron Richards, a Black settler in Freetown as the captain's apprentice "to prepare the road to progress," and before leaving, Cuffe founded the "Friendly Society for the Emigration of Free Negroes from America". After his return to America, "Cuffe began a speaking tour to introduce free Blacks to the notion of nation building in Africa."

The War of 1812 interrupted Cuffe's trade and emigration plans until 1815, at which time he paid $4,000 from personal funds to transport 38 African Americans to Sierra Leone, and he successfully secured homesteads for all of his Black American brethren at his expense. Failing health prevented any future trips and Cuffe died on September 9, 1817. Paul Cuffe's legacy is not as a wealthy Black man but as a wealthy Black man who fought for the betterment of his people and was always willing to back his convictions with self-sacrifice, discipline, determination, and financial resources.

DAVID WALKER

In 1829, David Walker published the first of four articles that he called "Walker's Appeal." In it he encouraged all slaves to become free by killing their masters. The South exploded in anger and offered a reward for Walker of $10,000 dead or alive. Laws were passed threatening to hang anyone with "Walker's Appeal" in their possession. Anti-slavery leaders of both races in the North and South rejected the violence advocated in Walker's publication and forced him to circulate it at his own risk and expense.

David Walker proclaimed to the slaves: "...it is no more harm for you to kill the man who is trying to kill you than it is for you to take a drink of water." Walker hated slavery despite the fact that he was born free as the product of a free mother and slave father. Afraid that his stirring publication meant eminent danger, Walker's wife and friends urged him to flee to Canada but he refused. Walker said: "I will stand my ground. Somebody must die in this cause. I may be doomed to the stake and the fire or to the scaffold tree, but it is not in me to falter if I can promote the work of emancipation."

Despite the great efforts of both the North and South to stop its publication, "Walker's Appeal" became one of the most widely read and circulated books ever written by a black person. David Walker was considered a hero by most abolitionists, who considered his book the boldest attack ever written against slavery.

Although the violent aspects of Walker's Appeal are most emphasized, he also offered whites an olive branch if they would end slavery: "Treat us like men, and there is no danger but we will all live in peace and happiness together. For we are not like you: hard hearted, unmerciful, and unforgiving. What a happy country this will be if Whites will listen." Walker viewed his publication as a religious document giving blacks an obligation from God to eradicate the evils of slavery. Walker said: "...answer God Almighty, had you not rather be killed than to be a slave to a tyrant who takes the life of your mother, wife, and children?"

He told the white slaveholders: "You may do your best to keep us in wretchedness and misery to enrich you and your children, but God will deliver us from under you."

David Walker was born in Wilmington, North Carolina on September 28, 1785. He was self-taught and read extensively the literature on slavery-especially on the history of resistance and oppression. In 1820, he moved to Boston, Massachusetts where he opened a secondhand clothing store. He began writing for a black newspaper called "The Freedom Journal" in 1827.

David Walker's Appeal was published "Walker's Appeal" on September 28, 1829. The full title is "Walker's Appeal in Four Articles: Together with a Preamble, to the Coloured Citizens of the World, but in Particular, and Very Expressly, to Those of the United States of America". Walker created such fear among slaveholding states that governors and city officials alike held emergency meetings to deal with its obvious implications. True to his word, Walker did not flee the country and was murdered in 1830. The "Appeal" was the inspiration for several slave rebellions including the terrifying slave rebellion of Nat Turner about one year after Walker's death.

David Walker's selfless devotion to the liberation of his people and his revolutionary spirit also served as an important model for future militants like Henry Highland Garnet who published Walker's "Appeal" and his own work entitled "Address to the Slaves of the United States" in a single volume in 1848.

17

Richard Allen and the AME Church

The African Methodist Episcopal Church (AME Church) was one of the first Black organizations dedicated to Black self-improvement and Pan-Africanist ideals. The AME Church was also distinguished by its commitment to political agitation, Black education, and social activism. The interest in education initially culminated in the founding of Wilberforce University in 1863, as the first Black College founded by Blacks. Numerous other AME Colleges soon followed. AME pastors were also responsible for numerous lawsuits against public school segregation, which eventually led to the 1954 case: "Brown vs. Eoard of Education." During the Civil Rights movement, the AME Church was very active, and in addition to a pragmatic gospel, the church addressed the housing, welfare, and unionization issues of new immigrants to northern cities. However, nothing more completely captures the spirit and embodiment of the AME Church than its founder and first bishop, Richard Allen.

Richard Allen was born into slavery in Philadelphia, Pennsylvania on February 14, 1760 and shortly thereafter his entire family was sold by a Philadelphia lawyer, Benjamin Chew, to a Delaware plantation owner, Stokely Sturgis. Although the slave master was unconverted, he allowed Richard Allen to attend Methodist meetings. In addition to their antislavery beliefs, Allen was especially impressed by their emphasis on a simple set of virtues including honesty, modesty, and sobriety and converted to Methodism at age 17. By age 20, Allen was able to convert his slave master and to convince him that slaveholding was wrong.

Allen was allowed to buy his freedom for $2000 by working a variety of odd jobs over the next five years. Once freed, "Allen traveled widely on the Methodist circuits, preaching, holding prayer meetings, and giving religious counsel to groups of White and Black Christians in the small towns and rural settlements of Maryland, Delaware, Pennsylvania, and New York." While in Philadelphia, Allen was asked by the elders at St. George Methodist Church to preach to their Black members. After the Black membership increased dramatically, Richard Allen determined that his calling was to minister to the "uneducated, poor, and unchurched community" and that he could best reach them in a separate Black church. However, the White Methodist elders ridiculed the whole idea with "very degrading and insulting language."

St. George's Black membership became so large that the church was forced to build a new seating gallery. When church authorities demanded that Blacks sit in the rear of the gallery, Allen and others decided they had been insulted enough: "We all went out of the church in a body and they were no more plagued with us." The Black Methodists agreed to purchase a blacksmith shop and to move it to a lot Allen had purchased with his own savings. Carpenters were hired to make the building suitable for church meetings and on April 9, 1794, Bishop Asbury dedicated the structure as "Bethel African Church." Bishop Asbury also ordained Allen as the first Black Methodist deacon and within four years the Bethel membership increased from 45 to 457 members. Richard Allen's success was the inspiration for many other Black Methodist groups to form African Methodist Churches throughout the Northeast especially in New York, Delaware, and Maryland.

Since Bethel African Church was still under White Methodist ecclesiastical jurisdiction, White Methodists sued for legal control of Bethel, but in 1807 the Pennsylvania Supreme Court ruled in Allen's favor. In 1816, Allen organized a national convention of Black Methodists, since many of them had similar White Methodist challenges. The convention delegates resolved that the churches they represent "should become one body under the name 'African Methodist Episcopal Church' in order to secure their privileges and promote union and harmony among themselves." Richard

Allen became the new denomination's first Bishop and retained that title until his death in 1831.

Richard Allen dedicated his entire life toward uplifting his fellow African Americans. He felt that true Christians had to stretch out their hands beyond the circle of family and friends "to comfort the poor neighbor, the stranger, the widow, and the orphan." He helped establish the Free African Society, the Bethel Benevolent Society, and the African Society for the Education of Youth "in order to support one another...from a love to the people of our complexion whom we behold with sorrow." Bethel Church became the scene of numerous Black conventions to discuss the abolition of slavery and racial discrimination, and Richard Allen was commonly recognized as the leader of free Northern Blacks. Allen also published "An Address to Those Who Keep Slaves" in which he attacked slavery and the arguments for it.

Allen spent the final years of his life vehemently opposing the American Colonization Society, which Whites organized in 1817 to support the emigration of free Blacks from America to Africa. The American Colonization Society argued that free Blacks would have to leave this country to find true freedom, since the Fugitive Slave Act allowed any White person to call a free Black a fugitive slave. Since African Americans could not testify in court and therefore could not defend themselves, they had to find someone White who could speak in their behalf or they would become enslaved. Richard Allen himself was once called a fugitive slave, but fortunately, he was so famous that he not only won his case but had his accuser thrown into jail for three months. The American Colonization Society also argued that African Americans could help civilize and convert their less fortunate African brothers. However, Allen angrily responded that American Blacks could not convert or civilize anyone since they were mostly illiterate and uneducated themselves. He felt the real purpose of the colonizationists was to expel the most vociferous opponents of slavery. Allen told the American Colonization Society: "We will never separate ourselves voluntarily from the slave population in this country; they are our brethren and we feel there is more virtue in suffering privations with them than fancied advantage for a season."

Richard Allen propelled the AME Church to the center of Black institutional activity during his lifetime. Allen's life, as much as his sermons, remained an effective example for the future leadership of the AME Church. Moreover, his leadership direction is responsible for the continued proliferation of AME membership throughout the 19th and 20th century, which today boasts a total of over 1.2 million members.

WAR OF 1812

African American soldiers and sailors played a tremendous role in helping America defeat the British during the Revolutionary War. Most northern states were so grateful for the contributions of Black soldiers that they abolished slavery shortly after the war. Even Virginia passed a law freeing all slaves who had participated in the Revolutionary War. However, peacetime produced a total amnesia to the contributions of Blacks in the military and a request for their participation was not made again until the War of 1812 (June 18, 1812-December 24, 1814).

After the Revolutionary War, southerners were determined to never again allow African Americans, neither free nor slave, to "gain dignity and prestige by fighting for the United States." They were instrumental in the passage by Congress of the Military Act (May 8, 1792), which called for the enrollment of "each and every able-bodied White male citizen between the ages of 18 and 45." When the Marine Corps was established by a congressional act on July 11, 1798, Secretary of War Henry Knox issued a directive that "No Negro, mulatto, or Indian is to be enlisted," and this directive was followed for the next 150 years. Only World War II manpower shortages forced the Marine Corps to change its 150-year policy and recruit African Americans. Secretary of the Navy Benjamin Stoddert followed the lead of the Army and Marine Corps and instructed his recruiters in August 1798 "...no Negroes, mulattos, or Indians."

During the early 1800s, the British had the most powerful Navy in the world, especially after defeating France's Napoleonic Navy. Still at war with Napoleon, a British naval blockade from Maine to Georgia was used to prevent American trading with French merchants. Moreover, because of a tremendous shortage of sailors, the British not only boarded and searched merchant vessels on the high seas but would frequently claim that American sailors were British deserters and force them to work on British ships (called impressment).

The impressment of three African American sailors from the American frigate "Chesapeake" on June 22, 1807 is called the first major incident leading to the War of 1812, and is frequently compared to the killing of Crispus Attucks which was called the first major incident leading to the Revolutionary War.

A group of expansionist congressmen called "War Hawks" convinced President James Madison to sign a declaration of war against Great Britain on June 18, 1812. In addition to conquering the British on the high seas, they hoped to expel the British from Canada, since most British troops were still fighting Napoleon. However, extreme racism left America ill prepared for this unpopular war. Not only did White men fail to enlist, but New England Whites also started a separatist movement and held a convention in Hartford, Connecticut in December 1814 to further solidify their demands. Moreover, the Canadian invasion was a total failure, and the British continued to defeat American Whites until they occupied Detroit and most of Ohio. JA Rogers states that the British practically wiped out American sea-borne trade and captured Florida and much of the South with Black volunteers whom they promised freedom. On August 24, 1814 the British Army captured Washington DC and burned many public buildings to the ground including the White House and Capital. The Encyclopedia Britannica says America was thoroughly defeated in this war while gaining none of the avowed aims and that only legend has converted defeat into the illusion of victory. Military historian Gary Donaldson states that only after the United States was brought to the edge of losing its independence were African Americans allowed in the military.

The White residents of both Pennsylvania and New York now welcomed Blacks into the military to defend their cities from the advancing enemy and even promised slaves freedom after three years of service. General Andrew Jackson begged Blacks in New Orleans to fight the British and promised them equal pay with Whites, 160 acres of land, and participation in all Black battalions led by Black officers to avoid White prejudices. Jackson said: "Through a mistake in policy, you have heretofore been deprived of participation in the glorious struggle for national rights in which our country is engaged. This no longer shall exist. As Americans, your country looks with confidence to her adopted children for a valorous support."

On March 3, 1813 the Navy officially authorized the recruitment of Blacks because of the severe manpower shortage, thus reversing their official exclusion since the congressional act of 1798. Experienced Black sailors who had previously worked on whaling boats and as merchant marines flocked to the Navy and were credited with much of America's success in defeating the British Navy in the Great Lakes region. Commodore Thomas McDonough said the accuracy of his Black gunners was responsible for his victory on Lake Champlain. Commodore Isaac Chancey said he had fifty Black crewmembers that were among his very best.

On September 10, 1813, Commodore Oliver Perry defeated the British fleet on Lake Erie after a savage three hour battle and acknowledged the contributions and individual bravery of his 100 Black seamen in his Battle Report and also noted: "They seemed to be absolutely insensitive to danger." Military historian Michael Lanning states: "The American naval victories in which Black sailors played such a critical role, finally forced the war-weary British to agree to a peace treaty." The "Treaty of Ghent" was signed on December 24, 1814 in Belgium restoring pre-war conditions.

Unaware that the war had ended, sixty British ships containing 12,000 men sailed up the Mississippi River on January 8, 1815 in an attempt to capture New Orleans. The men of the "Louisiana Battalion of Free Men of Color" were in the front line of American soldiers who dealt the British their worst defeat of the war, inflicting 4,000 casualties compared to only sixty of their own. After the battle, General Andrew Jackson praised the Black soldiers: "I was not ignorant that you possessed qualities most formidable to an invading enemy...the President of the United States shall hear how praise worthy was your conduct in the hour of danger." Jackson kept his promises of $124 and 160 acres of land to both White and Black soldiers. However, glory faded quickly for the

"Louisiana Battalion of Free Men of Color"; they were soon disbanded and again faced pre-war prejudices. In city celebrations of the "Battle of New Orleans" for the next 100 years, not a single Black person was allowed to participate in the festivities.

White America, again, quickly forgot the contributions of Blacks in the military. A War Department memorandum on March 3, 1815 discharged all Blacks from the military stating: "A Negro is deemed unfit to associate with the American soldier." The Navy issued orders in 1839 restricting Black enlistments to less than 5% and only in positions of cooks, mess boys, and servants, and this was signed by the same Isaac Chauncey who had highly praised his Black sailors during the War of 1812. Peacetime again became the chief promoter of racial exclusion in America and as always, when African Americans were no longer needed, they were also no longer wanted.

THE JOHN BROWN TEST

Dr. Leonard Jeffries recommends that before you call a white person a "true friend," that person should pass the "John Brown Test." Since history records numerous John Browns the question is, exactly which John Brown does Dr. Jeffries consider a good role model for white friendship? Rhode Island College changed its name to Brown University in 1804 to honor one person named John Brown. However, this John Brown made his fortune exchanging rum for slaves, so he couldn't possibly be the White friend role model. John Robert Brown (1909-1993) was Chief Justice for the Fifth Circuit Court of Appeals and played a pivotal role in championing and enforcing civil rights legislation in the South. He is most noted for ordering in 1962 that African-American James Meredith be enrolled in the all-white University of Mississippi. Most black people would be happy to have a White friend like John Robert Brown, but Leonard Jeffries says the "real" John Brown died at Harper's Ferry, West Virginia in 1859.

The "real" John Brown had an entire book written about him in 1909 by W.E. Burghardt DuBois which was most recently reprinted in 1996 by International Publishers. One of the greatest women in African American history, Harriet Tubman, regarded this John Brown and not President Abraham Lincoln as the true emancipator of her people. The "real" John Brown was born in Torrington, Connecticut on May 9, 1800 about four months before the attempted insurrection of slaves under Gabriel in Virginia in September of the same year. He was raised in Hudson, Ohio where his family migrated in 1805. By the age of 16, he had already joined the church and soon became such an experienced bible student that "when any person was reading he would correct the least mistake." His love for religion was exceeded only by his love for family where he fathered 20 well-disciplined, hard-working children. After seven of his children died before adulthood, he concluded that in some way his own sin and shortcomings were bringing upon him "the vengeful punishment of God." He felt his greatest sin was not doing enough "to increase the amount of human happiness."

In 1839, a turning point occurred in Brown's life when he was visited by a black preacher named Fayette. Fayette described slavery as "the foulest and filthiest blot on 19th century civilization." He added: "as a school of brutality and human suffering, of female prostitution and male debauchery; as a mockery of marriage and defilement of family life; as a darkening of reason, and spiritual death, slavery has no parallel." John Brown fell to his knees and "implored God's blessing on his purpose to make active war on slavery, and he bound his family in solemn and secret compact to labor for emancipation."

John Brown was convinced that the first step toward emancipation was education. He noted that all pro-slavery states were vehemently opposed to educating slaves and made this a capital offense.

John was also aware that slaveholders actively pursued African American schools and churches and burned them to the ground after Nate Turner's slave revolt on August 21, 1831. Brown felt that once the master-slave relationship was broken, Black people deserved their own state and educated blacks would be needed for self-government. He actively campaigned for the establishment of African American schools and even tried to establish a school himself in Hudson, Ohio. When Oberlin College opened its doors to "Negroes" in 1839, and appointed his father as a trustee, John Brown was overjoyed.

On August 1, 1846, Gerrit Smith, a wealthy New York abolition leader, offered free Blacks 100,000 acres of his land in North Elba, New York for farms. Because of the bleak climate and harsh soil, black farmers found it very difficult to succeed until John Brown volunteered to help. He went to Gerrit Smith at Petersboro, New York in April 1848 and said: "I am something of a pioneer...I will take one of your farms myself, clean it up and plant it, and show my Colored neighbors how such work should be done. I will look after them in all needful ways and be a kind of father to them."

In 1854, the government announced that Kansas would become a slave-free state open for settlement. Consequently, five of Brown's sons moved to Kansas in October 1854 but were appalled at what they discovered. Large pro-slavery gangs were traveling throughout Kansas killing anti-slavery farmers and burning their properties. When John Brown's sons informed him what was happening, he loaded a wagon full of weapons and headed for Kansas. In May 1856, shortly after John Brown's arrival in Kansas, two thousand pro-slavery Missourians surrounded Lawrence, Kansas, the capital city, and brutally killed many of the anti-slavery settlers and sacked and burned half the town. On the same day, Senator Brooks killed Senator Charles Sumner by a crushing blow to the head in the U.S. Senate Chamber for telling the truth about Kansas. John Brown was angry and "indignant that there had been no resistance; that Lawrence was not defended; and denounced the men as trembling cowards, or worse." In retaliation, Brown and his sons entered Missouri at night and dragged five of the pro-slavery ringleaders out of their cabins and hacked them to death with swords. This blow, called the Pottawatomie murders, is said to have freed Kansas by plunging it into civil war, and compelling men to fight for freedom, which they had vainly hoped to gain by political diplomacy. Kansas's anti-slavery settlers repelled Missouri's pro-slavery settlers' last invasion on September 15, 1856, and Kansas was finally declared a slave-free state. John Brown was now free to return to the East to resume his plan to free southern slaves by force.

Between 1857 and 1859, John Brown visited the homes of Frederick Douglas, Harriet Tubman, Henry Highland Garnet, Martin Delaney, and many other leading African American abolitionists to gain their support for his plan to free all southern slaves by force. All of the abolitionists were extremely impressed by John Brown's intense desire to end slavery. Although they believed in John Brown, most did not believe his plan was humanly possible. Nevertheless, only sickness prevented Harriet Tubman from joining John Brown on his southern invasion after she had actively recruited soldiers for his cause.

When told that he might die executing his plan, Brown exclaimed: "Did not my Master Jesus Christ come down from Heaven and sacrifice Himself upon the altar for the salvation of the race, and should I, a worm, not worthy to crawl under his feet, refuse to sacrifice myself?" On October 16, 1859, John Brown with an armed band of 16 Whites (including 2 of his sons) and 5 Blacks attacked the federal armory at Harper's Ferry, West Virginia. He had hoped that by capturing the armory arsenal, escaped slaves would join his rebellion, forming an "army of emancipation" with which to liberate their fellow slaves. Unfortunately, he was surrounded by U.S. Marines and overpowered. He was tried and convicted of slave insurrection and hanged on December 2, 1859. Many believe that Brown's attack helped immortalize him and hasten the Civil War, which did bring emancipation.

If Leonard Jeffries could find a single friend, Black or White, who even comes close to passing the "John Brown Test", he should consider himself truly blessed. The truth is, only one person in this country's history, either Black or White has ever passed the "John Brown Test", and he was the "REAL" John Brown.

18

Black People of the Old West

President Roosevelt called December 7, 1941, the day Pearl Harbor was bombed, as a day that will forever be recorded in infamy. For Black pioneers in the old west, February 2, 1848 will forever be recorded in infamy. This is the day the peace treaty was signed which ended the Mexican War and gave to the United States the territories of Texas, California, Nevada, Utah and parts of Arizona, Wyoming, Colorado, and New Mexico.

The African Americans who arrived with the earliest Spanish expeditions to California helped create a culture that accepted them as equals. Blacks purchased large segments of land and became successful businessmen with the establishment of hotels and trading centers. Los Angeles was founded by 26 people of African ancestry and only two Caucasians. Maria Rita Valdez, whose Black grandparents were among the founding members of Los Angeles, owned Rancho Rodeo de Las Aguas, today called Beverly Hills. Francisco Reyes, another Black resident, owned the San Fernando Valley. In the 1790's, he sold it and became mayor of Los Angeles. Pio Pico, whose grandmother was listed as mulatto in the 1790 census, was governor of California from 1845-1846 when the Mexican War started. Pico Boulevard in Los Angeles is named after this Black governor.

William Leidesdorff is one of San Francisco's most famous citizens. He was born in St. Croix, Virgin Islands to a Danish planter and his African wife. He sailed for California in 1841, after becoming a wealthy businessman, aboard his 160-ton schooner called "Julia Ann." He shortly thereafter became a landowner, having purchased a 35,000-acre estate in San Francisco and soon became treasurer of the San Francisco City Council. He helped set up the first public school system which was open to everyone, regardless of race, creed, or color. Leidesdorff opened the first hotel in San Francisco, introduced the first steamboat to the city, and organized its first horse race. Today a street in downtown San Francisco bears the name of this remarkable early Black citizen.

Things changed rapidly after February 2, 1848, when the United States assumed control of California. President Polk announced the discovery of gold in California in 1849, and the population soared 10 fold within two years. Although racial lines had been ignored before California became American territory, Black hatred and discrimination moved westward with the White wagon trains. Most White Californians were convinced that no matter how honest, reliable, hard working or wealthy a Black neighbor might be, he ought not be granted any rights a White man was bound to respect. In 1852, the legislature of California passed a law, deeply hated by Blacks, which prohibited any Black person from testifying in court. This prevented Black men from supporting their land claims, Black women from identifying rape assailants, and Black businessmen from suing those who had cheated or robbed them. Other anti Black laws produced segregated schools and prohibited Blacks from voting as well as from serving in the military.

In addition, the "fugitive slave law" was passed in 1852 by a 14 to 9 vote, which also permitted a slave owner to remain an indefinite time in the state, thus institutionalizing slavery despite its prohibition in the state constitution.

A Black exodus from California to Canada occurred in 1858, when the California legislature tried to pass a bill banning Black immigration. Blacks were terrified because Oregon's legislature passed a law the previous year, which provided for the expulsion of all Black people within 3 years. Any Black remaining after three years would be whipped every six months or forced into labor without pay. Oregon's exclusion provision was passed in 1857 and was not repealed until 1927.

Our Black ancestors in the old west could only dream about how wonderful their lives may have been if the Mexican government had won the war and had not signed the peace treaty on the infamous day of February 2, 1848.

19

Black Women of the Old West

Although our novels and movies are filled with heroes from the old west, African American heroes are virtually never mentioned. Moreover, historians have also contributed to this unjust and unbalanced recording of our glorious western saga by completely ignoring the many accomplishments of Black men and women, despite the fact they were accurately reported in newspapers, government records, military reports, and pioneer memoirs.

As members of a double minority, Black women have suffered an even greater historical injustice, although they were an integral part of the western fabric. Nothing more clearly demonstrates the contributions of Black women to the western tradition than the biographies of Biddy Bridget Mason, Clara Brown, and Mary Ellen Pleasant.

Biddy Bridget Mason (1815-1891) was born into slavery and given as a wedding gift to a Mormon couple in Mississippi named Robert and Rebecca Smith.

In 1847 at age 32, Biddy Mason was forced to walk from Mississippi to Utah tending cattle behind her master's 300-wagon caravan. After four years in Salt Lake City, Smith took the group to a new Mormon settlement in San Bernardino, California in search of gold.

When Biddy Mason discovered that the California State Constitution made slavery illegal, she had Robert Smith brought into court on a writ of habeas corpus, and the court freed all of Smith's slaves. Now free, Mason and her three daughters (probably fathered by Smith) moved to Los Angeles where they worked and saved enough money to buy a house at 331 Spring Street in downtown Los Angeles.

Knowing what it meant to be oppressed and friendless, Biddy Mason immediately began a philanthropic career by opening her home to the poor, hungry, and homeless.

Through hard work, saving, and investing carefully, she was able to purchase large amounts of real estate including a commercial building, which provided her with enough income to help build schools, hospitals, and churches.

Her most noted accomplishment was the founding of First African Methodist Episcopal (AME) Church, now the oldest church in Los Angeles, where she also operated a nursery and food pantry. Moreover, her generosity and compassion included personally bringing home cooked meals to men in state prison. In 1988, Mayor Tom Bradley had a tombstone erected at her unmarked gravesite and November 16, 1989 was declared "Biddy Mason Day". In addition, the highlights of her life were displayed on a wall of the Spring Center in downtown Los Angeles, an honor befitting Los Angeles's first Black female property owner and philanthropist.

Clara Brown (1806-1888) is another who dedicated her life to the betterment of others. She was born as a slave in Virginia and then sold at age three to the Brown family in Logan, Kentucky.

At age 35, her master died, and her slave husband, son, and daughter were sold at auction to different owners.

After 20 additional years in slavery, she was able to buy her freedom and immediately headed west to St. Louis. At age 55, she agreed to serve as cook and laundress in exchange for free transportation in a caravan headed for the gold mines of Colorado. Clara Brown established a laundry in Central City and as her resources expanded, she opened up her home, which served as a hospital, church, and hotel to the town's less fortunate.

Under her direction, the first Sunday school developed, and moreover, the whole town turned to her during illness because she was such a good nurse. Frequently, she even "grubstaked miners who had no other means of support while they looked for gold in the mountains and was repaid handsomely for her kindness and generosity by those who struck pay dirt." Far and wide, she was known as "Aunt Clara" and as "the Angel of the Rockies".

By the end of the Civil War, Clara Brown had accumulated several Colorado properties and over $10,000 in cash. Since slavery was over, she used her fortune to search for relatives in Virginia and Kentucky and returned with 34 of them including her daughter.

She continued her philanthropy among the needy for the rest of her life and also spent large sums of money helping other Blacks come west. Upon her death at age 82, the Colorado Pioneers Association buried her with honors, and a plaque was placed in the St. James Methodist Church stating that her house was the first home of the church.

Mary Ellen Pleasant (1814-1903), a former slave, moved to San Francisco in 1849 where she opened a successful boarding house, famous for cards, liquor, and beautiful women.

She was also a partner of Thomas Bell, cofounder of the first "Bank of California." As a businesswoman, she was called mercurial, cunning, cynical, and calculating, but personally she was softhearted and had a passion for helping the less fortunate who called her "the Angel of the West".

She was a leader in California for the protection of abused women and children and helped build and support numerous "safe havens" for them. Mary Ellen Pleasant hated slavery and frequently rode into the rural sections of California to rescue people held in bondage.

Because of Pleasant, the entire Black community of San Francisco received a warning from one judge for "the insolent, defiant, and dangerous way that they interfered with those who were arresting slaves." Mary Ellen Pleasant used most of her fortune to aid fugitive slaves. "She fed them, found occupations for them, and financially backed them in numerous small businesses." In 1858, she gave $30,000 to John Brown to help finance his raid at Harper's Ferry, Virginia. This White abolitionist had hoped to capture the national armory and distribute the weapons to slaves for a massive insurrection. During the Civil War, Pleasant raised money for the Union cause and continued to fight for civil rights. Her tombstone epitaph read: "Mother of Civil Rights in California" and "Friend of John Brown".

Brief biographies of Biddy Bridget Mason, Clara Brown, and Mary Ellen Pleasant serve to illustrate the enormous contributions and accomplishments of Black women in the old west. Era Bell Thompson in "American Daughter" clearly states the problem: "Black women were an integral part of the western and American tradition. It both impairs their sense of identity and unbalances the historical record to continue to overlook the role of Black women in the development of the American west."

20

African Americans and the Civil War

In a 1928 biography of Ulysses S. Grant, historian W.E. Woodward disavowed any contributions made by black Americans in the Civil War. He wrote: "The American Negroes are the only people in the history of the world, that ever became free without any effort of their own...The Civil War was not their business." Woodward dismissed the 200,000 African Americans who served in the war and the 28,000 who died fighting. White historians have always diminished the wartime contributions of African Americans (who have served honorably in every war since this country's inception), but no period seems more blatantly ignored than the Civil War. Freedom for Blacks was the lasting legacy of the Civil War, yet most history textbooks would have us believe that Black slaves sat around playing banjoes and awaiting Yankee soldiers to set them free. Nothing could be further from the truth!

The Civil War began on April 12, 1861 when the Confederate army attacked Fort Sumter. The North initially thought they would easily crush the South because of their 23,000,000 able-bodied white males verses only about 6,000,000 white males available to the South. The North was so certain of victory that they absolutely refused to allow any black people (free or slave) to participate. President Lincoln, however, had considerable difficulty in obtaining volunteers. Poor White men refused to fight in a war which, they believed, would liberate slaves who would take their jobs. They also felt that neither saving the Union nor ending slavery was adequate reason for risking their lives. In July 1862 President Lincoln asked for 300,000 men, but in five weeks less than 30,000 volunteered. On March 1, 1863, Congress passed the nation's first draft bill, the National Conscription Act, which was so unpopular that anti-draft riots broke out in several northern cities. Primarily, recently immigrated poor White males vented their anger against local defenseless African Americans. The New York Times wrote that people of African descent were "literally hunted down like wild beasts and when caught either stoned to death or hung from trees and lamp posts."

In addition to a manpower shortage, General Sherman told President Lincoln that "our men are not good soldiers. They brag but they don't perform." The New York World newspaper reported that "when the Confederate Calvary charged at Bull Run the Union soldiers ran in panic, leaving artillery, guns, ammunition, wagons, and equipment behind." Sir William Howard Russell, war correspondent of the London Times wrote: "Such cowardly scandalous behavior on the part of soldiers I should never have considered possible." The North was decisively defeated in its first three major battles at Bull Run, Wilson Creek, and Balls Bluff. Horace Greeley of the New York Tribute wrote Lincoln that "the larger part of the army is a confused mob, entirely demoralized." He further added that Lincoln should "make peace with the rebels at once and on their terms." Conceding victory to the Confederacy, Greeley published that "so short-lived has been the American Union that men who saw its rise may now see its fall."

In July 1862, Lincoln convinced his Cabinet that all was lost unless he could "win over the slaves of the South and have them fight on his side by offering them freedom." Lincoln himself wrote the original draft of the Emancipation Proclamation and called a special Cabinet meeting for its presentation. The Cabinet agreed that the proclamation was their last resort, but Secretary of War Seward asked Lincoln if he could wait for some type of Union victory prior to its release. Otherwise, Seward said: "It will be viewed as the last measure of an exhausted government; a cry for help; the government stretching forth its hands to Ethiopia, instead of Ethiopia stretching forth her hands to the government." The opportunity came with the marginal Federal victory at Antietam Creek in Maryland on September 17, 1862. One week after the Battle of Antietam, Lincoln released the Emancipation

Proclamation, which stated that all slaves in the Confederacy (or areas still in rebellion) would be "henceforth and forever free." In addition, this document also permitted for the first time, the recruitment of Black men into the army. As a result of these actions, large numbers of newly emancipated slaves all over the South began joining Federal forces as soldiers and laborers.

When it became clear to the Confederate forces in 1863 that their armies would be facing black soldiers in the field, they responded with a threat of death to all African Americans and their White commanding officers. These were not idle threats. At Fort Pillow, Tennessee in April 1864 about 300 Black Federal soldiers were massacred under the direction of Confederate General Nathan Bedford Forrest (who later founded the Ku Klux Klan). The Fort Pillow incident caused Black soldiers to fight more desperately throughout the remainder of the war. They either feared that capture meant certain death, or they intended to exact some revenge for the Fort Pillow atrocities or both.

On June 7, 1863 at Milliken's Bend, Louisiana, the Ninth and Eleventh Louisiana regiment won the Civil War's first significant battle secured by African Americans. Assistant Secretary of War Charles Dana reported that "a Confederate force of three thousand attacked the camp and initially forced the Negro troops to give way, but once reminded that those of their number who were captured were killed, they rallied with great fury and routed the enemy."

Although the Louisiana regiments fought the first major battles by African American soldiers in the Civil War, the Fifty-Fourth Massachusetts regiment gained the most widespread and lasting fame of the war during its assault on Confederate Fort Wagner in South Carolina. Most of the men of the Fifty-Fourth regiment were killed while attacking Fort Wagner, yet Northern politicians, newspapers, and military leaders hailed the Fifty-Fourth as a symbol of the country's greatest example of valor in combat. In 1989, Hollywood honored the Fifty-Fourth regiment in a feature film entitled "Glory" which earned an Oscar nomination for best picture.

Black soldiers participated in virtually every major battle once they were allowed to join the military and earned 23 Congressional

Metals of Honor. Senior Union commanders including Generals Daniel Ullman and Nathaniel Banks testified that "the brigades of Negroes behaved magnificently and fought splendidly, and they were far superior in discipline to the White troops and just as brave." On August 15, 1864 in an interview with John T. Mills, Lincoln defended the use of Black troops by stating that if the 200,000 Black soldiers had decided to fight for the Confederacy instead of the Union, he would have been "compelled to abandon the war in three weeks."

In summary, history textbooks should record that African American soldiers fought gallantly during the Civil War to end over 200 years of bondage. The Thirteenth Amendment (freeing all slaves) was only another testimony to the magnificent accomplishments of the Black soldiers on the Civil War's battlefields.

21

Black Cowboys

The deaths of Roy Rogers and Gene Autry saddened us all because many of us grew up watching these fictional cowboys help tame the old west. However, what's even sadder is that virtually none of us can name a single Black cowboy either real or fictional. The very word "cowboy" was initially only applied to Black men who took care of cows. Similarly, Black men who worked in the house were called "house boys." Nevertheless, once cowboys became the heroes of western novels and later television, Black people totally disappeared from the Old West.

Joseph G. McCoy created the need for "cowboys" when he established a market and railroad-shipping center at Abilene, Kansas. Before McCoy was able to convince the Union Pacific Railroad to extend its tracks into Abilene, ranchers in Texas had no way to get their cattle to beef hungry Eastern and Midwestern markets. Most of the cattle were merely slaughtered for their hides. It was estimated that over 4 million cattle grazed in Texas at the end of the Civil War. Once the marketplace for buyers and sellers of cattle was created, cattlemen had only to get their herds from Texas into the Abilene, Kansas cattle trains. The best known trail for delivering these cattle was called the Chisholm Trail. Its main stem ran from the Rio Grand through Austin, Waco, and Fort Worth, Texas before entering Oklahoma and finally Kansas.

A cattle crew of eleven men, the trail boss, eight cowboys, a wrangler and a cook, usually managed an average herd of 2,500 cattle. Approximately two to four Black cowboys were present on most cattle drives because among them were many of the best riders and ropers in the Midwest. Ironically enough, all cowhands-

whether White or Black-soon became known as cowboys which White Texans strongly resented. The eight cowboys usually rode in pairs with two in the front and rear and two on each side of the herd. Moreover, the cook was usually a retired Black cowboy and the wrangler was frequently a Black teenager who took care of the horses.

Ab Blocker, one of the most famous of the trail bosses, said he intentionally hired large numbers of Black cowboys because of their outstanding performances during the two to three month long arduous and dangerous trail drives. One Black cowboy actually saved his life. All the real cowboys-Black, Brown, Red, and White-shared the same jobs and dangers. They ate the same food and slept in the same area. Cowboys had to be willing to work almost day and night to the point of exhaustion and under the most strenuous conditions. They continuously risked death through drowning (at river crossings) and attacks from wild animals including wolves and snakes. They also faced illness produced by high winds and freezing thunderstorms.

This constant threat of danger developed an extreme comradery among cowboys on the trail. In fact, when a Black cowboy became the first person imprisoned in the new Abilene jail, his Black and White cowboy crew immediately broke him out and ran the sheriff out of town. At the end of their long cattle drives, a few Black cowboys remained on northern ranges to become horse breakers, ranch hands and even sheriffs or outlaws, but most of them drew their pay and rode back to Texas for yet another cattle drive.

Despite the legendary performances of great lawmen like Wyatt Earp and Batt Masterson, Black soldiers, known as the Buffalo Soldiers, were primarily responsible for keeping law and order in the Old West. Their peace keeping missions between cattlemen and farmers (who fought to keep cattle off of their crops) was primarily responsible for making expansion of the cattle empire possible. The Buffalo Soldiers were also the primary force that helped stop Indian attacks on cattlemen moving up the Chisholm Trail. The Congressional Act of July 28, 1866 established two Black infantry regiments and two Calvary regiments. All four saw continuous service in the West during the three decades following the Civil War. The Black Calvary fought in almost every part of the West from Mexico to Montana. Both General Miles and General Merritt praised their black troops as "courageous, skilled, intelligent, and brave in battle."

It should not be surprising that Black men were among the best horse riders in the Old West because they were traditionally responsible for the care and maintenance of horses while working as stable boys, trainers, and jockeys. In fact, thirteen of the fourteen jockeys who participated in the first running of the Kentucky Derby were Black. Moreover, from 1875 until 1902 Black jockeys won eleven Kentucky Derby titles. Isaac Murphy, who won the Kentucky Derby in 1884, 1890, and 1891, was recognized as America's finest rider during the last two decades of the 19th century. Forty years passed before Earl Sande tied his record of three Kentucky Derby titles. Black jockeys continued their outstanding performances until racism barred them from the racetracks and replaced them with White jockeys.

In July 1876, the booming new town of Deadwood, South Dakota, decided to have a roping contest to settle once and for all who was the best roping cowboy. Contestants came from miles around to win the $200 prize. A Black cowboy named Nat Love, who subsequently wrote his autobiography, was several minutes faster than his nearest competition.

With the roping contest completed, a dispute soon arose over who was the best marksman. Nat Love also won the subsequent shooting contest by placing all fourteen of his rifle shots in the bull's eye target at 150 yards. In addition to the prize money, Nat Love was given the title "Deadwood Dick" which he carried with "honor" ever after.

Bill Pickett is credited with having originated the sport of "bulldogging." Bulldogging is defined as "throwing a steer by seizing the horns and twisting the neck." According to Bill Pickett's boss, Zack Miller who owned the 101 Ranch, "Bill Pickett was the greatest sweat and dirt cowhand that ever lived-bar none." The Miller Brothers' 101 Ranch later became famous for putting on one of the finest rodeos in the world and played in such places as Chicago, New York, London, and Mexico City. One of their greatest attractions was Bill Pickett who would actually bring down steers with only his teeth.

As the agricultural frontier moved west, the open range was transformed into farms with barbed-wire boundaries, which significantly reduced the public domain for cattle trails. The long cattle drives also gradually declined as the railroads built branch lines into large Texas cities. By 1890, the legendary era of the cowboy was over, except in fictional novels where Black cowboys completely vanished from their role as self-reliant and masterful heroes of the Old West.

22

The Black Statue of Liberty

In 1798, Napoleon Bonaparte stated that history was only "a lie agreed upon." Nothing could be more illustrative than the history of the Statue of Liberty originally called "Liberty Enlightening the World." The liberation of African-American slaves was the only inspiration for the creation of a Statue of Liberation for Edouard Rene LeFebvre DeLaboulaye. He recruited a young sculptor, Frederick Auguste Bartholdi, to create a Black female slave statue holding a broken chain in her left hand and with broken chains of slavery at her feet.

The official web site of the Statue of Liberty states that the statue was given to the people of the United States by the people of France as an expression of friendship and to commemorate the centennial of American Independence (1776). The Encyclopedia Britannica states Bartholdi designed the Statue of Liberty as a monument to the Franco-American alliance of 1778. These are absolute and total lies! Edouard Rene LeFebvre DeLaboulaye, an internationally renowned lawyer and author of a three-volume history of the United States, first discussed the idea of a symbol to represent the end of U.S. slavery at a dinner party in 1865, at his country home near Versailles, France. In attendance at the dinner party were many abolitionists including Victor Hugo and Frederick Auguste Bartholdi, who had initially been retained to create a sculptured bust of Mr. DeLaboulaye.

Victor Hugo and Edouard DeLaboulaye were leaders of the French abolitionist movement. They hated slavery and were in strong support of John Brown when he attempted to arm slaves in West Virginia for rebellion by raiding the armory at Harpers

Ferry in 1859. After John Brown failed and was hanged, Hugo and DeLaboulaye took up a collection among the French people and presented a gold metal to John Brown's widow.

After Abraham Lincoln was elected president of the United States in 1861, the French liberals and abolitionists including Hugo, Bartholdi, and DeLaboulaye urged Lincoln to free the slaves even if civil war resulted. Lincoln was told: "You would become the first country in history to have fought a war against itself to free the internal slave and you would go down in history as a truly great country and a beacon of light to all freedom loving people." The French abolitionists saw the Emancipation Proclamation of 1863 as a worthless piece of paper since it only freed slaves in the Confederate controlled states where Lincoln had no jurisdiction and not in Union controlled states where Lincoln was still in authority. When the war ended in 1865, French abolitionists were extremely happy and in addition to again urging Lincoln to free all slaves, DeLaboulaye and Bartholdi requested permission to build and dedicate a monument or colossal statuary to that freeing of all slaves in America. When Abraham Lincoln was assassinated, DeLaboulaye again headed the abolitionists' committee that presented a gold metal to Mrs. Lincoln, just as he had done for the widow of John Brown.

In addition to a staunch abolitionist, Frederic Auguste Bartholdi (1834-1904) was an outstanding French sculptor. Bartholdi trained to be an architect in Alsace and Paris and then studied painting with Ary Scheffer and sculpture with J.F. Soitoux. Bartholdi's life and ideas changed dramatically after 1855 when he toured Egypt and witnessed the magnificent colossal monuments and statues created by the ancient Black Egyptians. Bartholdi's creation of a giant Black ex-slave female with broken chairs at her feet and left hand was readily accepted in France. Although liberals, freemasons, and businessmen with American interests were the most enthusiastic supporters of the project, by 1881 some 100,000 people and 181 towns throughout France had contributed money.

In 1871, Frederic Bartholdi at the urging of DeLaboulaye undertook a voyage to America to sale his idea of a colossal statue clearly symbolizing the end of chattel slavery in the United States. He was armed with a large terracotta statue and numerous drawings to clearly illustrate his proposed Statue of Liberty. The original African face of the Statue of Liberty was published in The New York Post dated June 17, 1986 as part of the centennial celebration. Bartholdi found little American support for his African slave model. In 1878, as the African head of Miss Liberty first went on display at the Universal Exposition in Paris, France, rampant reaction raged throughout the American South.

Bartholdi finally had to abandon his original ideas and changed the Statue of Liberty to the features we are now familiar with. The African face was re-sculptured into the face of his mother Madame Bartholdi. A tablet of law tucked into her folded arm that bears the date July 4, 1776, replaced the broken chains in the slave's left hand. Ironically, the chains were left at the feet but the meaning changed from broken American slavery to broken English tyranny.

On May 18, 1986 during the centennial celebration, The New York Times joined The New York Post in describing the original Statue of Liberty and the intention of DeLaboulaye and Bartholdi in presenting this statue to America. It's unconscionable that the Encyclopedia Britannica and the official Statue of Liberty literature can still lie and say that this is a monument celebrating American Independence of 1776 and/or the Franco-American alliance of 1778. Dr. Jack Felder sums it up clearly: "Once in place, Miss Liberty received a new meaning. She was hailed as the 'Mother of White Exiles,' greeting European immigrants seeking freedom in America. Nothing in the original conceptions of Bartholdi or DeLaboulaye envisioned this role for their stature."

23

Lynching

Lynching is defined as mob execution, usually by hanging, without the benefit of trial and often accompanied with torture and body mutilation. The usual scenario included a mob of up to 5,000 White men attacking a single, defenseless Black man and executing him for a crime he was never convicted of or even charged with in most cases. Lynching is considered one of the most horrific chapters in African American history and is only exceeded by slavery in cruelty and savagery toward another human being.

Lynching Statistics

Years	*Whites*	*Blacks*	*Total*
1882-1891	751	732	1,483
1892-1901	381	1,124	1,505
1902-1911	77	707	784
1912-1921	50	554	604
1922-1931	23	201	224
1932-1941	10	95	105
1942-1951	2	25	27
1952-1961	1	5	6
1962-1968	2	2	4
Totals	1,297	3,445	4,742

Ironically, the term "lynch" is derived from the name of Charles Lynch, a Virginia planter and patriot during the American Revolution, who directed violence toward White British loyalists. After the Civil War and emancipation, lynching became almost synonymous with hanging and torturing African American males. Between 1882 and 1930 more than 3,300 Black male victims were hanged, burned alive, castrated, and mutilated by mostly southern White mobs who have never faced any charges for these criminal acts. Coroners and law officials typically attributed the murders to "parties unknown." Most historians and sociologists agree that mob executions was really about social control and to maintain the status quo of White superiority and had little to due with crime control.

Ida B. Wells (1862-1931) could easily be called the mother of the anti-lynching movement. She was the first of eight children born to slave parents in Holly Springs, Mississippi. After emancipation, she attended several schools run by northern Methodist missionaries including Rust College. In 1879, after the yellow fever epidemic claimed the lives of both her parents, she moved to Memphis, Tennessee with the younger children and accepted a teaching position. Because of her great concern for racial injustice, Wells was invited to write for a local church paper. As her fame increased, she was asked to contribute to several Baptist newspapers. She eventually became editor and partner of the "Free Speech and Headlight" Baptist newspaper.

In 1892, the brutal lynching of three close friends in Memphis started Ida B. Wells on a militant, uncompromising, single-minded crusade against lynching from which she would never retreat. Her three friends committed the crime of opening a grocery store, which successfully competed with a White grocer directly across the street. For the crime of becoming too "uppity", a large White mob took the three proprietors from their grocery store, tortured and killed them. Ms. Wells wrote angry editorials in her newspaper encouraging Blacks to leave Memphis if possible and to boycott White businesses, which left several White companies including the newly opened streetcar line on the verge of bankruptcy.

Ida B. Wells decided to launch her anti-lynching movement on several fronts. She first wanted to explode the myth that lynching was primarily to protect White women from rape by Black men. She published detailed statistics on lynching, which demonstrated that less than one-fifth of the victims of lynch mobs were even accused of rape by their killers. She said that racist southern White mobs "cry rape" to brand their victims as "moral monsters" and to place them "beyond the pale of human sympathy." She wrote that while Southern White men raped Black women and children with impunity, they considered any liaison between a Black man and a White woman as involuntary by definition. She pointed out that children produced by White-Black relationships were called "mulatto" from the Spanish word for mule because racist Whites believed that mixed-race children, like the offspring of donkeys and horses, were an inferior breed that could not reproduce. When Ms. Wells suggested in print that White women were often willing participants with Black men, a large White mob destroyed the presses of her newspaper and would have killed her had she not been visiting friends in New York. Thomas Fortune invited her to stay in New York and write for the "New York Age". She was also allowed to exchange the circulation list of the "Free Speech" for a one fourth interest in the "Age" and immediately began to write a series on lynching.

The second approach of Ida B. Wells in her anti-lynching movement was to appeal to the Christian conscience of powerful non-southern Whites. She published two pamphlets ("Southern Horror" in 1892 and "A Red Book" in 1895) in hopes that extensive statistical analyses of lynching would clearly point out that the southern rape fantasy was merely "an excuse to get rid of Negroes who were acquiring wealth and property." She pointed out that the same lynch mob that killed a Nashville Black man accused of visiting a White woman left unharmed a White man convicted of raping an eight year old girl. Since Ms. Well's viewed lynching as primarily an economic issue, she hoped that economic pressure from the "ruling-class Whites" could produce southern social change. She began a lecture tour in the Northeast in 1892 and in 1894 she lectured in England where she helped organize the British Anti-Lynching Society. Ms. Wells was able to effect a curtailment of British investment in the South by suggesting that this could influence American sentiment. In 1895, Ida B. Wells toured the northern and western states organizing American anti-lynching societies.

Ida B. Wells told African Americans that her analysis of mob violence suggested that it abated whenever Blacks exercised "manly self-defense." In "Southern Horrors" she suggested, "a Winchester rifle should have a place of honor in every Black home." She also told Blacks that they must retaliate with their economic power. She urged Blacks to boycott White businesses or to migrate to Oklahoma since Black labor was the industrial strength of the South. She said: "The more the Afro-American yields and cringes and begs, the more he has to do so, the more he is insulted, outraged, and lynched."

Since Southern courts would not punish lynching participants, Ms. Wells lobbied for legislation that would make lynching a federal crime. In 1901, Ida B. Wells met with President William McKinley and pressed for his support with anti-lynching legislation. However, she could not get McKinley or Theodore Roosevelt to support an anti-lynching bill that was introduced in Congress in 1902. As one of the founding members of the NAACP in 1909, she made her anti-lynching campaign including anti-lynching legislation among the NAACP's highest priorities. The NAACP investigated specific incidents and published national statistics on lynching in an attempt to sway public support to put a stop to lynching. In 1918, the NAACP was able to get Republican Congressman Leonidas Dyer to introduce a bill that subjected lynch mobs to a charge of capital murder for their actions. The Dyer Bill passed in the House of Representatives but failed in the Senate because southern Democrats never allowed the bill out of committee. Congressman Dyer re-introduced the bill each year for the next ten years, but it never again passed either house.

As a result of the life-long crusade of Ida B. Wells against lynching, she became the inspiration for organizations throughout the country that opposed lynching. For example, The American Civil Liberties Union, The Commission on Interracial Cooperation, and The Communist Party of the United States all played a role in the anti-lynching campaign. Ironically, White middle class Southern women for whom lynching was suppose to protect, formed the Jessie Daniel Ames Association of Southern Women for the Prevention of Lynching in 1930. In honor of her legacy, a low-income housing project in Chicago was named after Ida B. Wells in 1941; and in 1990, the U.S. Postal Service issued an Ida B. Wells commemorative stamp. The "militant," "uncompromising," "outspoken," and "fearless" Ida B. Wells can surely look back upon her life as a genuine success in helping to end one of the most horrific chapters in African American history.

FIVE BLACK PRESIDENTS

Joel A. Rogers and Dr. Auset Bakhufu have both written books documenting that at least five former presidents of the United States had Black people among their ancestors. If one considers the fact that European men far outnumbered European women during the founding of this country, and that the rape and impregnation of an African female slave was not considered a crime, it is even more surprising that these two authors could not document Black ancestors among an ever larger number of former presidents. The presidents they name include Thomas Jefferson, Andrew Jackson, Abraham Lincoln, Warren Harding, and Calvin Coolidge.

The best case for Black ancestry is against Warren G. Harding, our 29th president from 1921 until 1923. Harding himself never denied his ancestry. When Republican leaders called on Harding to deny the "Negro" history, he said, "How should I know whether or not one of my ancestors might have jumped the fence." William Chancellor, a White professor of economics and politics at Wooster College in Ohio, wrote a book on the Harding family genealogy and identified Black ancestors among both parents of President Harding. Justice Department agents allegedly bought and destroyed all copies of this book. Chancellor also said that Harding's only academic credentials included education at Iberia College, which was founded in order to educate fugitive slaves.

Andrew Jackson was our 7th president from 1829 to 1837. The Virginia Magazine of History, Volume 29, says that Jackson was the son of a White woman from Ireland who had intermarried with a Negro. The magazine also said that his eldest brother had been sold as a slave in Carolina. Joel Rogers says that Andrew Jackson Sr. died long before President Andrew Jackson Jr. was born. He says the president's mother then went to live on the Crawford farm where there were Negro slaves and that one of these men was Andrew Jr's father. Another account of the "brother sold into slavery" story can be found in David Coyle's book entitled

"Ordeal of the Presidency" (1960). Thomas Jefferson was our 3rd president from 1801 to 1809. The chief attack on Jefferson was in a book written by Thomas Hazard in 1867 called "The Johnny Cake Papers." Hazard interviewed Paris Gardiner, who said he was present during the 1796 presidential campaign, when one speaker states that Thomas Jefferson was "a mean-spirited son of a half-breed Indian squaw and a Virginia mulatto father." In his book entitled "The Slave Children of Thomas Jefferson," Samuel Sloan wrote that Jefferson destroyed all of the papers, portraits, and personal effects of his mother, Jane Randolph Jefferson, when she died on March 31, 1776. He even wrote letters to every person who had ever received a letter from his mother, asking them to return that letter. Sloan says, "There is something strange and even psychopathic about the lengths to which Thomas Jefferson went to destroy all remembrances of his mother, while saving over 18,000 copies of his own letters and other documents for posterity." One must ask, "What is it he was trying to hide?"

Abraham Lincoln was our 16th president from 1861 to 1865. J. A. Rogers quotes Lincoln's mother, Nancy Hanks, as saying that Abraham Lincoln was the illegitimate son of an African man. William Herndon, Lincoln's law partner, said that Lincoln had very dark skin and coarse hair and that his mother was from an Ethiopian tribe. In Herndon's book entitled "The Hidden Lincoln" he says that Thomas Lincoln could not have been Abraham Lincoln's father because he was sterile from childhood mumps and was later castrated. Lincoln's presidential opponents made cartoon drawings depicting him as a Negro and nicknamed him "Abraham Africanus the First."

Calvin Coolidge was our 30th president, and he succeeded Warren Harding. He proudly admitted that his mother was dark because of mixed Indian ancestry. However, Dr. Bakhufu says that by 1800 the New England Indian was hardly any longer pure Indian, because they had mixed so often with Blacks. Calvin Coolidge's mother's maiden name was "Moor." In Europe the name "Moor" was given to all Black people just as the name Negro was used in America.

All of the presidents mentioned were able to pass for White and never acknowledged their Black ancestry. Millions of other children who were descendants of former slaves have also been able to pass for White. American society has had so much interracial mixing that books such as "The Bell Curve", discussing IQ evaluations based solely on race, are totally unrealistic.

BLACK INVENTORS

When the famous anthropologist Dr. Richard Leakey discovered bones in Africa in 1956, which were millions of years old, his accomplishment was belittled by people who regularly asked the question, "but what has Africa contributed to world progress?" He could not understand why people were so poorly informed, since he knew that the collective contributions of Black people to civilization, science, and invention are so extensive that it is not possible to live a full day in the United States, or any other part of the world without sharing in the benefits of those contributions. Still the genius of the Black imagination that has influenced every aspect of life in the United States and elsewhere is virtually unknown to most people.

Very few homes in America have as many as two books, which discuss the achievements of the Black race, either past or present. During the slave trade, many of the slaves from the former Songhay Empire were highly educated and were credited with teaching Caribbean and American farmers successful agricultural techniques. They also invented various tools and equipment to lessen the burden of their daily work. Most slave inventors were nameless, such as the slave owned by the Confederate President Jefferson Davis who designed the ship propeller used by the entire Confederate Navy.

Following the Civil War, the growth of industry in this country was tremendous and much of this was made possible with inventions by ethnic minorities. By 1913 over 1,000 inventions were patented by Black Americans. Among the most notable inventors were Jan Matzeliger, who developed the first machine to mass-produce shoes, and Elijah McCoy, who invented automatic lubrication devices for steam engines. Granville Woods had 35 patents to improve electric railway systems including the first system to allow moving trains to communicate. He even sued Alexander Graham Bell and Thomas Edison for stealing his patents and won both cases. Garrett Morgan developed the first automatic traffic signal and gas mask, and Norbert Rilleux who created the technique for converting sugar cane juice into white sugar crystals. Moreover, Rillieux was so brilliant that in 1854 he left Louisiana and went to France where he spent ten years working with the Champollions deciphering Egyptian hieroglyphics from the Rosetta Stone. Lewis Latimer created an inexpensive cotton-thread filament, which made electric light bulbs practical because Edison's original light bulb only burned for a few minutes. More recent inventors include McKinley Jones, who invented the movable refrigeration unit for food transport in trucks and trains and Lloyd Quarterman who with six other Black scientists, worked on the creation of the atomic bomb along (code named the Manhattan Project.) Quaterman also helped develop the first nuclear reactor, which was used in the atomically powered submarine called the Nautilus.

Lets conclude with two current contributors. It should not be surprising that we don't know about the wonderful contributions of Blacks in the past because we are not even made aware of the startling scientific achievements during our own lifetime. For example, Otis Bodkin invented an electrical device used in all guided missiles and all IBM computers, and Colonel Frederick Gregory, who was not only the first Black astronaut pilot but the person who also redesigned the cockpits for the last three space shuttles. Gregory was also on the team that pioneered the microwave instrumentation landing system. In 2000, Bendix Aircraft Company began a worldwide promotion of this microwave instrumentation landing system that can land planes without a pilot.

WEST POINT ACADEMY AND BLACK CADETS

President Thomas Jefferson under an 1802 Act of Congress, initially established the U.S. Military at West Point, New York, as a corps of engineers. General Sylvanus Thayer was appointed superintendent in 1814, and became known as the "Father of West Point" because of his academic expansion. Since members of Congress had to nominate West Point cadets, no African Americans were nominated until the Reconstruction period when Black voters elected Black Congressmen. The 13th, 14th, and 15th constitutional amendments made election of Black Congressmen possible. Emancipation was accomplished by the 13th amendment (1865); citizenship through the 14th amendment (1868); and the 15th amendment granted suffrage to Black males (1870).

African American Congressmen nominated 27 Blacks to West Point Academy between 1870 and 1887. Only 12 members of the group passed the academic and physical examinations for admission. Academically, they were examined in mathematics (including fractions and decimals) in addition to the rules of correct grammar. Candidates also had to demonstrate knowledge of "U.S. and world geography, by discussing various historical periods, wars, and U.S. administrations." The physical examination required the absence of infectious and chronic disease. During the four-year program, the cadets studied French, Spanish, chemistry, engineering, philosophy, law, mathematics (including calculus), mineralogy, and geology. Despite the many nominations, only three African Americans graduated from West Point Academy during its first 130 years of existence.

The first African American nominated to West Point was James Webster Smith who attended from 1870 until January 1874. James Smith was described as "a hot headed activist, bent on righting the wrongs of racial inequality." Smith was forced to repeat his first year at West Point because of an alleged lie in response to a charge of inattention in the ranks. After his fourth year, Smith wrote his patron, David Clark of Connecticut, complaining about the academy's mistreatment of Black cadets. His letters sparked a congressional board of inquiry, which eventually recommended the court martial of several White cadets. However, since one of the White cadets was the nephew of William Belknap, Secretary of War, the punishment was reduced to a mere reprimand. Smith's personal and public need to eradicate social injustice at West Point Academy resulted in extreme classmate hatred and the eventual dismissal of Smith from the academy for fighting after a court martial and three-week imprisonment.

Johnson Chesnut Whittaker was chosen to fill the vacancy created by James Smith's dismissal. Contrary to Smith, Whittaker was described as a quiet, shy, cowardly student who sought solace in the Bible. After completing four years and just prior to his final examinations, Whittaker was found on the floor of his room, "bleeding and insensible, bound hand and foot to his bedstead. His head was partly shaved, and his feet and hands slashed." Whittaker claimed that three masked men were responsible, and this created such uproar in the press that Congress initiated another investigation. A court of inquiry accused Whittaker of self-mutilation to avoid his final examinations. He received a court marital and was sentenced to a dishonorable discharge from the military and one year hard labor in prison. President Chester Arthur reversed the entire proceedings but did not allow him to finish West Point.

Henry Flipper, a former slave, was a roommate of both James Smith and Johnson Whittaker and was determined to finish West Point Academy at all costs. Henry received his appointment to West Point Academy upon the recommendation of Congressman James Freeman, who needed the Black vote for re-election. Despite threats, bribes as high as $5,000, and refusal of any cadets to speak to him for four years, Flipper became the first Black West Point graduate on June 14, 1877. Prominent Blacks throughout the nation were proud of Flipper's accomplishment and Charles Douglass, son of Frederick Douglass, sponsored a New York City reception in his honor.

On January 2, 1878 Flipper received his commission as second lieutenant and was assigned to the all Black 10th U.S. Calvary (called the Buffalo Soldiers) at Fort Sill, Oklahoma. Henry Flipper performed exceptionally well during his first four years and was well liked by everyone. He served admirably in a number of combat assignments on the frontier and also worked brilliantly as an engineer. He designed and perfected a drainage system that eliminated diseased stagnant rainwater (and subsequent malaria) that was plaguing the fort. Still known as "Flipper's Ditch", it became a national landmark in 1977. Unfortunately, he was transferred to Fort Davis, Texas in 1881 commanded by the racist Colonel William Shafter. Shafter disliked Blacks in general and the Buffalo Soldiers in particular. Shortly after Lieutenant Flipper's arrival, he was accused of stealing commissary funds. Flipper stated at his court martial that he hid the funds in his personal trunk because there was no secure place to keep the commissary funds and that Colonel Shafter was fully aware of this. Despite the fact that Colonel Shafter had Lucy Smith, Flipper's White housekeeper, laundress, and cook, searched and that $2,800 in commissary checks were found in her blouse, this fact was never mentioned at the trial. Moreover, the local town merchants, who highly admired Flipper, took up a collection and replaced all the missing funds. The court martial panel could not convict Flipper of embezzlement but were able to convict him of "conduct unbecoming an officer and gentleman." Although the Army's judge advocate general concluded that the conviction was racially motivated, President Chester Arthur refused to reverse his conviction, and Flipper was dishonorably discharged.

Henry Flipper used his outstanding education at West Point Academy to carve out a distinguished career as a civil and mining engineer, especially in and around Mexico, since he had learned fluent Spanish. He initially worked for an American mining company surveying land in Mexico. When Texas and Arizona joined the United States, Flipper translated Spanish land deeds and titles for the Land Grant Court and investigated their authenticity in Mexico City records. Flipper later joined the Justice Department and Senate Foreign Relations Committee as an expert on Mexican political developments. Subsequently, Secretary of Interior, Albert Fall, a close friend of Henry Flipper, chose him as chief civil engineer in determining the course for the Alaskan railroad lines.

Flipper unsuccessfully devoted his entire life to clearing his name. Four bills were introduced in Congress between 1903 and 1908 to clear Flipper, but racist southern politicians allowed the bills to die in committee. Despite all of his accomplishments, he died bitterly disappointed in 1940 at age 84. The redemption of Flipper's name was rekindled by a schoolteacher from Valdosta, Georgia named Ray MacColl who learned about Flipper while taking a Black history course and embarked on a tireless campaign to right what he regarded as a major injustice. Through MacColl's efforts, the Army's Board for the Correction of Military Records reviewed the circumstances of Flipper's discharge and changed his discharge from dishonorable to honorable in 1976. Moreover in 1977, exactly 100 years after his graduation, the Henry O. Flipper

Memorial Award was established at West Point Academy and is given annually to the cadet who best demonstrates leadership, self discipline, and perseverance. On February 11, 1978, his remains were moved from an unmarked grave in Atlanta and reburied, with full military honors in his hometown of Thomasville, Georgia.

On February 19, 1999, President Clinton granted Henry Flipper the first post-humorous pardon in American history, calling the pardon "an event that is 117 years overdue." Retired General Colin Powell, who attended the pardon ceremony, kept a picture of Flipper on the wall of his office at the Pentagon when he was Chairman of the Joint Chief of Staff. Powell wrote in his autobiography: "We knew that the path through the underbrush of prejudice and discrimination had been cleared by the sacrifices of nameless Blacks who had gone before us, the Henry Flippers...and to them we owed everything."

Henry Flipper is now a revered figure at West Point where a memorial bust is dedicated to him in the cadet library. Eighty Black cadets graduated in West Point Academy's class of 2000, and they should never forget that African Americans "stand tall because we stand on the shoulders of those who came before us." Pioneers are those with "arrows in their backs," and we must never stop honoring our pioneers.

BROWNSVILLE, TEXAS AND BLACK SOLDIERS

Despite stellar performances through five previous wars, Black servicemen in the early 1900s were hated by the South and despised and unappreciated by the North. Southerners hated Blacks in uniform because radical Republicans in Congress had used Black soldiers to police the South during Reconstruction and as added humiliation after their Civil War defeat. After Reconstruction, Black soldiers were sent to the Western frontier to fight "hostile Indians," but found the environment of White racism tremendously more hostile than the Native Americans. Nothing more typified American racial hatred for the Black soldier than the "Brownsville Affair."

During the summer of 1906 the first battalion of the 25th infantry regiment was transferred from Fort Niobrara in Nebraska to Fort Brown, a post near Brownsville, Texas at the mouth of the

Rio Grande River, to protect against Mexican revolutionaries. These 167 men had outstanding credentials for service, loyalty, discipline, and bravery during battles fought in Cuba and the Philippines. Six of these Black soldiers held the Medal of Honor and thirteen had been awarded citations for bravery in the Spanish-American War. More than half of the soldiers had been in uniform for more than five years; twenty five had served in active duty for more than ten years; and one had accrued more that twenty seven years. The citizens of Brownsville were appalled and wrote William Howard Taft, the Secretary of War, requesting that he keep the White 26th infantry at Fort Brown instead. The War Department refused to repeal the order and responded to the Brownsville citizens: "The fact is that a certain amount of race prejudice between Whites and Blacks seems to have become almost universal throughout the country, and no matter where colored troops are sent there are always some who make objections to their coming."

The Brownsville citizens immediately posted new signs announcing "NO NIGGERS OR DOGS ALLOWED" on saloons, restaurants, and all public and recreational facilities. However, since Brownsville is located near the Mexican border, most of the town's inhabitants were low paid Mexican workers, and these Hispanics welcomed the soldiers at their establishments. Consequently, Whites became very concerned that the assertive Black infantrymen might inspire Mexicans to challenge the status quo of White dominance and to resist local Jim Crow practices. As much as the White citizens of Brownsville hated Black soldiers, they saw an interracial alliance as an even greater threat to their town and felt compelled to eliminate the Black military presence by whatever means necessary.

Shortly after midnight on August 14, 1906 a group of men across the road from Fort Brown and dressed in army uniforms began firing shots randomly into buildings and at streetlights for about ten minutes. The random bullets killed a bartender, and seriously wounded a police lieutenant. Military rifle cartridges and clips from Springfield rifles recently issued to the 25th regiment were found at the scene. Several Brownsville citizens immediately claimed that they saw Blacks shooting. Major Penrose said it could not have been Black soldiers because all the battalion's soldiers were accounted for by company commanders at the 10:00 PM curfew check and again immediately after the shooting. The rifles were also checked and none had been recently fired. The Major stated that anyone could wear an army uniform because old uniforms were routinely discarded outside the fort and that ammunition and rifles were known to have been sold to the citizens of Brownsville by the White 26th regiment that occupied the fort before the Black soldiers. Brownsville Mayor, Fred Come, organized an investigating committee of local citizens who found witnesses who professed to have heard voices that sounded Black. Five witnesses said they saw Black soldiers but could not identify anyone, and they were not under oath. The committee prefaced their questions by stating: "We know that this outrage was committed by Negro soldiers. We want any information that will lead to a discovery of who did it." The committee did not call a single soldier to the inquiry.

After one day of testimony the committee sent a telegram to President Theodore Roosevelt stating: "Our women and children are terrified and our men practically under constant alarm and watchfulness. No community can stand this strain...we ask you to have the troops at once removed from Fort Brown and replaced by White soldiers." President Roosevelt ordered two investigations, one by Major August Blocksom and a second by General Ernest Garlington, a racist native of South Carolina. They took as evidence the testimony of White citizens and spent military cartridges and concurred that Black soldiers had committed the crime. They completely ignored the testimony of a civilian employee of the fort who swore that after the shooting he had seen four Brownsville citizens dressed in uniforms and carrying rifles. The officers concluded that the Black soldiers' denial of the shooting was proof of "collusion" and a "conspiracy-of-silence" and since no soldier would confess, they recommended dismissing the entire battalion. General Garlington added: "The secretive nature of the race, where crimes charged to members of their color are made, is well known."

President Theodore Roosevelt delayed his decision until after his re-election so as not to loose much needed Black support. Subsequently, on November 28, 1906, he ordered the discharge of all 167 soldiers of the first battalion without honor, and he denied the soldiers all back pay and pension benefits. The soldiers never received a formal trial or the benefit of legal counsel, and this remains the only example of mass punishment without the benefit of trial in U.S. military history. White people across the country celebrated Roosevelt's decision. The "New Orleans Picayune" reported: "Whatever may be the value of the Negro troops in time of war, the fact remains they are a curse to the country in time of peace." In December 1906 during the first congressional session after the Brownsville incident, Congressman John Garner of Texas, whose district included Brownsville, introduced a bill that "called for elimination of all Blacks currently in the military and barring Black enlistment." Although his bill was defeated, he re-introduced similar bills in each of the next three sessions. Franklin Roosevelt rewarded Garner's racial hatred by selecting him as his vice president in 1932 and 1936.

Senator Joseph Foraker of Ohio tried to rally support without success for the Black soldiers and even proposed a bill providing the men an opportunity to reenlist. Foraker's defense of the Brownsville soldiers and criticism of the White House "so infuriated Theodore Roosevelt that the President proceeded to "hound the Senator from public life." However, 66 years later (March 1971) Black California Congressman Augustus Hawkins introduced legislation to amend the records of the 25th regiment to "honorable discharge." On December 6, 1972, President Nixon signed a bill authorizing a one-time pension payment of $25,000 to 86 year old Dorsie Willis, the only survivor among those discharged, and thus partially corrected one of the greatest injustices in military history.

BLACK SCIENTISTS

In a review of historical literature, one is appalled by the absence of serious attention given to Black scientists by American historians. Yet, the collective contribution of Black Americans to science is so extensive that it is not possible to live a full day in any part of the United States or the world for that matter, without sharing in the benefits of their contributions in such fields as: biology, chemistry, physics, space and nuclear science.

The first scientific book ever written by an African American is believed to be the Astronomical Almanac published by Benjamin

Banneker in 1792; and he continued to publish this almanac for the next ten years. Banneker's almanac sold very well among White farmers and was extremely accurate in predicting: eclipses, high and low tides, positions of planets, times for sunrise and sunset, and many other useful items of information. Thomas Jefferson was so impressed by this self-taught mathematical genius that he sent a copy of Banneker's almanac to the Academy of Sciences in Paris to prove that the color of a person's skin had nothing to do with intelligence. Jefferson also had Benjamin Banneker appointed to the Federal Commission which planned and laid out Washington, D.C. When the head of the commission, Pierre L'Enfant, angrily quit and took all the plans back to France, Banneker was the only one able to reproduce the entire map and layout from memory; thus allowing our nation's capital to be completed.

The first national monument ever erected in honor of an African American was erected for George Washington Carver. A postage stamp was also issued in his honor. George Washington Carver, a former slave, was among the most outstanding agricultural scientists in the world. When the boll weevil completely destroyed the southern cotton industry, Carver saved the southern economy from financial ruin by convincing the farmers to grow peanuts instead. Moreover, his scientific research was able to create more than 300 products from the peanut and its shell. George Washington Carver was also an expert in detecting and treating plant diseases and was a collaborator for the U.S. Bureau of Plant Industry. Thomas Edison and Henry Ford both offered Carver large sums of money to work for them, but he never left his teaching position at Tuskegee Institute.

Percy Lavon Julian was one of America's premier chemists. His scientific work ranged from developing new substances that snuffed out gasoline and oil fires to synthesizing the drug Cortisone, which eases the pain of people with Rheumatoid Arthritis. Julian received 105 U.S. patents for chemical products and processes including two patents for his synthesis of male and female sex hormones called testosterone and progesterone. After working 17 years as Director of Research at the Glidden Chemical Company of Chicago, Illinois, he founded the Julian Laboratories Incorporated in 1954, with plants in Chicago, Illinois and Guatemala, Mexico. His plants became immensely successful and in 1961, Julian sold the Guatemala plant to the Upjohn Company, and the Chicago plant to Smith, Kline and French Company. Percy Julian succeeded as a major contributor to science despite the extreme hardships he endured because of his race, including the fact that he had to obtain his Ph.D. from the University of Vienna in Austria because American universities would not accept him.

Other famous African American scientists include Charles R. Drew who made possible the availability of stored blood plasma for blood transfusions. Dr. William Hinton devoted 30 years to research on syphilis. In 1935, the "Hinton Test" for syphilis was adopted by the entire state of Massachusetts, and in 1936 Hinton's book "Syphilis and its Treatment" became the first medical textbook written by an African American ever published.

Famous Black physicists include Dr. Lloyd Quarterman who helped develop the atomic bomb and the first nuclear reactor for atomic powered submarines. Christine Darden was the leading NASA researcher in supersonic aircraft with expertise in the area of reducing sonic boom.

Despite the fact that only about three percent of American scientists have been Black, they have made tremendous contributions for the benefit and betterment of mankind. It is truly a crime that the genius and imagination of the African American scientist is generally unknown to most Americans, both Black and White.

THE BLACK (NEGRO) WALL STREET

The "Black (Negro) Wall Street" was the name given to Greenwood Avenue of North Tulsa, Oklahoma during the early 1900's. Because of strict segregation, Blacks were only allowed to shop, spend, and live in a 35 square block area called the Greenwood District. The "circulation of Black dollars" only in the Black community produced a tremendously prosperous Black business district that was admired and envied by the whole country.

Oklahoma's first African American settlers were Indian slaves of the so-called "Five Civilized Tribes": Chickasaws, Choctaws, Cherokees, Creeks, and Seminoles. These tribes were forced to leave the Southeastern United States and resettle in Oklahoma in mid-winter over the infamous "Trail of Tears." After the Civil War, U.S.-Indian treaties provided for slave liberation and land allotments ranging from 40-100 acres, which helps explain why over 6,000 African-Americans lived in the Oklahoma territory by 1870. Oklahoma boasted of more all-Black towns and communities than any other state in the land, and these communities opened their arms to freed slaves from all across the country. Remarkably, at one time, there were over 30 African-American newspapers in Oklahoma.

Tulsa began as an outpost of the Creek Indians and as late as 1910, Walter White of the NAACP, described Tulsa as "the dead and hopeless home of 18,182 souls." Suddenly, oil was discovered and Tulsa rapidly grew into a thriving, bustling, enormously wealthy town of 73,000 by 1920 with bank deposits totaling over $65 million. However, Tulsa was a "tale of two cities isolated and insular," one Black and one White. Tulsa was so racist and segregated that it was the only city in America that boasted of segregated telephone booths.

Since African Americans could neither live among Whites as equals nor patronize White businesses in Tulsa, Blacks had to develop a completely separate business district and community, which soon became prosperous and legendary. Black dollars invested in the Black community also produced self-pride, self-sufficiency, and self-determination. The business district, beginning at the intersection of Greenwood Avenue and Archer Street, became so successful and vibrant that Booker T. Washington during his visit bestowed the moniker: "Negro Wall Street." By 1921, Tulsa's African-American population of 11,000 had its own bus line, two high schools, one hospital, two newspapers, two theaters, three drug stores, four hotels, a public library, and thirteen churches. In addition, there were over 150 two and three story brick commercial buildings that housed clothing and grocery stores, cafes, rooming houses, nightclubs, and a large number of professional offices including doctors, lawyers, and dentists. Tulsa's progressive African American community boasted some of the city's most elegant brick homes, well furnished with china, fine linens, beautiful furniture, and grand pianos. Mary Elizabeth

Parrish from Rochester, New York wrote: "In the residential section there were homes of beauty and splendor which would please the most critical eye." Well known African American personalities often visited the Greenwood district including: educators Mary McCloud Bethune and W.E.B. DuBois, scientist George Washington Carver, opera singer Marian Anderson, blues singer Dinah Washington, and noted Chicago chemist Percy Julian.

T.P. Scott wrote in "Negro City Directory": "Early African American business leaders in Tulsa patterned the development of Tulsa's thriving Greenwood district after the successful African American entrepreneurial activity in Durham, North Carolina." After the Civil War, former slaves moved to Durham from the neighboring farmlands and found employment in tobacco processing plants. By 1900, a large Black middle class had developed which began businesses that soon grew into phenomenally successful corporations, especially North Carolina Mutual Life Insurance Company. Charles Clinton Spaulding was so successful with the North Carolina Mutual Life Insurance Company that he was able to create a real estate company, a textile and hosiery mill, and the "Durham Negro Observer" newspaper. Durham Blacks also created a hospital, Mechanics and Farmers Bank (1908), North Carolina Training College (1910), Banker's Fire Insurance Company (1920), and the National Negro Finance Company (1922). However, living conditions in Durham were so substandard and working conditions so poor that the 1920 mortality rate among Blacks in Durham was three times higher than the White rate. As of 1926, 64% of all African Americans in Durham died before the age of 40. These perilous working and living conditions were not present in Tulsa.

On May 31, 1921, the successful Black Greenwood district was completely destroyed by one of the worse race riots in U.S. history. A 19 year old Black male accidentally stumbled on a jerky elevator and bumped the 17-year-old White elevator operator who screamed. The frightened young fellow was seen running from the elevator by a group of Whites and by late afternoon the "Tulsa Tribune" reported that the girl had been raped. Despite the girl's denial of any wrongdoing, the boy was arrested and a large mob of 2,000 White men came to the jail to lynch the prisoner. About seventy five armed African Americans came to the jail to offer assistance to the sheriff to protect the prisoner. The sheriff not only refused the assistance but also deputized the White mob to disarm the Blacks. With a defenseless Black community before them, the White mob advanced to the Greenwood district where they first looted and then burned all Black businesses, homes, and churches.

Any Black resisters were shot and thrown into the fires. When the National Guard arrived, they assisted the others by arresting all Black men, women, and children, and herding them into detention centers at the Baseball Park and Convention Hall. As many as 4,000 Blacks were held under armed guard in detention. Dr. Arthur C. Jackson, a nationally renowned surgeon and called by the Mayo brothers (of Mayo Clinic fame) "the most able Negro surgeon in America," was shot at the Convention Hall and allowed to bleed to death.

The "Chicago Tribute" Newspaper reported that Whites also used private airplanes to drop kerosene and dynamite on Black homes. By the next morning the entire Greenwood district was reduced to ashes and not one White was even accused of any wrongdoing, much less arrested.

The race riot of Tulsa, Oklahoma was not an isolated event in American history. On May 28, 1917, a White mob of over 3,000 in East St. Louis, Illinois ravaged African American stores, homes, and churches. Eyewitnesses reported that over one hundred Blacks were gunned down as they left their burning homes including a small Black child who was shot and thrown back into the burning building to die. Seven White police officers charged with murder by the Illinois Attorney General were collectively fined $150. During the "Red Summer" of 1919, over twenty-five race riots, where White mobs attacked black neighborhoods. were recorded.

In the 1919 race riot at Elaine, Arkansas, White mobs killed over 200 African Americans and burned their homes and businesses. Federal troops arrested hundreds of Blacks trying to protect their possessions and forcibly held them in basements of the city's public schools. Twelve Blacks were indicted (no Whites) and convicted of inciting violence and sentenced to die. The NAACP persuaded the U.S. Supreme Count for the first time in history to reverse a racially biased Southern court.

Director John Singleton exposed the horror of the Rosewood, Florida massacre of 1922 in his film entitled "Rosewood." A White mob burned down the entire town and tried to kill all of its Black inhabitants. In April 1994, the Florida legislature passed the "Rosewood Bill," which awarded $150,000 to each of the riot's nine eligible Black survivors.

After the Tulsa riot, the White inhabitants tried to buy the Black property and force Black people out of town. No Tulsa bank or lending institution would make loans in the riot-marred Greenwood district, and the city refused all outside assistance. However, racial pride and self-determination would not permit the Greenwood owners to sell, and they doggedly spend the entire winter in tents donated by the American Red Cross.

Rebuilding was a testament to the courage and stamina of Tulsa's pioneers in their struggle for freedom. Most of the buildings along the first block of Greenwood Avenue were rebuilt within one year. Henry Whitlow wrote: "A little over a decade after the riot, everything was more prosperous than before." In 1926, W.E.B. DuBois visited Tulsa and wrote: "Black Tulsa is a happy city. It has new clothes. It is young and gay and strong. Five little years ago, fire and blood and robbery leveled it to the ground. Scars are there, but the city is impudent and noisy. It believes in itself. Thank God for the grit of Black Tulsa." Like Black Tulsa, African Americans can continue to survive by self-pride, self-help, and self-determination.

MARCUS MOSIAH GARVEY

Marcus Mosiah Garvey (1887-1940) arrived in the United States from Jamaica almost penniless in 1916, but within six years he boasted of an organization with branches worldwide that had over six million registered members. He was almost worshipped by the Black masses throughout the world for his vision to organize the Black race through race pride, education, self-reliance, economic development, and the desire to build a strong African motherland controlled by Africans. Garvey wrote: "I read Booker T. Washington's 'Up From Slavery' and then my doom-if I may so call it-of being a race leader dawned upon me. I asked, Where is the Black man's government? Where is his king and kingdom?

Where is his president, his country, his ambassadors, his army, his navy, and his men of big affairs? I could not find them. I decided, I will help to make them."

Marcus Garvey founded the Universal Negro Improvement Association (UNIA) in Harlem in 1918. By 1924, there were over 700 branches in 38 states and over 200 branches throughout the world, as far away as South Africa at a time when there was no E-mail, television, or even radio to advertise. Those who could not hear Garvey directly received his views through his newspaper called the "Negro World", which boasted a circulation as high as 200,000 by 1924. The most recent speeches of Marcus Garvey were published in addition to articles on race pride, self-reliance, and anti-colonialism. In 1919, the UNIA and "Negro World" were blamed for the numerous violent colonial uprisings in Jamaica, Grenada, Belize, Trinidad, and Tobago. British and French authorities deported all UNIA organizers and banned the "Negro World" from all their colonies, but seamen continued to smuggle the paper throughout the world. In 1921, the U.S. Marines invaded a UNIA meeting in the Dominican Republic and arrested every man, woman, and child in attendance. In Rhodesia (Zimbabwe), in 1927, an African was given life imprisonment for smuggling in only three copies of the newspaper. Although the "Negro World" was banned in Kenya, Jomo Kenyatta, the first president of independent Kenya, told how "someone who could understand English would read Garvey's 'Negro World' message to a group of Africans until they were able to memorize it. They would then spread the message far and wide throughout the countryside."

"Race first" was the first major theme of Garvey in his attempt to restore race pride and to destroy the inferiority complex of Black people. Garvey demanded that Black people have Black heroes: "Take down the pictures of White men and women from your walls and elevate your own men and women to that place of honor. Mothers! Give your children dolls that look like them to play with and cuddle." He demanded that his followers abandon skin lighteners and hair straighteners. Garvey said: "God made no mistake when he made us Black with kinky hair...take the kinks out of your minds instead of your hair." In religion, Garvey insisted that Black people should worship images of God and angels that look like them. Marcus Garvey also thought history was extremely important and told his audiences: "We have a beautiful history, and we shall create another one in the future. When savages, heathens, and pagans inhabited Europe, Africa was peopled with a race of cultured Black men, who were masters in art, science, and literature. Whatsoever a Black man has done, a Black man can do."

"Self-reliance and economic development" was Garvey's second major theme. He founded the "Negro Factories Corporation" in 1919, with the ultimate objective of "manufacturing every marketable commodity" and establishing factories throughout the world, which could also employ and train thousands of Black workers. Garvey was proud that his corporate stock was only available to Black people. Yet, he still raised enough money in New York City alone to operate three grocery stores, two restaurants, a printing plant, a steam laundry, and a men's and women's manufacturing department that made uniforms, hats, and shirts for such groups as his Black Cross Nurses. Similar enterprises occurred throughout the United States, Central America, and the West Indies. In order to distribute these products worldwide, Marcus Garvey's organization raised enough money within one year (1919) in $5 stock certificates to purchase three ships, which he called the "Black Star Line." Hugh Mulzac, a black ship's officer, said that hundreds of thousands of people throughout the Western Hemisphere welcomed them as conquering heroes wherever they docked. He wrote: "Thousands of peasants came down from the hills on horses, donkeys, and in makeshift carts, showering us with flowers, fruits, and gifts...we had the first ship they had ever seen entirely owned and operated by colored men."

"Africa for Africans at home and abroad" was another very strong message from Marcus Garvey. He believed that if Black people could not develop a strong country in Africa as a protective base, then White people would eventually destroy all Blacks especially African Americans; just as they had done to the Tasmanians, native Australians, and native Americans. Garvey partitioned the League of Nations, after World War I, to give the African colonies of Germany back to native Africans and to allow the UNIA to serve as custodian. He also negotiated with Liberia for land that could serve as a beachhead for trained African Americans to spread modern technology and scientific skills throughout Africa. Garvey sent thousands of dollars of equipment to Liberia in preparation of transferring his headquarters to Monrovia, but was blocked at the last minute by extreme pressure from the neighboring British and French colonies. Garvey never gave up his dream of an independent African continent and even created the red, black, and green flag in addition to a national anthem for his future African Republic.

The UNIA held a total of eight international conventions but none was more spectacular than the first, which was held from August 1-31, 1920. Over 25,000 Black delegates from around the world packed Madison Square Garden, and the surrounding New York streets. Delegates reported to the convention on the problems of their native country and many of their grievances were contained in the "Declaration of Rights of the Negro People of the World." The major demands included: "All persons of African descent anywhere in the world should be accepted as free citizens of Africa; Africans must set out to win justice by whatsoever means possible; Blacks must not be tried by all-White judges and juries; Use of the word 'nigger' must cease; Black history must be taught to Black children; and there must be no taxation without representation."

Black intellectuals, especially W.E.B. DuBois, joined the NAACP and other Garvey haters and demanded that the U.S. Attorney General have Garvey arrested and deported back to Jamaica. They were exceptionally jealous of Garvey's ability to amass millions of Black supporters and raise millions of dollars while refusing to accept any money from Whites. In 1922, Garvey was arrested and charged with mail fraud while promoting stock for the Black Star Line.

The trial was a complete mockery of justice. Even the judge, Julian Mack, was a member of the NAACP, which instigated Garvey's deportation. Garvey was given the maximum five-year prison sentence, but worldwide protests forced President Calvin Coolidge to commute his sentence after two years and have him deported. Marcus Garvey moved from Jamaica to London in 1935 and died of a stroke on June 10, 1940.

Upon his death, the man who had led the largest, most widespread, most powerful, and most influential movement among people of African descent in world history was completely ignored by our textbooks. Fortunately, his spirit lives through the millions of people he has uplifted. For example, Elijah Muhammad was a former UNIA member and while creating the "Nation of Islam," he adopted many of Garvey's ideas like race first, self-reliance, and a separate Black nation. Ho Chi Minh of Vietnam in his youth was a seaman and once spent several months in New York regularly attending UNIA meetings. Kwame Nkrumah, the first President of Ghana, attended many UNIA meetings as a student in New York and so admired Garvey that he named Ghana's shipping company the "Black Star Line" after Garvey's line. Tony Martin says: "No power could prevent the influence which Marcus Garvey has continued to exert on organizations and individuals since his death. As he himself was so fond of saying, 'Truth crushed to earth shall rise again' and 'Up you mighty race you can accomplish what you will.'"

ARTHUR ALFONSO SCHOMBURG

When Arthur Schomburg was a child, his peers frequently teased him about having no history. White classmates told him that Black people had never accomplished anything of note and never would. The young Schomburg asked his teacher where he might find books on Black history and was told there is no such thing. As an extended rebuttal to this teacher, he dedicated his entire life to collecting everything he possibly could that was written by people of African descent. Today the "Schomburg Center for Research in Black Culture" located at 135th Street and Lenox Avenue in Harlem (New York City) has over 150,000 volumes of Black history and nearly five million artifacts, photographs, magazines, and manuscripts from throughout the world and has become the mecca for anyone needing to document or research Black history.

Arthur Alfonso Schomburg (1874-1938) has been called the "Sherlock Holmes of Negro History" because of his uncanny ability to locate extremely rare or "presumed lost" material written by people of African decent. Russell L. Adams states that " at the

Schomburg Center, a reader may see copies of the 1792-93 almanacs of Benjamin Banneker; 'Clotel', the first novel published by an African American; early editions of the poems of Phyllis Wheatley; the addresses and broadsides of free men of color in their conventions of protest; and many other extremely rare Black publications, such as sermons on slavery by ex-slaves." John W. Cromwell, while president of the American Negro Academy, wrote Schomburg on June 17, 1928 highly praising and complimenting him: "You possess some magnetic influence drawing you to these treasures that elude the eager quest of others. How can I adequately express to you my indebtedness for your rescue of Banneker from the seclusion in which he has been for 120 years and the many other valuable manuscripts you have located."

Unlike most of his American bibliophile colleagues, Schomburg wanted to collect material from all great men of color worldwide. At his own expense, he often took extended vacations to Europe, Africa, and South America in search of books, pamphlets, manuscripts, and etchings. In Seville, Spain, he dug into the original records of the West Indies, which were loosely collected there since Western slavery had originated on the Iberian Peninsula. While in Spain, he also definitely established the fact that two of Spain's noted painters, Juan Pareja and Sebastian Gomez, were men of color. Similarly important discoveries were made in France, Germany, and England. In Africa, he found such things as Zulu nursery rhymes printed in the Bantu language, and books on anthropology, folklore, sociology, and customs of the Congo, Guinea, and Ashanti.

In 1925, Schomburg wrote an essay which was published in "The New Negro" by Alain Locke explaining why he made such tremendous personal sacrifices in time and money: "History must restore what slavery took away...History must become less a matter of argument and more a matter of record. There is the definite desire and determination to have a history: well documented, widely known (at least within race circles), and administered as a stimulating and inspiring tradition for the coming generations."

The "coming generations" to significantly benefit from Schomburg's repository of information include such leaders as

Kwame Nkrumah of Ghana, Nnamdi Azikiwe of Nigeria, and Tom Mboya of Kenya which indicates the importance of Schomburg's collection in the African decolonization process that began in the 1950s. In the United States the collection was a prominent anchor for the black intellectual and cultural ferment of the 1960s. John Henrik Clarke, one of our foremost historians, says he provided Malcolm X with research material from the Schomburg collection in his numerous televised debates with Ivy League professors. Dr. Clarke also says he met Schomburg at the age of 18 and credits him with providing the written material that enabled his self-education. More recently, Kareem Abdul Jabbar says it took months of research at the Schomburg Center to permit him to complete his recently published book entitled: Black Profiles in Courage.

Arthur Alfonso Schomburg was born on January 24, 1874 in San Juan, Puerto Rico to a Black mother and White father, who abandoned the household. Schomburg was primarily self-taught but attended public school in Puerto Rico and attended St. Thomas College in the Virgin Islands. He arrived in New York in April 1891 as a black militant fighting for the independence of Cuba and Puerto Rico, but never stopped collecting books and other materials on African history. In 1911, Schomburg and John Bruce founded the influential "Negro Society for Historical Research" and in 1922 he was elected president of the "American Negro Academy", the first major organization of the black intelligentsia. J.A. Rogers says, "Schomburg was a walking encyclopedia. Ask him almost any fact about the Negro, and he would be almost sure to know something about it offhand." In 1926 he received the "Harmon Award" for his work on Negro education.

Schomburg also wrote extensively for magazines and newspapers. His most popular articles include "The Collected Poems of Phyllis Wheatley"; "The Life of Placido"; "Racial Identity-Help to the Study of Negro History"; "Spanish Painters of the School of Seville"; and "Notes on Panama". He was also one of the writers included in an anthology of Negro literature by V.F. Calverton in 1929.

By 1926 Schomburg had collected over 5,000 items including books, documents, and manuscripts which were purchased for

$10,000 by the Carnegie Corporation and donated to the public library in Harlem that was renamed the "Department of Negro Literature and History." In 1932, the Carnegie Corporation provided a grant to the New York Public Library to hire Schomburg as curator of the materials he had collected. He remained curator until his death on June 10, 1938.

The collection of Arthur Schomburg is now housed in the "Schomburg Center for Research in Black Culture" which serves as a monument to his influence on the Black experience in American and throughout the world. Schomburg's obsession with making black history "less a matter of argument and more a matter of record" and to "restore what slavery took away" makes this self-taught lonely visionary of indomitable spirit one whom the world of black scholarship will forever be immensely indebted.

DR. CARTER GOODWIN WOODSON

Carter Goodwin Woodson (1875-1950) wrote: "If a race has no history, if it has no worthwhile tradition, it becomes a negligible factor in the thought of the world, and it stands in danger of being exterminated." Woodson saw the educational system of his generation as solely dedicated to the glorification of Europeans and their achievements. Consequently, he dedicated his entire life to informing the masses, both black and white, about the magnificent history and "worthwhile traditions" of people of African descent.

Dr. Carter G. Woodson has been called the "Father of Negro History" because of his pioneering efforts to systematically and continuously have the accomplishments of Black people taught in our school systems. In 1915, he organized the "Association for the Study of Negro Life and History" and in 1916 started the "Journal of Negro History." In 1926, he initiated the observance of "Negro History Week" which was later expanded to "Black History Month". Dr. Woodson felt that any African American only exposed to the white educational system without any exposure to positive black achievements was "mis-educated and completely useless to his race."

The founding of the "Association for the Study of Negro Life and History" in 1915 was one of Woodson's most important accomplishments. Centered in Washington D.C., this association gathered as many books on black history and achievements as possible and many of these books were later used as textbooks in all grades of schools from elementary to the university. Dr. Woodson also published voluminously to help fill the initial textbook void. His most popular books include: "A Century of Negro Education," "History of the Negro Church," "The Rural Negro," "Education of the Negro Prior to 1861," "Mis-Education of the Negro," "African Backgrounds Outlined," "African Heroes and Heroines," and "The Negro in Our History." Dr. Woodson also collected vast quantities of original documents by people of African descent, which might otherwise have been lost.

Dr. Woodson's "Journal of Negro History" which soon became established as one of the most scholarly and authoritative journals in America. The journal received contributions from some of America's foremost scholars, both Black and White, with many of its articles widely quoted in the leading educational centers of Europe, Asia, Africa, Latin America, and the United States. Woodson hoped that articles from his journal would help black students develop a more self-respecting view of themselves. J.A. Rogers says: "Woodson's outspokenness at the manner in which Negroes were being taught to despise themselves by their teachers brought him several powerful enemies among leading Negro educators; but undaunted, he attacked them fearlessly until they were forced to his point of view."

"Negro History Week" was initiated in 1926 with Carter G. Woodson as the principal founder. "Negro History Week" forced both Black and White schools and colleges throughout the nation to gather and present information on "Negro" history and achievements, which they had never done before. Woodson once said at the annual meeting of the Georgia Teachers' and Educational Association: "I lament the teachers' ignorance of their rich heritage...Few of our college presidents could make more than 10% on an examination in Negro history."

Dr. Woodson was extremely critical of the so-called "highly educated"; that is, "the Negroes who have put on the finishing touches of our best colleges." He wrote: "The same educational process which inspires and stimulates the oppressor with the thought that he is everything and has accomplished everything worthwhile, depresses and crushes at the same time the spark of genius in the Negro by making him feel that his race does not amount to much and never will measure up to the standards of other peoples. The Negro thus educated is a hopeless liability of the race." Woodson frequently told his audiences that it took him over 20 years to "get over" his Harvard education. He felt "modern education" meant bringing a person's mind under the control of his oppressor. He wrote that once a black person's mind is controlled, you won't have to tell him to go to the back door because he will already know his "proper place." He continued: " In fact, if there is no back door, he will cut one out for his special benefit. His education makes it necessary."

Dr. Woodson had even less respect for the black professional class, believing it to be more culturally backward and less race conscious than the masses. In 1930, he analyzed 25,000 Black professionals including doctors, dentists, and lawyers and concluded that they were more interested in making money than contributing to the advancement of their professions or to their race. He wrote that Black professionals were less likely than their White counterparts to keep up with the professional literature in their fields and that Black professional associations tended to emphasize social rather than professional advancement. Although Black professionals were dependent upon the Black working class to earn a living, Woodson saw the Black professional as "just as much class prejudice against the poor Negro as his White professional counterpart" and the least socially responsible among all Black people. Woodson viewed the Black physician as the worst. He wrote that Black physicians, when attending meetings of the National Medical Association were more interested in discussing the merits or demerits of the latest Cadillac than discussing the proper treatment for Tuberculosis or Typhoid Fever." He said that most successful Black physicians "frittered away much of their energy in quest of material things like fine cars, fine homes, and a fine time." Woodson once told a group of professionals: "You spend millions yearly to straighten your hair and bleach your skin and some of you go so far as to have your noses lifted in the hope of looking like the White man. Well, monkeys too have straight hair and thin lips."

Dr. Carter Goodwin Woodson was born on December 19, 1875 in New Canton, Virginia to parents who were former slaves. Woodson was the eldest of nine children and was forced to work in the coal mines of West Virginia at an early age to help his parents make ends meet. This precluded his attending school until he was twenty years old. However, his love of knowledge was so great that despite the hard work he studied by himself at night and was especially fond of Greek and Latin classics. When he finally was able to go to school, he scored so high on the high school entrance examination that he was given an advanced standing and thus earned a diploma in only 18 months. Woodson then went on to obtain his bachelor's degree and master's degree at the University of Chicago. He completed studies for his Ph.D. at Harvard University in 1912, and then went to Sorbonne, Paris where he was one of the most brilliant students in "French languages and literature" for that year. After teaching several years in West Virginia, he went to the Philippines as a teacher and five months later was promoted to "Supervisor of Education" where he served for three years. He subsequently returned to the United States to become dean of the School of Liberal Arts at Howard University and later, dean of the West Virginia Collegiate Institute.

Carter Goodwin Woodson would be proud to know that black history is now a well-established, legitimate, and respected subject of study, and that historians are finally acknowledging his pioneering contributions. Dr. Woodson was tremendously effective in helping to improve the self-respect of Black people and giving them a brighter, more optimistic outlook. As he so eloquently said: "If you read the history of Africa, the history of your ancestors-people of whom you should feel proud-you will realize that they have a history that is worthwhile. They have traditions that have value of which you can boast and upon which you can base a claim for the right to share in the blessings of democracy."

BLACKS IN THE MILITARY

Television images of General Colin Powell in specific and Black, well trained, energetic soldiers in general are a great source of pride for most African Americans. These television images represent the fruits of over two hundred years of struggle by

African Americans for equality, integration, and respect in the military service. There is probably no irony in American history more pointed than the American Black soldier fighting and dying for basic American democracy and freedom, while being denied most of those same freedoms at home and in the military since the founding of this country.

Until recently African Americans begged for the privilege to fight and die for this country in hopes that a more equitable society would await them at the end of the war. However, Black soldiers and sailors were strictly prohibited from participation in virtually every American war until a severe manpower shortage made this country desperate. In 1792, laws were passed by Congress to exclude Blacks from the Army and Marines. The Marine Corp did not accept an African American for its first 150 years of existence, up to and including World War II, when White politicians and generals finally became desperate enough to encourage Black military participation. Black soldiers were frequently poorly trained, unequally paid and equipped, and forced to participate in all Black regiments with White southern officers in charge.

When Blacks were allowed to participate in American wars, they invariably performed exceptionally well. Over 5,000 African Americans, both slave and free, served in the army during the Revolutionary War, and almost all of them received their freedom in appreciation after the war. In fact, most northern states abolished slavery because of their contribution. The outstanding contributions of over 200,000 African American soldiers and sailors during the Civil War led to the 13th Amendment freeing all slaves.

Between 1869 and 1890 Black soldiers in the West, nicknamed the Buffalo Soldiers, won 14 Congressional Metals of Honor, 9 Certificates of Merit and 29 Orders of Honorable Mention while fighting Native Americans. President Theodore Roosevelt credits these same Buffalo Soldiers for saving his famous "Rough Riders" from extermination in Cuba during the Spanish American War of 1898.

About 160,000 of the 200,000 African Americans sent to Europe during World War I were forced to work as laborers in unloading ships and building roads. The remaining soldiers were not even allowed to fight along side White American soldiers but rather were assigned by General Pershing to French Divisions. These Black soldiers had to fight in French uniforms with French weapons and French leadership until the end of World War I. Over 3,000 casualties were sustained by these Black soldiers, who subsequently were awarded over 540 metals by the French government including the Legion of Honor-for gallantry in action.

The plight of Blacks in the military did not improve significantly until President Franklin Roosevelt and President Harry Truman made concessions to Black leaders in exchange for Black votes. On October 15, 1940, Roosevelt announced that Blacks would be trained as pilots, that Black reserve officers would be called to active duty, and that Colonel Benjamin Davis would be named the first Black brigadier general.

In 1948, Truman was even more desperate for Black votes and issued Executive Order 9981, ending military segregation and demanding "equality of treatment and opportunity for all persons in the Armed Services without regard to race, color, religion or national origin." After two hundred years of struggle, African Americans can now look upon Black military men and officers with a great since of pride and accomplishment.

WORLD WAR II ATROCITIES AND BLACK SERVICEMEN

Most Americans would never believe that the United States government was involved in atrocities. After all, doesn't the U.S. currency have "IN GOD WE TRUST" written all over it. Moreover, most Americans still don't believe that the U.S. government funded a "NO TREATMENT" syphilis study in Tuskegee, Alabama for 40 years or that hundreds of Vietnamese were massacred at "My Lai." Authors Carroll Case, "The Slaughter," and Robert Allen, "The Port Chicago Mutiny," have written even less believable stories about the U.S. Military's treatment towards Blacks.

Black servicemen found life exceptionally difficult during World War II. Racism was rampant, segregation made everything separate and extremely unequal, and opportunities for advancement for Blacks were non-existent. In fact, Black servicemen were considered "inferior and ill qualified" according to an Army War College committee study in 1940, which also concluded that Blacks were "far below the Whites in capacity to absorb instruction."

Initially, the Army assigned Black soldiers to labor and support units, and the Navy made Black sailors either messman (waiting tables) or ammunition loaders. African American servicemen were not allowed into combat until manpower shortages became severe. In fact, General Patton vehemently refused to allow any Blacks to serve under his command under any circumstances. Despite legendary acts of heroism which often cost their lives, not a single Black person received the Metal of Honor during World War II and Lieutenant General (retired) William McCaffrey says the reason was simple: "Everyone in the Army then was a racist." Fifty years later the Department of Defense decided that seven Black soldiers deserved the Metal of Honor. On January 13, 1997, President Clinton presented the Metal of Honor to the only survivor, Vernon Baker, and to the families of the others stating: "They were denied their nation's highest honor, but their deeds could not be denied."

African American servicemen were severely punished for military and civil crimes and rarely received a fair trial under military justice. All but three of the twenty one American soldiers executed for capital crimes during World War II were Black. The Army hung six African Americans after a hastily conducted military police investigation accused them of raping a White nurse in New Guinea. The soldiers went to their deaths proclaiming their innocence. Brigadier General Benjamin Davis made an inspection tour of army camps throughout the United States in 1943 and concluded: "There is still great dissatisfaction on the part of the Colored soldier.

The War Department offers him nothing but humiliation and mistreatment and has even introduced Jim Crow practices in areas, both at home and abroad, where they have not hitherto been practiced." African American anger and frustration with lack of opportunity and discrimination resulted in numerous work stoppages and riots. For example, in 1944 Black sailors rioted after racial harassment from White Marines on the island of Guam turned violent, and Black soldiers of the 364th infantry also rioted in Phoenix, Arizona for alleged mistreatment. In March 1945, members of a Black construction battalion at Port Hueneme, California protested nonviolently against their White commander's racism by refusing to eat for two days.

Carroll Case in "The Slaughter" claims the worse military atrocity occurred at Camp Van Dorn in southern Mississippi in 1943, where over 1,200 Black soldiers of the 364th infantry were murdered with machine guns by White military police. Although the Army has no record of this incident, Case says he has thousands of sworn affidavits from eyewitnesses including one of the military police involved in the shooting. The fate of the 364th was sealed after racial violence erupted in Phoenix, Arizona on Thanksgiving night in 1942 according to Carroll Case. Approximately one hundred men took part in a shootout with a detachment of White military police resulting in fifteen casualties. Inspector General Peterson labeled this incident as "having all the earmarks of a mutiny." Sixteen men of the 364th were tried by general court martial and sentenced to fifty years hard labor. As punishment, the remaining members of the 364th were sent to an extremely racist base called Fort Van Dorn near Centerville, Mississippi.

Even the sidewalks were segregated in Centerville, Mississippi and the "uppity" 364th outraged the citizens by demanding equal treatment. On Sunday May 30, 1944, an MP stopped a soldier and ordered him back to base because a button on his uniform was missing. When the soldier objected, the local sheriff shot and killed the soldier and asked the MP if "any other Nigger needed killing." After word of the soldier's death reached the base, riots ensued which resulted in the death of twenty five additional Black soldiers. There is no official documentation of either incident according to Case, but several soldiers wrote letters detailing the events. Another major disturbance occurred one month later involving three thousand soldiers and the 99th infantry division had to be called to stop the violence. Carroll Case says the Army then ordered the 364th quarantined to their barracks where later that night, they were slaughtered by White MPs with machine guns. The bodies were loaded in boxcars and taken to the south gate of the base where they were dumped into a large bulldozed trench. Case says all records after this blood bath were destroyed but that he has even interviewed men in the laundry room who remembered receiving the blood soaked linen from the barracks.

Port Chicago was a naval ammunition base located about 30 miles from San Francisco on the Sacramento River. The ammunition depot at Port Chicago was one of the main sources of supply for the Pacific fleet because the dock facilities could handle the largest ammunition carriers in the Navy. All the men who actually handled the ammunition and bombs were Black, and all commissioned officers were White. Explosives were transferred from boxcars to ship holds 24 hours a day, and the work was hard and dangerous. Some ships received over 8,500 tons of ammunition and bombs.

Black sailors complained that neither they nor their officers had received any training in handling the explosives. They felt the explosives were dangerous and needed better supervision. When the Coast Guard inspected the port and complained about unsafe practices, they were asked to leave. The naval officers told the Black sailors that the bombs could never explode because the firing pins and fuses had been removed. On July 17, 1944, a gigantic explosion estimated equivalent to a five-kiloton atomic bomb, instantly killed 202 Black ammunition loaders and destroyed two cargo ships. The small town of Port Chicago and the base itself, both over a mile away, were severely damaged. This was by far the worst home-front disaster of World War II. A subsequent naval investigation held the Black sailors 100% responsible for the explosion citing rough ammunition handling.

When Port Chicago was rebuilt, fifty sailors refused to return to ammunition loading, because of inadequate training and a lack of safety provisions for hazardous duty. The fifty sailors were convicted of mutiny and sentenced to hard labor for fifteen years with dishonorable discharges. Not until after the war, January 1946, was future Supreme Court Justice Thurgood Marshall able to appeal the verdict and influence the Navy to return the men to active duty. However, the mutiny convictions were never removed from their records. In May 1998, several Black Congressmen made a written appeal to President Clinton to reverse the mutiny convictions and clear the names of these courageous men.

Even more intriguing is the current belief that the Port Chicago explosion was not an accident at all. Many claim to have irrefutable evidence that the U.S. military used Port Chicago to evaluate the damage of an atomic bomb delivered by ship and concluded that air explosions would produce far more destruction. The atomic bombs under consideration were called Mark I (little boy), Mark II, and Mark III (fat boy). Mark II was allegedly tested on the hapless souls at Port Chicago and abandoned because the damage radius was inadequate. Subsequently, the two atomic bombs destined for Japan (Mark I and Mark III) were delivered to an island near Port Chicago and loaded onto B-29 bombers for aerial delivery.

In 1948, President Truman needed the Black vote and consequently decided to "do the right thing" and conclude his presidency in an "honorable way". On July 26, 1948, Truman issued executive order 9981 which declared: "...there shall be equality of treatment and opportunity for all persons in the armed forces without regard to race, color, religion, or national origin." Perhaps the American government should also "do the right thing" and acknowledge and apologize for the numerous atrocities during World War II involving Black servicemen.

BLACK NATIONALISM

Black Nationalism is defined as "a complex set of beliefs emphasizing the need for the cultural, political, and economic separation of African Americans from White society." The philosophy of Black Nationalism is a direct response to racial discrimination and the overt hostility of White society toward anyone of African descent. Black Nationalist beliefs were strongest during slavery and again with Marcus Garvey at the beginning of the 20th century. Since most Black Nationalists believed that White society would never treat African Americans fairly, they demanded a territorial base either in Africa or in America, completely governed by Black men.

As the philosophy of Black Nationalism expanded, Black pride, solidarity, and self-reliance became issues just as important as the demand for a territorial base. For example, in the 18th century, Boston's free Blacks demanded that Crispus Attucks, the first to die in the American Revolution, become a symbol of African American contributions to the Revolutionary War. Crispus Attucks Day (March 5) was celebrated for decades before it was replaced by July 4th. During the 19th century, Paul Cuffe, the richest Black man in America, employed only African Americans to demonstrate their ability to the skeptical White world. In the 1920s, Marcus Garvey demanded distinctly Black standards of beauty and refused any advertisements in his newspaper "The Negro World" for hair straighteners or skin whiteners. He insisted on highlighting the accomplishments of Blacks throughout the world and that Black people chose Black heroes. He even demanded that Black churches depict all religious figures as Black, including Jesus Christ.

During the Civil Rights Movement of the 1960s, many young Blacks became impatient with its slow progress and passive non-violent philosophy and again embraced Black Nationalism. Stokely Carmichael (Kwame Ture) and the Student Nonviolent Coordinating Committee (SNCC) soon had most Black youths proclaiming the slogans "Black is Beautiful" and "Black Power." Bobby Seale and Huey Newton founded the "Black Panther Party" in 1966 and advocated militant self defense in addition to Black Nationalism. Elijah Muhammad (a former Garveyite) and Malcolm X emphasized religious justification for racially separate enterprises, especially in business. When the young Black leaders of the Civil Rights Movement looked for the "Father of Black Nationalism", they chose a name that history had almost forgotten: Martin Robison Delany.

Martin Robison Delany (1812-1885) was a highly intelligent, well-educated Black Nationalist with an immense and outspoken love for his people. Delany strenuously rejected the notion of Black inferiority and proposed emigration rather than the continuous submission to racial humiliation by White society. Although his father, Samuel Delany, was a slave, Martin was born free because his mother, Pati Peace Delany, was free. The Delany children mastered reading and education so quickly that West Virginian Whites became threatened and forced them to move to Pittsburgh, Pennsylvania in 1822.

In 1831, Martin completed the Reverend Lewis Woodson School for Negroes and later completed enough medical study in the offices of abolitionist medical doctors to make a comfortable living as a medical practitioner. In 1850 he became the first Black admitted to Harvard Medical School but was asked to leave after one year because Dean Oliver Holmes considered him a "distraction to education".

Martin Delany hated slavery and while still practicing medicine, he published the "Mystery", the first Black-owned newspaper "West of the Alleghenies". He published his abolitionist newspaper from 1843-47 and when finances forced him to close, he joined Frederick Douglass as coeditor of the newly founded "North Star". Delany demanded liberty for Blacks as a human right. He also exhorted Blacks to elevate themselves by becoming skilled workers and landowning farmers. Martin Delany emphasized Black self-reliance through education, independent thought, and self respect. He felt that Blacks would only gain "the world's applause" by obtaining wealth through successful businesses.

When Congress passed the Fugitive Slave Act, Delany gave up all hope that this country would ever ameliorate the condition of his people. He moved his family to Canada and became a full time advocate for emigration to Africa. Delany organized three emigration conventions (in 1854, 1856, and 1858). In July 1859, Martin Delany sailed to Western Africa and on December 27, 1859, he signed a treaty with the king of Abeokuta (Nigeria). The treaty "permitted African Americans associated with Delany to settle in unused tribal lands in exchange for sharing their skills and education with the Yoruba people." Happy with his African treaty, Delany then sailed for Britain to obtain financial support.

In London, Martin Delany was able to convince cotton dealers and philanthropists that Christian colonies in Africa could easily compete with slave cotton from the South. Delany helped found the "African Aid Society," which agreed to lend two thirds of the money needed by the first group of settlers who were expected to leave the U.S. in June 1861. Unfortunately, before the first settlers could leave, the Civil War began, and Delany decided to cancel the first group's departure.

After four years of bloodshed, Martin Delany was able to convince President Lincoln to allow him to recruit an all Black army with Black officers, which would terrorize the South by arming all slaves and encouraging them to fight for their own emancipation. Delany was commissioned as a Major in the Union Army, the first Black field officer, but the war ended before he could implement his plan to arm all slaves. After the war, Delany was labelled as a "race agitator" for telling freed slaves to "trust only Blacks" and "to break the peace of society and force their way by insurrection to a position he is ambitious they should attain to."

African Methodist Episcopal Church (AME) Bishop Daniel Payne wrote that "Delany was too intensely African to be popular...had his love for humanity been as great as his love for his race, his influence might have equalled that of Fredrick Douglass." Martin Delany's emphasis on race pride and self-reliance and his stressing of the importance of "elevating the race" clearly makes him the "Father of Black Nationalism."

24

The Thirteenth Tribe

RISE

"In Khazaria, sheep, honey, and Jews exist in large quantities." Muqaddasi, Descriptio Imperii Moslemici (tenth century). impetus of the Muslim Holy War was spent, the Caliphate was rocked by internal dissensions, and the Arab invaders retraced their steps across the Caucasus without having gained a permanent foothold in the north, whereas the Khazars became more powerful than they had previously been.

A few years later, probably AD 740, the King, his court and the military ruling class embraced the Jewish faith, and Judaism became the state religion of the Khazars. No doubt their contemporaries were as astonished by this decision as modern scholars were when they came across the evidence in the Arab, Byzantine, Russian and Hebrew sources. One of the most recent comments is to be found in a work by the Hungarian Marxist historian, Dr Antal Bartha. His book on *The Magyar Society in the Eighth and Ninth Centuries*4 has several chapters on the Khazars, as during most of that period the Hungarians were ruled by them. Yet their conversion to Judaism is discussed in a single paragraph, with obvious embarrassment. It reads:

Our investigations cannot go into problems pertaining to the history of ideas, but we must call the reader's attention to the matter of the Khazar kingdom's state religion. It was the Jewish faith which became the official religion of the ruling strata of society. Needless to say, the acceptance of the Jewish faith as the state religion of an ethnically non-Jewish people could be the subject of interesting speculations. We shall, however, confine ourselves to the remark that this official conversion – in defiance of Christian proselytizing by Byzantium, the Muslim influence from the East, and in spite of the political pressure of these two powers – to a religion which had no support from any political power, but was persecuted by nearly all – has come as a surprise to all historians concerned with the Khazars, and cannot be considered as accidental, but must be regarded as a sign of the independent policy pursued by that kingdom.

Which leaves us only slightly more bewildered than before. Yet whereas the sources differ in minor detail, the major facts are beyond dispute.

What is in dispute is the fate of the Jewish Khazars after the destruction of their empire, in the twelfth or thirteenth century. On this problem the sources are scant, but various late mediaeval Khazar settlements are mentioned in the Crimea, in the Ukraine, in Hungary, Poland and Lithuania. The general picture that emerges from these fragmentary pieces of information is that of a migration of Khazar tribes and communities into those regions of Eastern Europe – mainly Russia and Poland – where, at the dawn of the Modern Age, the greatest concentrations of Jews were found. This has lead several historians to conjecture that a substantial part, and perhaps the majority of eastern Jews – and hence of world Jewry – might be of Khazar, and not of Semitic Origin.

The far-reaching implications of this hypothesis may explain the great caution exercised by historians in approaching this subject – if they do not avoid it altogether. Thus in the 1973 edition of the *Encyclopaedia Judaica* the article "Khazars" is signed by Dunlop, but there is a separate section dealing with "Khazar Jews after the Fall of the Kingdom", signed by the editors, and written with the obvious intent to avoid upsetting believers in the dogma of the Chosen Race:

> The Turkish-speaking Karaites [a fundamentalist Jewish sect] of the Crimea, Poland, and elsewhere have affirmed a connection with the Khazars, which is perhaps confirmed by evidence from folklore and anthropology as well as language. There seems to be a considerable amount of evidence attesting to the continued presence in Europe of descendants of the Khazars.

How important, in quantitative terms, is that "presence" of the Caucasian sons of Japheth in the tents of Shem? One of the most radical propounders of the hypothesis concerning the Khazar origins of Jewry is the Professor of Mediaeval Jewish History at Tel Aviv University, A. N. Poliak. His book *Khazaria* (in Hebrew) was published in 1944 in Tel Aviv, and a second edition in 1951.5 In his introduction he writes that the facts demand – a new approach, both to the problem of the relations between the Khazar Jewry and other Jewish communities, and to the question of how far we can go in regarding this [Khazar] Jewry as the nucleus of the large Jewish settlement in Eastern Europe... The descendants of this settlement – those who stayed where they were, those who emigrated to the United States and to other countries, and those who went to Israel – constitute now the large majority of world Jewry.

This was written before the full extent of the holocaust was known, but that does not alter the fact that the large majority of surviving Jews in the world is of Eastern European – and thus perhaps mainly of Khazar – origin. If so, this would mean that their ancestors came not from the Jordan but from the Volga, not from Canaan but from the Caucasus, once believed to be the cradle of the Aryan race; and that genetically they are more closely related to the Hun, Uigur and Magyar tribes than to the seed of Ab raham, Isaac and Jacob. Should this turn out to be the case, then the term "anti-Semitism" would become void of meaning, based on a misapprehension shared by both the killers and their victims. The story of the Khazar Empire, as it slowly emerges from the past, begins to look like the most cruel hoax which history has ever perpetrated.

Thus Cassel,6 a nineteenth-century orientalist, implying that the Khazars shared, for similar reasons, a similar fate. Yet the Hun presence on the European scene lasted a mere eighty years, (From circa 372, when the Huns first started to move westward from the steppes north of the Caspian, to the death of Attila in 453), whereas the kingdom of the Khazars held its own for the best part of four centuries. They too lived chiefly in tents, but they also had large urban settlements, and were in the process of transformation from a tribe of nomadic warriors into a nation of farmers, cattle-breeders, fishermen, vine-growers, traders and skilled craftsmen. Soviet archaeologists have unearthed evidence for a relatively advanced civilization which was altogether different from the "Hun whirlwind". They found the traces of villages extending over several miles,7 with houses connected by galleries to huge cattlesheds, sheep-pens and stables (these measured 3–31/2 ' 10–14 metres and were supported by columns.8 Some remaining ox-ploughs showed remarkable craftsmanship; so did the preserved artefacts – buckles, clasps, ornamental saddle plates. Of particular interest were the foundations, sunk into the ground, of houses built in a circular shape.9 According to the Soviet archaeologists, these were found all over the territories inhabited by the Khazars, and were of an earlier date than their "normal", rectangular buildings. Obviously the round-houses symbolize the transition from portable, dome-shaped tents to permanent dwellings, from the nomadic to a settled, or rather semi-settled, existence. For the contemporary Arab sources tell us that the Khazars only stayed in their towns – including even their capital, Itil – during the winter; come spring, they packed their tents, left their houses and sallied forth with their sheep or cattle into the steppes, or camped in their cornfields or vineyards.

The excavations also showed that the kingdom was, during its later period, surrounded by an elaborate chain of fortifications, dating from the eighth and ninth centuries, which protected its northern frontiers facing the open steppes. These fortresses formed a rough semicircular arc from the Crimea (which the Khazars ruled for a time) across the lower reaches of the Donetz and the Don to the Volga; while towards the south they were protected by the Caucasus, to the west by the Black Sea, and to the east by the "Khazar Sea", the Caspian. ("To this day, the Muslims, recalling the Arab terror of the Khazar raids, still call the Caspian, a sea as shifting as the nomads, and washing to their steppe-land parts, *Bahr-ul-Khazar* – "the Khazar Sea"." (W. E. 0. Allen, *A History of the Georgian People*, London 1952).) However, the northern chain of fortifications marked merely an inner ring, protecting the stable core of the Khazar country; the actual boundaries of their rule over the tribes of the north fluctuated according to the fortunes of war. At the peak of their power they controlled or exacted tribute from some thirty different nations and tribes inhabiting the vast territories between the Caucasus, the Aral Sea, the Ural Mountains, the town of Kiev and the Ukrainian steppes. The people under Khazar suzerainty included the Bulgars, Burtas, Ghuzz, Magyars (Hungarians), the Gothic and Greek colonies of the Crimea, and the Slavonic tribes in the north-western woodlands. Beyond these extended dominions, Khazar armies also raided Georgia and Armenia and penetrated into the Arab Caliphate as far as Mosul. In the words of the Soviet archaeologist M. I. Artamonov:

Until the ninth century, the Khazars had no rivals to their supremacy in the regions north of the Black Sea and the adjoining steppe and forest regions of the Dnieper. The Khazars were the supreme masters of the southern half of Eastern Europe for a century and a hall, and presented a mighty bulwark, blocking the Ural-Caspian gateway from Asia into Europe. During this whole period, they held back the onslaught of the nomadic tribes from the East. Taking a bird's-eye view of the history of the great nomadic empires of the East, the Khazar kingdom occupies an intermediary position in time, size, and degree of civilization between the Hun and Avar Empires which preceded, and the Mongol Empire that succeeded it.

But who were these remarka le people – remarkable as much by their power and achievements as by their conversion to a religion of outcasts? The descriptions that have come down to us originate in hostile sources, and cannot be taken at face value. "As to the Khazars," an Arab chronicler11 writes, "they are to the north of the inhabited earth towards the 7th clime, having over their heads the constellation of the Plough. Their land is cold and wet. Accordingly their complexions are white, their eyes blue, their hair flowing and predominantly reddish, their bodies large and their natures cold. Their general aspect is wild."

After a century of warfare, the Arab writer obviously had no great sympathy for the Khazars. Nor had the Georgian or Armenian scribes, whose countries, of a much older culture, had been repeatedly devastated by Khazar horsemen. A Georgian chronicle, echoing an ancient tradition, identifies them with the hosts of Gog and Magog – "wild men with hideous faces and the manners of wild beasts, eaters of blood". An Armenian writer refers to "the horrible multitude of Khazars with insolent, broad, lashless faces and long falling hair, like women". Lastly, the Arab geographer Istakhri, one of the main Arab sources, has this to say:

"The Khazars do not resemble the Turks. They are black-haired, and are of two kinds, one called the Kara-Khazars, [Black Khazars] who are swarthy verging on deep black as if they were a kind of Indian, and a white kind [Ak-Khazars], who are strikingly handsome.".

This is more flattering, but only adds to the confusion. For it was customary among Turkish peoples to refer to the ruling classes or clans as "white", to the lower strata as "black". Thus there is no reason to believe that the "White Bulgars" were whiter than the "Black Bulgars", or that the "White Huns" (the Ephtalites) who invaded India and Persia in the fifth and sixth centuries were of fairer skin than the other Hun tribes which invaded Europe. Istakhri's blackskinned Khazars – as much else in his and his colleagues' writings – were based on hearsay and legend; and we are none the wiser regarding the Khazars' physical appearance, or their ethnic Origins.

The last question can only be answered in a vague and general way. But it is equally frustrating to inquire into the origins of the Huns, Alans, Avars, Bulgars, Magyars, Bashkirs, Burtas, Sabirs, Uigurs, Saragurs, Onogurs, Utigurs, Kutrigurs, Tarniaks, Kotragars, Khabars, Zabenders, Pechenegs, Ghuzz, Kumans, Kipchaks, and dozens of other tribes or people who at one time or another in the lifetime of the Khazar kingdom passed through the turnstiles of those migratory playgrounds. Even the Huns, of whom we know much more, are of uncertain origin; their name is apparently derived from the Chinese *Hiung-nu*, which designates warlike nomads in general, while other nations applied the name Hun in a similarly indiscriminate way to nomadic hordes of all kinds, including the "White Huns" mentioned above, the Sabirs, Magyars and Khazars. (It is amusing to note that while the British in World War I used the term "Hun" in the same pejorative sense, in my native Hungary schoolchildren were taught to look up to "our glorious Hun forefathers" with patriotic pride An exclusive rowing club in Budapest was called "Hunnia", and Attila is still a popular first name). In the first century AD, the Chinese drove these disagreeable Hun neighbours westward, and thus started one of those periodic avalanches which swept for many centuries from Asia towards the West. From the fifth century onward, many of these westward-bound tribes were called by the generic name of "Turks". The term is also supposed to be of Chinese origin (apparently derived from the name of a hill) and was subsequently used to refer to all tribes who spoke languages with certain common characteristics – the "Turkic" language group. Thus the term Turk, in the sense in which it was used by mediaeval writers – and often also by modern ethnologists – refers primarily to language and not to race. In this sense the Huns and Khazars were "Turkic" people. (But not the Magyars, whose language belongs to the Finno-Ugrian language group). The Khazar language was supposedly a Chuvash dialect of Turkish, which still survives in the Autonomous Chuvash Soviet Republic, between the Volga and the Sura. The Chuvash people are actually believed to be descendants of the Bulgars, who spoke a dialect similar to the Khazars. But all these connections are rather tenuous, based on the more or less speculative deductions of oriental philologists. All we can say with safety is that the Khazars were a "Turkic" tribe, who erupted from the Asian steppes, probably in the fifth century of our era.

The origin of the name Khazar, and the modern derivations to which it gave rise, has also been the subject of much ingenious speculation. Most likely the word is derived from the Turkish root *gaz,* "to wander", and simply means "nomad". Of greater interest to the non-spe7 cialist are some alleged modern derivations from it: among them the Russian Cossack and the Hungarian Huszar – both signifying martial horsemen; (Huszar is probably derived via the Serbo-Croat from Greek references to Khazars), and also the German *Ketzer* – heretic, i.e., Jew. If these derivations are correct, they would show that the Khazars had a considerable impact on the imagination of a variety of peoples in the Middle Ages.

Some Persian and Arab chronicles provide an attractive combination of legend and gossip column. They may start with the Creation and end with stop-press titbits. Thus Yakubi, a ninth-century Arab historian, traces the origin of the Khazars back to Japheth, third son of Noah. The Japheth motive recurs frequently in the literature, while other legends connect them with Abraham or Alexander the Great.

One of the earliest factual references to the Khazars occurs in a Syriac chronicle by "Zacharia Rhetor", (It was actually written by an anonymous compiler and named after an earlier Greek historian whose work is summarized in the compilation), dating from the middle of the sixth century. It mentions the Khazars in a list of people who inhabit the region of the Caucasus. Other sources indicate that they were already much in evidence a century earlier, and intimately connected with the Huns. In AD 448, the Byzantine Emperor Theodosius II sent an embassy to Attila which included a famed rhetorician by name of Priscus. He kept a minute account not only of the diplomatic negotiations, but also of the court intrigues and goings-on in Attila's sumptuous banqueting hall – he was in fact the perfect gossip columnist, and is still one of the main sources of information about Hun customs and habits. But Priscus also has anecdotes to tell about a people subject to the Huns whom he calls Akatzirs – that is, very likely, the Ak-Khazars, or "White" Khazars (as distinct from the "Black" Kara-Khazars). (The "Akatzirs" are also mentioned as a nation of warriors by Jordanes, the great Goth historian, a century later, and the so-called "Geographer of Ravenna" expressly identifies them with the Khazars.

This is accepted by most modern authorities. [A notable exception was Marquart, but see Dunlop's refutation of his views, *op. cit.*, pp. 7f.] Cassel, for instance, points out that Priscus's pronunciation and spelling follows the Armenian and Georgian: Khazir). The Byzantine Emperor, Priscus tells us, tried to win this warrior race over to his side, but the greedy Khazar chieftain, named Karidach, considered the bribe offered to him inadequate, and sided with the Huns. Attila defeated Karidach's rival chieftains, installed him as the sole ruler of the Akatzirs, and invited him to visit his court. Karidach thanked him profusely for the invitation, and went on to say that "it would be too hard on a mortal man to look into the face of a god. For, as one cannot stare into the sun's disc, even less could one look into the face of the greatest god without suffering injury." Attila must have been pleased, for he confirmed Karidach in his rule.

Priscus's chronicle confirms that the Khazars appeared on the European scene about the middle of the fifth century as a people under Hunnish sovereignty, and may be regarded, together with the Magyars and other tribes, as a later offspring of Attila's horde.

The collapse of the Hun Empire after Attila's death left a power-vacuum in Eastern Europe, through which once more, wave after wave of nomadic hordes swept from east to west, prominent among them the Uigurs and Avars. The Khazars during most of this period seemed to be happily occupied with raiding the rich trans-Caucasian regions of Georgia and Armenia, and collecting precious plunder. During the second half of the sixth century they became the dominant force among the tribes north of the Caucasus. A number of these tribes – the Sabirs, Saragurs, Samandars, Balanjars, etc. – are from this date onward no longer mentioned by name in the sources: they had been subdued or absorbed by the Khazars. The toughest resistance, apparently, was offered by the powerful Bulgars. But they too were crushingly defeated (circa 641), and as a result the nation split into two: some of them migrated westward to the Danube, into the region of modern Bulgaria, others north-eastward to the middle Volga, the latter remaining under Khazar suzerainty. We shall frequently encounter both Danube Bulgars and Volga Bulgars in the course of this narrative.

But before becoming a sovereign state, the Khazars still had to serve their apprenticeship under another short-lived power, the so-called West Turkish Empire, or Turkut kingdom. It was a confederation of tribes, held together by a ruler: the Kagan or Khagan (Or Kaqan or Khaqan or Chagan, etc. Orientalists have strong Idiosyncrasies about spelling. I shall stick to Kagan as the least offensive to Western eyes. The h in Khazar, however, is general usage), – a title which the Khazar rulers too were subsequently to adopt. This first Turkish state – if one may call it that – lasted for a century (circa 550-650) and then fell apart, leaving hardly any trace. However, it was only after the establishment of this kingdom that the name "Turk" was used to apply to a specific nation, as distinct from other Turkic-speaking peoples like the Khazars and Bulgars. (This, however, did not prevent the name "Turk" still being applied indiscriminately to any nomadic tribe of the steppes as a euphemism for Barbarian, or a synonym for "Hun". It led to much confusion in the interpretation of ancient sources). The Khazars had been under Hun tutelage, then under Turkish tutelage. After the eclipse of the Turks in the middle of the seventh century it was their turn to rule the "Kingdom of the North", as the Persians and Byzantines came to call it. According to one tradition,15 the great Persian King Khusraw (Chosroes) Anushirwan (the Blessed) had three golden guest-thrones in his palace, reserved for the Emperors of Byzantium, China and of the Khazars. No state visits from these potentates materialized, and the golden thrones – if they existed – must have served a purely symbolic purpose. But whether fact or legend, the story fits in well with Emperor Constantine's official account of the triple gold seal assigned by the Imperial Chancery to the ruler of the Khazars.

Thus during the first few decades of the seventh century, just before the Muslim hurricane was unleashed from Arabia, the Middle East was dominated by a triangle of powers: Byzantium, Persia, and the West Turkish Empire. The first two of these had been waging intermittent war against each other for a century, and both seemed on the verge of collapse; in the sequel, Byzantium recovered, but the Persian kingdom was soon to meet its doom, and the Khazars were actually in on the kill. They were still nominally under the suzerainty of the West Turkish kingdom, within which they represented the strongest effective force, and to which they were soon to succeed; accordingly, in 627, the Roman Emperor Heraclius concluded a military alliance with the Khazars – the first of several to follow – in preparing his decisive campaign against Persia. There are several versions of the role played by the Khazars in that campaign which seems to have been somewhat inglorious – but the principal facts are well established. The Khazars provided Heraclius with 40000 horsemen under a chieftain named Ziebel, who participated in the advance into Persia, but then – presumably fed up with the cautious strategy of the Greeks – turned back to lay siege on Tiflis; this was unsuccessful, but the next year they again joined forces with Heraclius, took the Georgian capital, and returned with rich plunder. Gibbon has given a colourful description (based on Theophanes) of the first meeting between the Roman Emperor and the Khazar chieftain.

... To the hostile league of Chosroes with the Avars, the Roman emperor opposed the useful and honourable alliance of the Turks. (By "Turks", as the sequel shows, he means the Khazars). At his liberal invitation, the horde of Chozars transported their tents from the plains of the Volga to the mountains of Georgia; Heraclius received them in the neighbourhood of Tiflis, and the khan with his nobles dismounted from their horses, if we may credit the Greeks, and fell prostrate on the ground, to adore the purple of the Caesar. Such voluntary homage and important aid were entitled to the warmest acknowledgements; and the emperor, taking off his own diadem, placed it on the head of the Turkish prince, whom he saluted with a tender embrace and the appellation of son. After a sumptuous banquet, he presented Ziebel with the plate and ornaments, the gold, the gems, and the silk, which had been used at the Imperial table, and, with his own hand, distributed rich jewels and earrings to his new allies. In a secret interview, he produced a portrait of his daughter Eudocia, condescended to flatter the barbarian with the promise of a fair and august bride, and obtained an immediate succour of forty thousand horse...

Eudocia (or Epiphania) was the only daughter of Heraclius by his first wife. The promise to give her in marriage to the "Turk" indicates once more the high value set by the Byzantine Court on the Khazar alliance. However, the marriage came to naught because Ziebel died while Eudocia and her suite were on their way to him. There is also an ambivalent reference in Theophanes to the effect that Ziebel "presented his son, a beardless boy" to the Emperor – as a *quid pro quo*?

There is another picturesque passage in an Armenian chronicle, quoting the text of what might be called an Order of Mobilization issued by the Khazar ruler for the second campaign against Persia: it was addressed to "all tribes and peoples [under Khazar authority], inhabitants of the mountains and the plains, living under roofs or the open sky, having their heads shaved or wearing their hair long".

This gives us a first intimation of the heterogeneous ethnic mosaic that was to compose the Khazar Empire. The "real Khazars" who ruled it were probably always a minority – as the Austrians were in the Austro-Hungarian monarchy.

The Persian state never recovered from the crushing defeat inflicted on it by Emperor Heraclius in 627. There was a revolution; the King was slain by his own son who, in his turn, died a few months later; a child was elevated to the throne, and after ten years of anarchy and chaos the first Arab armies to erupt on the scene delivered the *coup de grace* to the Sassanide Empire. At about the same time, the West Turkish confederation dissolved into its tribal components. A new triangle of powers replaced the previous one: the Islamic Caliphate – Christian Byzantium and the newly emerged Khazar Kingdom of the North. It fell to the latter to bear the brunt of the Arab attack in its initial stages, and to protect the plains of Eastern Europe from the invaders.

In the first twenty years of the Hegira – Mohammed's flight to Medina in 622, with which the Arab calendar starts – the Muslims had conquered Persia, Syria, Mesopotamia, Egypt, and surrounded the Byzantine heartland (the present-day Turkey) in a deadly semi-circle, which extended from the Mediterranean to the Caucasus and the southern shores of the Caspian. The Caucasus was a formidable natural obstacle, but no more forbidding than the Pyrenees; and it could be negotiated by the pass of Dariel (Now called the Kasbek pass), or bypassed through the defile of Darband, along the Caspian shore.

This fortified defile, called by the Arabs *Bab al Abwab*, the Gate of Gates, was a kind of historic turnstile through which the Khazars and other marauding tribes had from time immemorial attacked the countries of the south and retreated again. Now it was the turn of the Arabs. Between 642 and 652 they repeatedly broke through the Darband Gate and advanced deep into Khazaria, attempting to capture Balanjar, the nearest town, and thus secure a foothold on the European side of the Caucasus. They were beaten back on every occasion in this first phase of the Arab-Khazar war; the last time in 652, in a great battle in which both sides used artillery (catapults and ballistae). Four thousand Arabs were killed, including their commander, Abdal-Rahman ibn-Rabiah; the rest fled in disorder across the mountains.

For the next thirty or forty years the Arabs did not attempt any further incursions into the Khazar stronghold. Their main attacks were now aimed at Byzantium. On several occasions (AD

669, 673-8, 717-18), they laid siege to Constantinople by land and by sea; had they been able to outflank the capital across the Caucasus and round the Black Sea, the fate of the Roman Empire would probably have been sealed. The Khazars, in the meantime, having subjugated the Bulgars and Magyars, completed their western expansion into the Ukraine and the Crimea. But these were no longer haphazard raids to amass booty and prisoners; they were wars of conquest, incorporating the conquered people into an empire with a stable administration, ruled by the mighty Kagan, who appointed his provincial governors to administer and levy taxes in the conquered territories. At the beginning of the eighth century their state was sufficiently consolidated for the Khazars to take the offensive against the Arabs.

From a distance of more than a thousand years, the period of intermittent warfare that followed (the so-called 'second Arab war", 722-37) looks like a series of tedious episodes on a local scale, following the same, repetitive pattern: the Khazar cavalry in their heavy armour breaking through the pass of Dariel or the Gate of Darband into the Caliph's domains to the south; followed by Arab counter-thrusts through the same pass or the defile, towards the Volga and back again. Looking thus through the wrong end of the telescope, one is reminded of the old jingle about the noble Duke of York who had ten thousand men; "he marched them up to the top of the hill. And he marched them down again." In fact, the Arab sources (though they often exaggerate) speak of armies of 100000, even of 300000, men engaged on either side – probably outnumbering the armies which decided the fate of the Western world at the battle of Tours about the same time.

The death-defying fanaticism which characterized these wars is illustrated by episodes such as the suicide by fire of a whole Khazar town as an alternative to surrender; the poisoning of the water supply of Bab al Abwab by an Arab general; or by the traditional exhortation which would halt the rout of a defeated Arab army and make it fight to the last man: "To the Garden, Muslims, not the Fire" – the joys of Paradise being assured to every Muslim soldier killed in the Holy War.

At one stage during these fifteen years of fighting the Khazars overran Georgia and Armenia, inflicted a total defeat on the Arab army in the battle of Ardabil (AD 730) and advanced as far as Mosul and Dyarbakir, more than half-way to Damascus, capital of the Caliphate. But a freshly raised Muslim army stemmed the tide, and the Khazars retreated homewards across the mountains. The next year Maslamah ibn-Abd-al-Malik, most famed Arab general of his time, who had formerly commanded the siege of Constantinople, took Balanjar and even got as far as Samandar, another large Khazar town further north. But once more the invaders were unable to establish a permanent garrison, and once more they were forced to retreat across the Caucasus. The sigh of relief experienced in the Roman Empire assumed a tangible form through another dynastic alliance, when the heir to the throne was married to a Khazar princess, whose son was to rule Byzantium as Leo the Khazar.

The last Arab campaign was led by the future Caliph Marwan II, and ended in a Pyrrhic victory. Marwan made an offer of alliance to the Khazar Kagan, then attacked by surprise through both passes. The Khazar army, unable to recover from the initial shock, retreated as far as the Volga. The Kagan was forced to ask for terms; Marwan, in accordance with the routine followed in other conquered countries, requested the Kagan's conversion to the True Faith. The Kagan complied, but his conversion to Islam must have been an act of lip-service, for no more is heard of the episode in the Arab or Byzantine sources – in contrast to the lasting effects of the establishment of Judaism as the state religion which took place a few years later. (The probable date for the conversion is around AD 740 – see below). Content with the results achieved, Marwan bid farewell to Khazaria and marched his army back to Transcaucasia – without leaving any garrison, governor or administrative apparatus behind. On the contrary, a short time later he requested terms for another alliance with the Khazars against the rebellious tribes of the south.

It had been a narrow escape. The reasons which prompted Marwan's apparent magnanimity are a matter of conjecture – as so much else in this bizarre chapter of history. Perhaps the Arabs realized that, unlike the relatively civilized Persians, Armenians or Georgians, these ferocious Barbarians of the North could not be ruled by a Muslim puppet prince and a small garrison. Yet

Marwan needed every man of his army to quell major rebellions in Syria and other parts of the Omayad Caliphate, which was in the process of breaking up. Marwan himself was the chief commander in the civil wars that followed, and became in 744 the last of the Omayad Caliphs (only to be assassinated six years later when the Caliphate passed to the Abbasid dynasty). Given this background, Marwan was simply not in a position to exhaust his resources by further wars with the Khazars. He had to content himself with teaching them a lesson which would deter them from further incursions across the Caucasus. Thus the gigantic Muslim pincer movement across the Pyrenees in the west and across the Caucasus into Eastern Europe was halted at both ends about the same time. As Charles Martel's Franks saved Gaul and Western Europe, so the Khazars saved the eastern approaches to the Volga, the Danube, and the East Roman Empire itself. On this point at least, the Soviet archaeologist and historian, Artamonov, and the American historian, Dunlop, are in full agreement. I have already quoted the latter to the effect that but for the Khazars, "Byzantium, the bulwark of European civilization to the East, would have found itself outflanked by the Arabs", and that history might have taken a different course.

Artamonov is of the same opinion: Khazaria was the first feudal state in Eastern Europe, which ranked with the Byzantine Empire and the Arab Caliphate... It was only due to the powerful Khazar attacks, diverting the tide of the Arab armies to the Caucasus, that Byzantium withstood them...

Lastly, the Professor of Russian History in the University of Oxford, Dimitry Obolensky:19 "The main contribution of the Khazars to world history was their success in holding the line of the Caucasus against the northward onslaught of the Arabs."

Marwan was not only the last Arab general to attack the Khazars, he was also the last Caliph to pursue an expansionist policy devoted, at least in theory, to the ideal of making Islam triumph all over the world. With the Abbasid caliphs the wars of conquest ceased, the revived influence of the old Persian culture created a mellower climate, and eventually gave rise to the splendours of Baghdad under Harun al Rashid. During the long lull between the first and second Arab wars, the Khazars became involved in one of the more lurid episodes of Byzantine history, characteristic of the times, and of the role the Khazars played in it.

In AD 685 Justinian II, Rhinotmetus, became East Roman Emperor at the age of sixteen. Gibbon, in his inimitable way, has drawn the youth's portrait:

His passions were strong; his understanding was feeble; and he was intoxicated with a foolish pride... His favourite ministers were two beings the least susceptible of human sympathy, a eunuch and a monk; the former corrected the emperor's mother with a scourge, the latter suspended the insolvent tributaries, with their heads downwards, over a slow and smoky fire.

After ten years of intolerable misrule there was a revolution, and the new Emperor, Leontius, ordered Justinian's mutilation and banishment:

The amputation of his nose, perhaps of his tongue, was imperfectly performed; the happy flexibility of the Greek language could impose the name of Rhinotmetus ("Cut-off Nose"); and the mutilated tyrant was banished to Chersonae in Crim-Tartary, a lonely settlement where corn, wine and oil were imported as foreign luxuries. (The treatment meted out to Justinian was actually regarded as an act of leniency: the general tendency of the period was to humanize the criminal law by substituting mutilation for capital punishment – amputation of the hand [for thefts] or nose [fornication, etc], being the most frequent form. Byzantine rulers were also given to the practice of blinding dangerous rivals, while magnanimously sparing their lives).

During his exile in Cherson, Justinian kept plotting to regain his throne. After three years he saw his chances improving when, back in Byzantium, Leontius was de-throned and also had his nose cut off. Justinian escaped from Cherson into the Khazar-ruled town of Doros in the Crimea and had a meeting with the Kagan of the Khazars, King Busir or Bazir. The Kagan must have welcomed the opportunity of putting his fingers into the rich pie of Byzantine dynastic policies, for he formed an alliance with Justinian and gave him his sister in marriage. This sister, who was baptized by the name of Theodora, and later duly crowned, seems to have been the only decent person in this series of sordid intrigues, and to bear genuine love for her noseless husband (who was still only in his early thirties). The couple and their band of followers were now moved to the town of Phanagoria (the present Taman) on the eastern shore of the strait of Kerch, which had a Khazar governor.

Here they made preparations for the invasion of Byzantium with the aid of the Khazar armies which King Busir had apparently promised. But the envoys of the new Emperor, Tiberias III, persuaded Busir to change his mind, by offering him a rich reward in gold if he delivered Justinian, dead or alive, to the Byzantines. King Busir accordingly gave orders to two of his henchmen, named Papatzes and Balgitres, to assassinate his brother-in-law. But faithful Theodora got wind of the plot and warned her husband. Justinian invited Papatzes and Balgitres separately to his quarters, and strangled each in turn with a cord. Then he took ship, sailed across the Black Sea into the Danube estuary, and made a new alliance with a powerful Bulgar tribe. Their king, Terbolis, proved for the time being more reliable than the Khazar Kagan, for in 704 he provided Justinian with 15000 horsemen to attack Constantinople. The Byzantines had, after ten years, either forgotten the darker sides of Justinian's former rule, or else found their present ruler even more intolerable, for they promptly rose against Tiberias and reinstated Justinian on the throne. The Bulgar King was rewarded with "a heap of gold coin which he measured with his Scythian whip" and went home (only to get involved in a new war against Byzantium a few years later).

Justinian's second reign (704-711) proved even worse than the first; "he considered the axe, the cord and the rack as the only instruments of royalty".22 He became mentally unbalanced, obsessed with hatred against the inhabitants of Cherson, where he had spent most of the bitter years of his exile, and sent an expedition against the town. Some of Cherson's leading citizens were burnt alive, others drowned, and many prisoners taken, but this was not enough to assuage Justinian's lust for revenge, for he sent a second expedition with orders to raze the city to the ground. However, this time his troops were halted by a mighty Khazar army; whereupon Justinian's representative in the Crimea, a certain Bardanes, changed sides and joined the Khazars. The demoralized Byzantine expeditionary force abjured its allegiance to Justinian and elected Bardanes as Emperor, under the name of Philippicus. But since Philippicus was in Khazar hands, the insurgents had to pay a heavy ransom to the Kagan to get their new Emperor back. When the expeditionary force returned to Constantinople, Justinian and his son were assassinated and Philippicus, greeted as a liberator, was installed on the throne only to be deposed and blinded a couple of years later. The point of this gory tale is to show the influence which the Khazars at this stage exercised over the destinies of the East Roman Empire – in addition to their role as defenders of the Caucasian bulwark against the Muslims. Bardanes-Philippicus was an emperor of the Khazars' making, and the end of Justinian's reign of terror was brought about by his brotherin-law, the Kagan. To quote Dunlop: "It does not seem an exaggeration to say that at this juncture the Khaquan was able practically to give a new ruler to the Greek empire."

From the chronological point of view, the next event to be discussed should be the conversion of the Khazars to Judaism, around AD 740. But to see that remarkable event in its proper perspective, one should have at least some sketchy idea of the habits, customs and everyday life among the Khazars prior to the conversion. Alas, we have no lively eyewitness reports, such as Priscus's description of Attila's court. What we do have are mainly second-hand accounts and compilations by Byzantine and Arab chroniclers, which are rather schematic and fragmentary – with two exceptions. One is a letter, purportedly from a Khazar king, to be discussed in Chapter 2; the other is a travelogue by an observant Arab traveller, Ibn Fadlan, who – like Priscus – was a member of a diplomatic mission from a civilized court to the Barbarians of the North.

The court was that of the Caliph al Muktadir, and the diplomatic mission travelled from Baghdad through Persia and Bukhara to the land of the Volga Bulgars. The official pretext for this grandiose expedition was a letter of invitation from the Bulgar king, who asked the Caliph (a) for religious instructors to convert his people to Islam, and (b) to build him a fortress which would enable him to defy his overlord, the King of the Khazars. The invitation – which was no doubt prearranged by earlier diplomatic contacts – also provided an opportunity to create goodwill among the various Turkish tribes inhabiting territories through which the mission had to pass, by preaching the message of the Koran and distributing huge amounts of gold bakhshish.

The opening paragraphs of our traveller's account read (The following quotations are based on Zeki Validi Togan's German translation of the Arabic text and the English translation of extracts by Blake and Frye, both slightly paraphrased in the interest of readability):

This is the book of Ahmad ibn-Fadlan ibn-al-Abbas, ibn-Rasid, ibn-Hammad, an official in the service of [General] Muhammed ibn-Sulayman, the ambassador of [Caliph] al Muktadir to the King of the Bulgars, in which he relates what he saw in the land of the Turks, the Khazars, the Rus, the Bulgars, the Bashkirs and others, their varied kinds of religion, the histories of their kings, and their conduct in many walks of life.

The letter of the King of the Bulgars reached the Commander of the Faithful, al Muktadir; he asked him therein to send him someone to give him religious instruction and acquaint him with the laws of Islam, to build him a mosque and a pulpit so that he may carry out his mission of converting the people all over his country; he also entreated the Caliph to build him a fortress to defend himself against hostile kings (i.e., as later passages show, the King of the Khazars). Everything that the King asked for was granted by the Caliph. I was chosen to read the Caliph's message to the King, to hand over the gifts the Caliph sent him, and to supervise the work of the teachers and interpreters of the Law... (There follow some details about the financing of the mission and names of participants.] And so we started on Thursday the 11th Safar of the year 309 [June 21, AD 921) from the City of Peace [Baghdad, capital of the Caliphate].

The date of the expedition, it will he noted, is much later than the events described in the previous section. But as far as the customs and institutions of the Khazars' pagan neighbours are concerned, this probably makes not much difference; and the glimpses we get of the life of these nomadic tribes convey at least some idea of what life among the Khazars may have been during that earlier period – before the conversion – when they adhered to a form of Shamanism similar to that still practised by their neighbours in Ibn Fadlan's time. The progress of the mission was slow and apparently uneventful until they reached Khwarizm, the border province of the Caliphate south of the Sea of Aral. Here the governor in charge of the province tried to stop them from proceeding further by arguing that between his country and the kingdom of the Bulgars there were "a thousand tribes of disbelievers" who were sure to kill them. In fact his attempts to disregard the Caliph's instructions to let the mission pass might have been due to other motives: he realized that the mission was indirectly aimed against the Khazars, with whom he maintained a flourishing trade and friendly relations. In the end, however, he had to give in, and the mission was allowed to proceed to Gurganj on the estuary of the Amu-Darya. Here they hibernated for three months, because of the intense cold – a factor which looms large in many Arab travellers' tales:

The river was frozen for three months, we looked at the landscape and thought that the gates of the cold Hell had been opened for us. Verily I saw that the market place and the streets were totally empty because of the cold... Once, when I came out of the bath and got home, I saw that my beard had frozen into a lump of ice, and I had to thaw it in front of the fire. I stayed for some days in a house which was inside of another house [compound?] and in which there stood a Turkish felt tent, and I lay inside the tent wrapped in clothes and furs, but nevertheless my cheeks often froze to the cushion...

Around the middle of February the thaw set in. The mission arranged to join a mighty caravan of 5000 men and 3000 pack animals to cross the northern steppes, and bought the necessary supplies: camels, skin boats made of camel hides for crossing rivers, bread, millet and spiced meat for three months. The natives warned them about the even more frightful cold in the north, and advised them what clothes to wear:

So each of us put on a Kurtak, [camisole] over that a woollen Kaftan, over that a buslin, [fur-lined coat] over that a burka [fur coat]; and a fur cap, under which only the eyes could be seen; a simple pair of underpants, and a lined pair, and over them the trousers; house shoes of kaymuht [shagreen leather] and over these also another pair of boots; and when one of us mounted a camel, he was unable to move because of his clothes. Ibn Fadlan, the fastidious Arab, liked neither the climate nor the people of Khwarizm:

They are, in respect of their language and constitution, the most repulsive of men. Their language is like the chatter of starlings. At a day's journey there is a village called Ardkwa whose inhabitants are called Kardals; their language sounds entirely like the croaking of frogs.

They left on March 3 and stopped for the night in a caravanserai called Zamgan – the gateway to the territory of the Ghuzz Turks. From here onward the mission was in foreign land, "entrusting our fate to the all-powerful and exalted God". During one of the frequent snowstorms, Ibn Fadlan rode next to a Turk, who complained: "What does the Ruler want from us? He is killing us with cold. If we knew what he wants we would give it to him." Ibn Fadlan:

"All he wants is that you people should say: "There is no God save Allah". The Turk laughed: "If we knew that it is so, we should say so."

There are many such incidents, which Ibn Fadlan reports without appreciating the independence of mind which they reflect. Nor did the envoy of the Baghdad court appreciate the nomadic tribesmen's fundamental contempt for authority. The following episode also occurred in the country of the powerful Ghuzz Turks, who paid tribute to the Khazars and, according to some sources, were closely related to them:

The next morning one of the Turks met us. He was ugly in build, dirty in appearance, contemptible in manners, base in nature; and we were moving through a heavy rain. Then he said: "Halt." Then the whole caravan of 3000 animals and 5000 men halted. Then he said: "Not a single one of you is allowed to go on." We halted then, obeying his orders. (Obviously the leaders of the great caravan had to avoid at all costs a conflict with the Ghuzz tribesmen). Then we said to him: "We are friends of the Kudarkin [Viceroy]". He began to laugh and said: "Who is the Kudarkin? I shit on his beard." Then he said: "Bread." I gave him a few loaves of bread. He took them and said: "Continue your journey; I have taken pity on you."

The democratic methods of the Ghuzz, practised when a decision had to be taken, were even more bewildering to the representative of an authoritarian theocracy: They are nomads and have houses of felt. They stay for a while in one place and then move on. One can see their tents dispersed here and there all over the place according to nomadic custom. Although they lead a hard life, they behave like donkeys that have lost their way. They have no religion which would link them to God, nor are they guided by reason; they do not worship anything. Instead, they call their headmen lords; when one of them consults his chieftain, he asks: "O lord, what shall I do in this or that matter?" The course of action they adopt is decided by taking counsel among themselves; but when they have decided on a measure and are ready to carry it through, even the humblest and lowliest among them can come and disrupt that decision.

The sexual mores of the Ghuzz – and other tribes — were a remarkable mixture of liberalism and savagery:

Their women wear no veils in the presence of their men or strangers. Nor do the women cover any parts of their bodies in the presence of people. One day we stayed at the place of a Ghuzz and were sitting around; his wife was also present. As we conversed, the woman uncovered her private parts and scratched them, and we all saw it. Thereupon we covered our faces and said: "May God forgive me." The husband laughed and said to the interpreter: "Tell them we uncover it in your presence so that you may see and restrain yourselves; but it cannot be attained. This is better than when it is covered up and yet attainable." Adultery is alien to them; yet when they discover that someone is an adulterer they split him in two halves. This they do by bringing together the branches of two trees, tie him to the branches and then let both trees go, so that the man tied to them is torn in two.

He does not say whether the same punishment was meted out to the guilty woman. Later on, when talking about the Volga Bulgars, he describes an equally savage method of splitting adulterers into two, applied to both men and women. Yet, he notes with astonishment, Bulgars of both sexes swim naked in their rivers, and have as little bodily shame as the Ghuzz. As for homosexuality – which in Arab countries was taken as a matter of course – Ibn Fadlan says that it is "regarded by the Turks as a terrible sin". But in the only episode he relates to prove his point, the seducer of a "beardless youth" gets away with a fine of 400 sheep.

Accustomed to the splendid baths of Baghdad, our traveller could not get over the dirtiness of the Turks. "The Ghuzz do not wash themselves after defacating or urinating, nor do they bathe after seminal pollution or on other occasions. They refuse to have anything to do with water, particularly in winter...". When the Ghuzz commander-in-chief took off his luxurious coat of brocade to don a new coat the mission had brought him, they saw that his underclothes were "fraying apart from dirt, for it is their custom never to take off the garment they wear close to their bodies until it disintegrates". Another Turkish tribe, the Bashkirs, "shave their beards and eat their lice. They search the folds of their undergarments and crack the lice with their teeth". When Ibn Fadlan watched a Bashkir do this, the latter remarked to him: "They are delicious".

All in all, it is not an engaging picture. Our fastidious traveller's contempt for the barbarians was profound. But it was only aroused by their uncleanliness and what he considered as indecent exposure of the body; the savagery of their punishments and sacrificial rites leave him quite indifferent. Thus he describes the Bulgars' punishment for manslaughter with detached interest, without his otherwise frequent expressions of indignation: "They make for him [the delinquent] a box of birchwood, put him inside, nail the lid on the box, put three loaves of bread and a can of water beside it, and suspend the box between two tall poles, saying: "We have put him between heaven and earth, that he may be exposed to the sun and the rain, and that the deity may perhaps forgive him." And so he remains suspended until time lets him decay and the winds blow him away."

He also describes, with similar aloofness, the funeral sacrifice of hundreds of horses and herds of other animals, and the gruesome ritual killing of a Rus (Rus: the Viking founders of the early Russian settlements – see below, Chapter III.) slave girl at her master's bier. About pagan religions he has little to say. But the Bashkirs' phallus cult arouses his interest, for he asks through his interpreter one of the natives the reason for his worshipping a wooden penis, and notes down his reply: "Because I issued from something similar and know of no other creator who made me." He then adds that 'some of them [the Bashkirs] believe in twelve deities, a god for winter, another for summer, one for the rain, one for the wind, one for the trees, one for men, one for the horse, one for water, one for the night, one for the day, a god of death and one for the earth; while that god who dwells in the sky is the greatest among them, but takes counsel with the others and thus all are contented with each other's doings... We have seen a group among them which worships snakes, and a group which worships fish, and a group which worships cranes..."

Among the Volga Bulgars, Ibn Fadlan found a strange custom: When they observe a man who excels through quickwittedness and knowledge, they say: "for this one it is more befitting to serve our Lord." They seize him, put a rope round his neck and hang him on a tree where he is left until he rots away.

Commenting on this passage, the Turkish orientalist Zeki Validi Togan, undisputed authority on Ibn Fadlan and his times, has this to say:25 "There is nothing mysterious about the cruel treatment meted out by the Bulgars to people who were overly clever. It was based on the simple, sober reasoning of the average citizens who wanted only to lead what they considered to be a normal life, and to avoid any risk or adventure into which the "genius" might lead them." He then quotes a Tartar proverb: "If you know too much, they will hang you, and if you are too modest, they will trample on you." He concludes that the victim 'should not be regarded simply as a learned person, but as an unruly genius, one who is too clever by half". This leads one to believe that the custom should be regarded as a measure of social defence against change, a punishment of non-conformists and potential innovators. (In support of his argument, the author adduces Turkish and Arabic quotations in the original, without translation – a nasty habit common among modern experts in the field.) But a few lines further down he gives a different interpretation:

Ibn Fadlan describes not the simple murder of too-clever people, but one of their pagan customs: human sacrifice, by which the most excellent among men were offered as sacrifice to God.

This ceremony was probably not carried out by common Bulgars, but by their Tabibs, or medicine men, i.e. their shamans, whose equivalents among the Bulgars and the Rus also wielded power of life and death over the people, in the name of their cult. According to Ibn Rusta, the medicine men of the Rus could put a rope round the neck of anybody and hang him on a tree to invoke the mercy of God. When this was done, they said: "This is an offering to God."

Perhaps both types of motivation were mixed together: 'since sacrifice is a necessity, let's sacrifice the trouble-makers".

We shall see that human sacrifice was also practised by the Khazars – including the ritual killing of the king at the end of his reign. We may assume that many other similarities existed between the customs of the tribes described by Ibn Fadlan and those of the Khazars. Unfortunately he was debarred from visiting the Khazar capital and had to rely on information collected in territories under Khazar dominion, and particularly at the Bulgar court.

It took the Caliph's mission nearly a year (from June 21, 921, to May 12, 922) to reach its destination, the land of the Volga Bulgars. The direct route from Baghdad to the Volga leads across the Caucasus and Khazaria – to avoid the latter, they had to make the enormous detour round the eastern shore of the "Khazar Sea", the Caspian. Even so, they were constantly reminded of the proximity of the Khazars and its potential dangers.

A characteristic episode took place during their sojourn with the Ghuzz army chief (the one with the disreputable underwear). They were at first well received, and given a banquet. But later the Ghuzz leaders had second thoughts because of their relations with the Khazars. The chief assembled the leaders to decide what to do:

The most distinguished and influential among them was the Tarkhan; he was lame and blind and had a maimed hand. The Chief said to them: "These are the messengers of the King of the Arabs, and I do not feel authorized to let them proceed without consulting you." Then the Tarkhan spoke: "This is a matter the like of which we have never seen or heard before; never has an ambassador of the Sultan travelled through our country since we and our ancestors have been here. Without doubt the Sultan is deceiving us; these people he is really sending to the Khazars, to stir them up against us. The best will be to cut each of these messengers into two and to confiscate all their belongings." Another one said: "No, we should take their belongings and let them run back naked whence they came." Another said: "No, the Khazar king holds hostages from us, let us send these people to ransom them."

They argued among themselves for seven days, while Ibn Fadlan and his people feared the worst. In the end the Ghuzz let them go; we are not told why. Probably Ibn Fadlan succeeded in persuading them that his mission was in fact directed against the Khazars. The Ghuzz had earlier on fought with the Khazars against another Turkish tribe, the Pechenegs, but more recently had shown a hostile attitude; hence the hostages the Khazars took.

The Khazar menace loomed large on the horizon all along the journey. North of the Caspian they made another huge detour before reaching the Bulgar encampment somewhere near the confluence of the Volga and the Kama. There the King and leaders of the Bulgars were waiting for them in a state of acute anxiety. As soon as the ceremonies and festivities were over, the King sent for Ibn Fadlan to discuss business. He reminded Ibn Fadlan in forceful language ("his voice sounded as if he were speaking from the bottom of a barrel") of the main purpose of the mission to wit, the money to be paid to him 'so that I shall be able to build a fortress to protect me from the Jews who subjugated me". Unfortunately that money – a sum of four thousand dinars – had not been handed over to the mission, owing to some complicated matter of red tape; it was to be sent later on. On learning this, the King – "a personality of impressive appearance, broad and corpulent" – seemed close to despair. He suspected the mission of having defrauded the money:

"What would you think of a group of men who are given a sum of money destined for a people that is weak, besieged, and oppressed, yet these men defraud the money?" I replied: "This is forbidden, those men would be evil." He asked: "Is this a matter of opinion or a matter of general consent?" I replied: "A matter of general consent." Gradually Ibn Fadlan succeeded in convincing the King that the money was only delayed, (Apparently it did arrive at some time, as there is no further mention of the matter). but not to allay his anxieties. The King kept repeating that the whole point of the invitation was the building of the fortress "because he was afraid of the King of the Khazars". And apparently he had every reason to be afraid, as Ibn Fadlan relates:

The Bulgar King's son was held as a hostage by the King of the Khazars. It was reported to the King of the Khazars that the Bulgar King had a beautiful daughter. He sent a messenger to sue for her. The Bulgar King used pretexts to refuse his consent. The Khazar sent another messenger and took her by force, although he was a Jew and she a Muslim; but she died at his court. The Khazar sent another messenger and asked for the Bulgar King's other daughter. But in the very hour when the messenger reached him, the Bulgar King hurriedly married her to the Prince of the Askil, who was his subject, for fear that the Khazar would take her too by force, as he had done with her sister. This alone was the reason which made the Bulgar King enter into correspondence with the Caliph and ask him to have a fortress built because he feared the King of the Khazars.

It sounds like a refrain. Ibn Fadlan also specifies the annual tribute the Bulgar King had to pay the Khazars: one sable fur from each household in his realm. Since the number of Bulgar households (i.e., tents) is estimated to have been around 50000, and since Bulgar sable fur was highly valued all over the world, the tribute was a handsome one.

What Ibn Fadlan has to tell us about the Khazars is based – as already mentioned – on intelligence collected in the course of his journey, but mainly at the Bulgar court. Unlike the rest of his narrative, derived from vivid personal observations, the pages on the Khazars contain second-hand, potted information, and fall rather flat. Moreover, the sources of his information are biased, in view of the Bulgar King's understandable dislike of his Khazar overlord-while the Caliphate's resentment of a kingdom embracing a rival religion need hardly be stressed.

The narrative switches abruptly from a description of the Rus court to the Khazar court:

Concerning the King of the Khazars, whose title is Kagan, he appears in public only once every four months. They call him the

Great Kagan. His deputy is called Kagan Bek; he is the one who commands and supplies the armies, manages the affairs of state, appears in public and leads in war. The neighbouring kings obey his orders. He enters every day into the presence of the Great Kagan, with deference and modesty, barefooted, carrying a stick of wood in his hand. He makes obeisance, lights the stick, and when it has burned down, he sits down on the throne on the King's right. Next to him in rank is a man called the K-nd-r Kagan, and next to that one, the Jawshyghr Kagan.

It is the custom of the Great Kagan not to have social intercourse with people, and not to talk with them, and to admit nobody to his presence except those we have mentioned. The power to bind or release, to mete out punishment, and to govern the country belongs to his deputy, the Kagan Bek.

It is a further custom of the Great Kagan that when he dies a great building is built for him, containing twenty chambers, and in each chamber a grave is dug for him. Stones are broken until they become like powder, which is spread over the floor and covered with pitch. Beneath the building flows a river, and this river is large and rapid. They divert the river water over the grave and they say that this is done so that no devil, no man, no worm and no creeping creatures can get at him. After he has been buried, those who buried him are decapitated, so that nobody may know in which of the chambers is his grave. The grave is called "Paradise" and they have a saying: "He has entered Paradise". All the chambers are spread with silk brocade interwoven with threads of gold. It is the custom of the King of the Khazars to have twenty-five wives; each of the wives is the daughter of a king who owes him allegiance. He takes them by consent or by force. He has sixty girls for concubines, each of them of exquisite beauty.

Ibn Fadlan then proceeds to give a rather fanciful description of the Kagan's harem, where each of the eighty-five wives and concubines has a "palace of her own", and an attendant or eunuch who, at the King's command, brings her to his alcove "faster than the blinking of an eye.

After a few more dubious remarks about the "customs" of the Khazar Kagan (we shall return to them later), Ibn Fadlan at last provides some factual information about the country:

The King has a great city on the river Itil [Volga] on both banks. On one bank live the Muslims, on the other bank the King and his court. The Muslims are governed by one of the King's officials who is himself a Muslim. The law-suits of the Muslims living in the Khazar capital and of visiting merchants from abroad are looked after by that official. Nobody else meddles in their affairs or sits in judgment over them.

Ibn Fadlan's travel report, as far as it is preserved, ends with the words: The Khazars and their King are all Jews. (This sounds like an exaggeration in view of the existence of a Muslim community in the capital. Zeki Validi accordingly suppressed the word "all". We must assume that "the Khazars" here refers to the ruling nation or tribe, within the ethnic mosaic of Khazaria, and that the Muslims enjoyed legal and religious autonomy, but were not considered as "real Khazars".) The Bulgars and all their neighbours are subject to him. They treat him with worshipful obedience. Some are of the opinion that Gog and Magog are the Khazars.

Ihave quoted Ibn Fadlan's odyssey at some length, not so much because of the scant information he provides about the Khazars themselves, but because of the light it throws on the world which surrounded them, the stark barbarity of the people amidst whom they lived, reflecting their own past, prior to the conversion. For, by the time of Ibn Fadlan's visit to the Bulgars, Khazaria was a surprisingly modern country compared to its neighbours. The contrast is evidenced by the reports of other Arab historians, (The following pages are based on the works of lstakhri, al-Masudi, Ibn Rusta and Ibn Hawkal), and is present on every level, from housing to the administration of justice. The Bulgars still live exclusively in tents, including the King, although the royal tent is "very large, holding a thousand people or more".26 On the other hand, the Khazar Kagan inhabits a castle built of burnt brick, his ladies are said to inhabit "palaces with roofs of teak",27 and the Muslims have several mosques, among them "one whose minaret rises above the royal castle".

In the fertile regions, their farms and cultivat ed areas stretched out continuously over sixty or seventy miles. They also had extensive vineyards. Thus Ibn Hawkal: "In Kozr [Khazaria] there is a certain city called Asmid [Samandar] which has so many orchards and gardens that from Darband to Serir the whole country is covered with gardens and plantations belonging to this city. It is said that there are about forty thousand of them. Many of these produce grapes."

The region north of the Caucasus was extremely fertile. In AD 968 Ibn Hawkal met a man who had visited it after a Russian raid: "He said there is not a pittance left for the poor in any vineyard or garden, not a leaf on the bough... [But] owing to the excellence of their land and the abundance of its produce it will not take three years until it becomes again what it was." Caucasian wine is still a delight, consumed in vast quantities in the Soviet Union. However, the royal treasuries' main source of income was foreign trade. The sheer volume of the trading caravans plying their way between Central Asia and the Volga-Ural region is indicated by Ibn Fadlan: we remember that the caravan his mission joined at Gurganj consisted of "5000 men and 3000 pack animals". Making due allowance for exaggeration, it must still have been a mighty caravan, and we do not know how many of these were at any time on the move. Nor what goods they transported – although textiles, dried fruit, honey, wax and spices seem to have played an important part. A second major trade route led across the Caucasus to Armenia, Georgia, Persia and Byzantium. A third consisted of the increasing traffic of Rus merchant fleets down the Volga to the eastern shores of the Khazar Sea, carrying mainly precious furs much in demand among the Muslim aristocracy, and slaves from the north, sold at the slave market of Itil. On all these transit goods, including the slaves, the Khazar ruler levied a tax of ten per cent. Adding to this the tribute paid by Bulgars, Magyars, Burtas and so on, one realizes that Khazaria was a prosperous country – but also that its prosperity depended to a large extent on its military power, and the prestige it conveyed on its tax collectors and customs officials.

Apart from the fertile regions of the south, with their vineyards and orchards, the country was poor in natural resources. One Arab historian (Istakhri) says that the only native product they exported was isinglass. This again is certainly an exaggeration, yet the fact remains that their main commercial activity seems to have consisted in re-exporting goods brought in from abroad. Among these goods, honey and candle-wax particularly caught the Arab chroniclers' imagination. Thus Muqaddasi: "In Khazaria, sheep, honey and Jews exist in large quantities." It is true that one source – the Darband *Namah* – mentions gold or silver mines in Khazar territory, but their location has not been ascertained. On the other hand, several of the sources mention Khazar merchandise seen in Baghdad, and the presence of Khazar merchants in Constantinople, Alexandria and as far afield as Samara and Fergana.

Thus Khazaria was by no means isolated from the civilized world; compared to its tribal neighbours in the north it was a cosmopolitan country, open to all sorts of cultural and religious influences, yet jealously defending its independence against the two ecclesiastical world powers. We shall see that this attitude prepared the ground for the *coup de theatre* – or *coup d'tat* – which established Judaism as the state religion.

The arts and crafts seem to have flourished, including haute couture. When the future Emperor Constantine V married the Khazar Kagan's daughter (see above, section 1), she brought with her dowry a splendid dress which so impressed the Byzantine court that it was adopted as a *male* ceremonial robe; they called it tzitzakion, derived from the Khazar-Turkish pet-name of the Princess, which was Chichak or "flower" (until she was baptized Eirene). "Here," Toynbee comments, "we have an illuminating fragment of cultural history."31 When another Khazar princess married the Muslim governor of Armenia, her cavalcade contained, apart from attendants and slaves, ten tents mounted on wheels, "made of the finest silk, with gold-and silver-plated doors, the floors covered with sable furs. Twenty others carried the gold and silver vessels and other treasures which were her dowry".32 The Kagan himself travelled in a mobile tent even more luxuriously equipped, carrying on its top a pomegranate of gold.

Khazar art, like that of the Bulgars and Magyars, was mainly imitative, modelled on Persian-Sassanide patterns. The Soviet archaeologist Bader33 emphasized the role of the Khazars in the spreading of Persian-style silver-ware towards the north. Some of these finds may have been re-exported by the Khazars, true to their role as middlemen; others were imitations made in Khazar workshops – the ruins of which have been traced near the ancient

Khazar fortress of Sarkel. (Unfortunately, Sarkel, the most important Khazar archaeological site has been flooded by the reservoir of a newly built hydro-electric station). The jewellery unearthed within the confines of the fortress was of local manufacture.34 The Swedish archaeologist T. J. Arne mentions ornamental plates, clasps and buckles found as far as Sweden, of Sassanide and Byzantine inspiration, manufactured in Khazaria or territories under their influence.

Thus the Khazars were the principal intermediaries in the spreading of Persian and Byzantine art among the semi-barbaric tribes of Eastern Europe. After his exhaustive survey of the archaeological and documentary evidence (mostly from Soviet sources), Bartha concludes:

The sack of Tiflis by the Khazars, presumably in the spring of AD 629, is relevant to our subject... [During the period of occupation] the Kagan sent out inspectors to supervise the manufacture of gold, silver, iron and copper products. Similarly the bazaars, trade in general, even the fisheries, were under their control... [Thus] in the course of their incessant Caucasian campaigns during the seventh century, the Khazars made contact with a culture which had grown out of the Persian Sassanide tradition. Accordingly, the products of this culture spread to the people of the steppes not only by trade, but by means of plunder and even by taxation.... All the tracks that we have assiduously followed in the hope of discovering the origins of Magyar art in the tenth century have led us back to Khazar territory.

The last remark of the Hungarian scholar refers to the spectacular archaeological finds known as the "Treasure of Nagyszentmiklos" (see frontispiece). The treasure, consisting of twentythree gold vessels, dating from the tenth century, was found in 1791 in the vicinity of the village of that name. (It now belongs to Rumania and is called Sinnicolaul Mare). Bartha points out that the figure of the "victorious Prince" dragging a prisoner along by his hair, and the mythological scene at the back of the golden jar, as well as the design of other ornamental objects, show close affinities with the finds in Novi Pazar in Bulgaria and in Khazar Sarkel. As both Magyars and Bulgars were under Khazar suzerainty for protracted periods, this is not very surprising, and the warrior, together with the rest of the treasure, gives us at least some idea of the arts practised within the Khazar Empire (the Persian and Byzantine influence is predominant, as one would expect). (The interested reader will find an excellent collection of photographs in Gyula László's The Art of the Migration Period [although his historical comments have to be treated with caution]).

One school of Hungarian archaeologists maintains that the tenth century gold-and silversmiths working in Hungary were actually Khazars.37 As we shall see later on (see III, 7, 8), when the Magyars migrated to Hungary in 896 they were led by a dissident Khazar tribe, known as the Kabars, who settled with them in their new home. The Kabar-Khazars were known as skilled gold and silversmiths; the (originally more primitive) Magyars only acquired these skills in their new country. Thus the theory of the Khazar origin of at least some of the archaeological finds in Hungary is not implausible – as will become clearer in the light of the Magyar-Khazar nexus discussed later on.

Whether the warrior on the golden jar is of Magyar or Khazar origin, he helps us to visualise the appearance of a cavalryman of that period, perhaps belonging to an elite regiment. Masudi says that in the Khazar army 'seventhousand of them (Istakhri has 12000). ride with the King, archers with breast plates, helmets, and coats of mail. Some are lancers, equipped and armed like the Muslims... None of the kings in this part of the world has a regular standing army except the King of the Khazars." And Ibn Hawkal: "This king has twelve thousand soldiers in his service, of whom when one dies, another person is immediately chosen in his place."

Here we have another important clue to the Khazar dominance: a permanent professional army, with a Praetorian Guard which, in peacetime, effectively controlled the ethnic patchwork, and in times of war served as a hard core for the armed horde, which, as we have seen, may have swollen at times to a hundred thousand or more. (According to Masudi, the "Royal Army" consisted of Muslims who "immigrated from the neighbourhood of Kwarizm. Long ago, after the appearance of Islam, there was war and pestilence in their territory, and they repaired to the Khazar king... When the king of the Khazars is at war with the Muslims, they have a separate place in his army and do not fight the people of their own faith" [Quoted by Dunlop (1954), p. 206]. That the army "consisted" of Muslims is of course an exaggeration, contradicted by Masudi himself a few lines later, where he speaks of the Muslim contingent having a "separate place" in the Khazar army. Also, lbn Hawkal says that "the king has in his train 4000 Muslims and this king has 2000 soldiers in his service". The Kwarizmians probably formed a kind of Swiss Guard within the army, and their compatriots" talk of "hostages" [see above, section 10] may refer to them. Vice versa, the Byzantine Emperor Constantine Porphyrogenitus had a corps d'élite of Khazar guardsmen stationed at the gates of his palace. This was a privilege dearly bought: "These guards were so well remunerated that they had to purchase their posts for considerable sums, on which their salaries represented an annuity varying from about 2.25 to 4 per cent." [Constantine, De Ceremoniis, pp. 692-3]. For example, "a Khazar who received 7.4s. had paid for enrolment 302.8s." [Bury, p. 228n])

The capital of this motley empire was at first probably the fortress of Balanjar in the northern foothills of the Caucasus; after the Arab raids in the eighth century it was transferred to Samandar, on the western shore of the Caspian; and lastly to Itil in the estuary of the Volga.

We have several descriptions of Itil, which are fairly consistent with each other. It was a twin city, built on both sides of the river. The eastern half was called Khazaran, the western half Itil; (The town was in different periods also mentioned under different names, e.g., al-Bayada, "The White City") the two were connected by a pontoon bridge. The western half was surrounded by a fortified wall, built of brick; it contained the palaces and courts of the Kagan and the Bek, the habitations of their attendants (Masudi places these buildings on an island, close to the west bank, or a peninsula.) and of the "pure-bred Khazars". The wall had four gates, one of them facing the river. Across the river, on the east bank, lived "the Muslims and idol worshippers";38 this part also housed the mosques, markets, baths and other public amenities. Several Arab writers were impressed by the number of mosques in the Muslim quarter and the height of the principal minaret. They also kept stressing the autonomy enjoyed by the

Muslim courts and clergy. Here is what al-Masudi, known as "the Herodotus among the Arabs", has to say on this subject in his oft-quoted work *Meadows of Gold Mines and Precious Stones*:

The custom in the Khazar capital is to have seven judges. Of these two are for the Muslims, two are for the Khazars, judging according to the Torah (Mosaic law), two for the Christians, judging according to the Gospel and one for the Saqualibah, Rus and other pagans, judging according to pagan law... In his [the Khazar King's] city are many Muslims, merchants and craftsmen, who have come to his country because of his justice and the security which he offers. They have a principal mosque and a minaret which rises above the royal castle, and other mosques there besides, with schools where the children learn the Koran.

In reading these lines by the foremost Arab historian, written in the first half of the tenth century, (Supposedly between AD 943 and 947), one is tempted to take a perhaps too idyllic view of life in the Khazar kingdom. Thus we read in the article "Khazars" in the : "In a time when fanaticism, ignorance and anarchy reigned in Western Europe, the Kingdom of the Khazars could boast of its just and broad-minded administration." (*Jewish Encyclopaedia,* published 1901-6. In the *Encyclopaedia Judaica,* 1971, the article on the Khazars by Dunlop is of exemplary objectivity).

This, as we have seen, is partly true; but only partly. There is no evidence of the Khazars engaging in religious persecution, either before or after the conversion to Judaism. In this respect they may be called more tolerant and enlightened than the East Roman Empire, or Islam in its early stages. On the other hand, they seem to have preserved some barbaric rituals from their tribal past. We have heard Ibn Fadlan on the killings of the royal gravediggers. He also has something to say about another archaic custom regicide: "The period of the king's rule is forty years. If he exceeds this time by a single day, his subjects and attendants kill him, saying "His reasoning is already dimmed, and his insight confused"."

Istakhri has a different version of it:

When they wish to enthrone this Kagan, they put a silken cord round his neck and tighten it until he begins to choke. Then they ask him: "How long doest thou intend to rule?" If he does not die before that year, he is killed when he reaches it. Bury is doubtful whether to believe this kind of Arab traveller's lore, and one would indeed be inclined to dismiss it, if ritual regicide had not been such a widespread phenomenon among primitive (and not-so-primitive) people. Frazer laid great emphasis on the connection between the concept of the King's divinity, and the sacred obligation to kill him after a fixed period, or when his vitality is on the wane, so that the divine power may find a more youthful and vigorous incarnation. (Frazer wrote a special treatise on these lines on "The Killing of the Khazar Kings" [Folklore, XXVIII, 1917]).

It speaks in Istakhri's favour that the bizarre ceremony of "choking" the future King has been reported in existence apparently not so long ago among another people, the Kok-Turks. Zeki Validi quotes a French anthropologist, St Julien, writing in 1864:

When the new Chief has been elected, his officers and attendants... make him mount his horse. They tighten a ribbon of silk round his neck, without quite strangling him; then they loosen the ribbon and ask him with great insistence: "For how many years canst thou be our Khan?" The king, in his troubled mind, being unable to name a figure, his subjects decide, on the strength of the words that have escaped him, whether his rule will be long or brief.40

We do not know whether the Khazar rite of slaying the King (if it ever existed) fell into abeyance when they adopted Judaism, in which case the Arab writers were confusing past with present practices as they did all the time, compiling earlier travellers' reports, and attributing them to contemporaries. However that may be, the point to be retained, and which seems beyond dispute, is the divine role attributed to the Kagan, regardless whether or not it implied his ultimate sacrifice. We have heard before that he was venerated, but virtually kept in seclusion, cut off from the people, until he was buried with enormous ceremony. The affairs of state, including leadership of the army, were managed by the Bek (sometimes also called the Kagan Bek), who wielded all effective power. On this point Arab sources and modern historians are in agreement, and the latter usually describe the Khazar system of government as a "double kingship", the Kagan representing divine, the Bek secular, power.

The Khazar double kingship has been compared – quite mistakenly, it Seems – with the Spartan dyarchy and with the superficially similar dual leadership among various Turkish tribes. However, the two kings of Sparta, descendants of two leading families, wielded equal power; and as for the dual leadership among nomadic tribes, (Alföldi has suggested that the two leaders were the commanders of the two wings of the horde [quoted by Dunlop, p. 159, n. 123]), there is no evidence of a basic division of functions as among the Khazars. A more valid comparison is the system of government in Japan, from the Middle Ages to 1867, where secular power was concentrated in the hands of the shogun, while the Mikado was worshipped from afar as a divine figurehead.

Cassel has suggested an attractive analogy between the Khazar system of government and the game of chess. The double kingship is represented on the chess-board by the King (the Kagan) and the Queen (the Bek). The King is kept in seclusion, protected by his attendants, has little power and can only move one short step at a time. The Queen, by contrast, is the most powerful presence on the board, which she dominates. Yet the Queen may be lost and the game still continued, whereas the fall of the King is the ultimate disaster which instantly brings the contest to an end.

The double kingship thus seems to indicate a categorical distinction between the sacred and the profane in the mentality of the Khazars. The divine attributes of the Kagan are much in evidence in the following passage from Ibn Hawkal (Ibn Hawkal, another much-travelled Arab geographer and historian, wrote his Oriental Geography around AD 977. The passage here quoted is virtually a copy of what Istakhri wrote forty years earlier, but contains less obscurities, so I have followed Ouseley's translation [1800] of Ibn Hawkal):

The Khacan must be always of the Imperial race [Istakhri: "... of a family of notables"].41a No one is allowed to approach him but on business of importance: then they prostrate themselves before him, and rub their faces on the ground, until he gives orders for their approaching him, and speaking. When a Khacan... dies, whoever passes near his tomb must go on foot, and pay his respects at the grave; and when he is departing, must not mount on horseback, as long as the tomb is within view.

So absolute is the authority of this sovereign, and so implicitly are his commands obeyed, that if it seemed expedient to him that one of his nobles should die, and if he said to him, "Go and kill yourself," the man would immediately go to his house, and kill himself accordingly. The succession to the Khacanship being thus established in the same family [Istakhri: "in a family of notables who possess neither power nor riches"];41b when the turn of the inheritance arrives to any individual of it, he is confirmed in the dignity, though he possesses not a single dirhem [coin]. And I have heard from persons worthy of belief, that a certain young man used to sit in a little shop at the public marketplace, selling petty articles [Istakhri: 'selling bread"]; and that the people used to say, "When the present Khacan shall have departed, this man will succeed to the throne" [Istakhri: "There is no man worthier of the Khaganate than he"].41c But the young man was a Mussulman, and they give the Khacanship only to Jews.

The Khacan has a throne and pavilion of gold: these are not allowed to any other person. The palace of the Khacan is loftier than the other edifices.

The passage about the virtuous young man selling bread, or whatever it is, in the bazaar sounds rather like a tale about Harun al Rashid. If he was heir to the golden throne reserved for Jews, why then was he brought up as a poor Muslim? If we are to make any sense at all of the story, we must assume that the Kagan was chosen on the strength of his noble virtues, but chosen among members of the "Imperial Race" or "family of notables". This is in fact the view of Artamonov and Zeki Validi. Artamonov holds that the Khazars and other Turkish people were ruled by descendants of the Turkut dynasty, the erstwhile sovereigns of the defunct Turk Empire (cf. above, section 3). Zeki Validi suggests that the "Imperial Race" or "family of notables", to which the Kagan must belong, refers to the ancient dynasty of the Asena, mentioned in Chinese sources, a kind of desert aristocracy, from which Turkish and Mongol rulers traditionally claimed descent. This sounds fairly plausible and goes some way towards reconciling the contradictory values implied in the narrative just quoted: the noble youth without a dirhem to his name – and the pomp and circumstance surrounding the golden throne. We are witnessing the overlap of two traditions, like the optical interference of two wave-patterns on a screen: the asceticism of a tribe of hard-living desert nomads, and the glitter of a royal court prospering on its commerce and crafts, and striving to outshine its rivals in Baghdad and Constantinople. After all, the creeds professed by those sumptuous courts had also been inspired by ascetic desert-prophets in the past.

All this does not explain the startling division of divine and secular power, apparently unique in that period and region. As Bury wrote:43

"We have no information at what time the active authority of the Chagan was exchanged for his divine nullity, or why he was exalted to a position resembling that of the Emperor of Japan, in which his existence, and not his government, was considered essential to the prosperity of the State."

A speculative answer to this question has recently been proposed by Artamonov. He suggests that the acceptance of Judaism as the state religion was the result of a *coup d'état*, which at the same time reduced the Kagan, descendant of a pagan dynasty whose allegiance to Mosaic law could not really be trusted, to a mere figurehead. This is a hypothesis as good as any other – and with as little evidence to support it. Yet it seems probable that the two events – the adoption of Judaism and the establishment of the double kingship – were somehow connected. (Before the conversion the Kagan was still reported to play an active role – as, for instance, in his dealings with Justinian. To complicate matters further, the Arab sources sometimes refer to the "Kagan" when they clearly mean the "Bek" (as "kagan" was the generic term for "ruler" among many tribes), and they also use different names for the Bek, as the following list shows [after Minorsky, Hudud al Alam, p. 451:

Const. Porphyr. Khaqan Bek

Ibn Rusta Khazar Khaqan Aysha

Masudi Khaqan Malik

Istakhri Malik Khazar Khaqan Khazar*

Ibn Hawkal Khaqan Khazar Malik Khazar or Bek

Gardezi Khazar Khaqan Abshad

* The order of the rulers appears to have been changed]

THE religion of the Hebrews",writes Bury, "had exercised a profound influence on the creed of Islam, and it had been a basis for Christianity; it had won scattered proselytes; but the conversion of the Khazars to the undiluted religion of Jehova is unique in history." 1 What was the motivation of this unique event? It is not easy to get under the skin of a Khazar prince – covered, as it was, by a coat of mail. But if we reason in terms of power-politics, which obeys essentially the same rules throughout the ages, a fairly plausible analogy offers itself.

At the beginning of the eighth century the world was polarized between the two super-powers representing Christianity and Islam. Their ideological doctrines were welded to power-politics pursued by the classical methods of propaganda, subversion and military conquest. The Khazar Empire represented a Third Force, which had proved equal to either of them, both as an adversary and an ally. But it could only maintain its independence by accepting neither Christianity nor Islam – for either choice would have automatically subordinated it to the authority of the Roman Emperor or the Caliph of Baghdad.

There had been no lack of efforts by either court to convert the Khazars to Christianity or Islam, but all they resulted in was the exchange of diplomatic courtesies, dynastic inter-marriages and shifting military alliances based on mutual self-interest. Relying on its military strength, the Khazar kingdom, with its hinterland of vassal tribes, was determined to preserve its position as the Third Force, leader of the uncommitted nations of the steppes. At the same time, their intimate contacts with Byzantium and the Caliphate had taught the Khazars that their primitive shamanism was not only barbaric and outdated compared to the great monotheistic creeds, but also unable to confer on the leaders the spiritual and legal authority which the rulers of the two theocratic world powers, the Caliph and the Emperor, enjoyed. Yet the conversion to either creed would have meant submission, the end of independence, and thus would have defeated its purpose. What could have been more logical than to embrace a third creed, which was uncommitted towards either of the two, yet represented the venerable foundation of both? The apparent logic of the decision is of course due to the deceptive clarity of hindsight. In reality, the conversion to Judaism required an act of genius. Yet both the Arab and Hebrew sources on the history of the conversion, however varied in detail, point to a line of reasoning as indicated above. To quote Bury once more:

> There can be no question that the ruler was actuated by political motives in adopting Judaism. To embrace Mohammadanism would have made him the spiritual dependent of the Caliphs, who attempted to press their faith on the Khazars, and in Christianity lay the danger of his becoming an ecclesiastical vassal of the Roman Empire. Judaism was a reputable religion with sacred books which both Christian and Mohammadan respected; it elevated him above the heathen barbarians, and secured him against the interference of Caliph or Emperor. But he did not adopt, along with circumcision, the intolerance of the Jewish cult. He allowed the mass of his people to abide in their heathendom and worship their idols.

Though the Khazar court's conversion was no doubt politically motivated, it would still be absurd to imagine that they embraced overnight, blindly, a religion whose tenets were unknown to them. In fact, however, they had been well acquainted with Jews and their religious observances for at least a century before the conversion, through the continued influx of refugees from religious persecution in Byzantium, and to a lesser extent from countries in Asia Minor conquered by the Arabs. We know that Khazaria was a relatively civilized country among the Barbarians of the North, yet not committed to either of the militant creeds, and so it became a natural haven for the periodic exodus of Jews under Byzantine rule, threatened by forced conversion and other pressures. Persecution in varied forms had started with Justinian I (527-65), and assumed particularly vicious forms under Heraclius in the seventh century, Leo III in the eighth, Basil and Leo IV in the ninth, Romanus in the tenth. Thus Leo III, who ruled during the two decades immediately preceding the Khazar conversion to Judaism, "attempted to end the anomaly [of the tolerated status of Jews] at one blow, by ordering all his Jewish subjects to be baptized".3 Although the implementation of the order seemed to have been rather ineffective, it led to the flight of a considerable number of Jews from Byzantium. Masudi relates:

In this city [Khazaran-Itil] are Muslims, Christians, Jews and pagans. The Jews are the king, his attendants and the Khazars of his kind. [i.e., presumably the ruling tribe of "White Khazars"] The king of the Khazars had already become a Jew in the Caliphate of Harun al-Rashid [i.e., between AD 786 and 809; but it is generally assumed that Masudi used a convenient historical landmark and that the conversion took place around AD 740.] and he was joined by Jews from all lands of Islam and from the country of the Greeks [Byzantium]. Indeed the king of the Greeks at the present time, the Year of the Hegira 332 [AD 943-4] has converted the Jews in his kingdom to Christianity by coercion... Thus many Jews took flight from the country of the Greeks to Khazaria...

The last two sentences quoted refer to events two hundred years after the Khazar conversion, and show how persistently the waves of persecution followed each other over the centuries. But the Jews were equally persistent. Many endured torture, and those who did not have the strength to resist returned later on to their faith – "like dogs to their vomit", as one Christian chronicler gracefully put it.4 Equally picturesque is the description of a Hebrew writer5 of one method of forced conversion used under the Emperor Basil against the Jewish community of Oria in southern Italy:

How did they force them? Anyone refusing to accept their erroneous belief was placed in an olive mill under a wooden press, and squeezed in the way olives are squeezed in the mill.

Another Hebrew source6 remarks on the persecution under the Emperor Romanus (the "Greek King"to whom Masudi refers): "And afterwards there will arise a King who will persecute them not by destruction, but mercifully by driving them out of the country.".The only mercy shown by history to those who took to flight, or were driven to it, was the existence of Khazaria, both before and after the conversion. Before, it was a refugee haven; after, it became a kind of National Home. The refugees were products of a superior culture, and were no doubt an important factor in creating that cosmopolitan, tolerant outlook which so impressed the Arab chroniclers quoted before. Their influence – and no doubt their proselytizing zeal [This was an age when converting unbelievers by force or persuasion was a foremost concern. That the Jews, too, indulged in it is shown by the fact that, since the rule of Justinian, Byzantine law threatened severe punishments for the attempt to convert Christians to Judaism, while for Jews "molesting"converts to Christianity the penalty was death by fire (Sharf, p.25).] – would have made itself felt first and foremost at the court and among leading notables. They may have combined in their missionary efforts theological arguments and messianic prophecies with a shrewd assessment of the political advantages the Khazars would derive from adopting a "neutral"religion.

The exiles also brought with them Byzantine arts and crafts, superior methods in agriculture and trade, and the square Hebrew alphabet. We do not know what kind of script the Khazars used before that, but the Fihrist of Ibn Nadim,7 a kind of universal bibliography written circa AD 987, informs us that in his time the Khazars used the Hebrew alphabet. It served the dual purpose of scholarly discourse in Hebrew (analogous to the use of mediaeval Latin in the West) and as a written alphabet for the various languages spoken in Khazaria (analogous to the use of the Latin alphabet for the various vernaculars in Western Europe). From Khazaria the Hebrew script seemed to have spread into neighbouring countries.

Thus Chwolson reports that "inscriptions in a non-Semitic language (or possibly in two different non-Semitic languages) using Hebrew characters were found on two gravestones from Phanagoria and Parthenit in the Crimea; they have not been deciphered yet." [These inscriptions are a category apart from the forgeries of Firkovitch, notorious among historians (see Appendix III). – Poliak (4/3) quoting Chwolson, D.A. (1865).] (The Crimea was, as we have seen, intermittently under Khazar rule; but it also had an old-established Jewish community, and the inscriptions may even pre-date the conversion.) Some Hebrew letters (*shin* and *tsadei*) also found their way into the Cyrillic alphabet,9 and furthermore, many Polish silver coins have been found, dating from the twelfth or thirteenth century, which bear Polish inscriptions in Hebrew lettering (e.g., Leszek krol Polski – Leszek King of Poland), side by side with coins inscribed in the Latin alphabet. Poliak comments:

"These coins are the final evidence for the spreading of the Hebrew script from Khazaria to the neighbouring Slavonic countries. The use of these coins was not related to any question of religion. They were minted because many of the Polish people were more used to this type of script than to the Roman script, not considering it as specifically Jewish."

Thus while the conversion was no doubt inspired by opportunistic motives – conceived as a cunning political manoeuvre – it brought in its wake cultural developments which could hardly have been foreseen by those who started it. The Hebrew alphabet was the beginning; three centuries later the decline of the Khazar state is marked by repeated outbreaks of a messianic Zionism, with pseudo-Messiahs like David El-Roi (hero of a novel by Disraeli) leading quixotic crusades for the re-conquest of Jerusalem. [See below, Chapter IV, II.] After the defeat by the Arabs in 737, the Kagan's forced adoption of Islam had been a formality almost instantly revoked, which apparently left no impression on his people. In contrast to this, the voluntary conversion to Judaism was to produce deep and lasting effects.

The circumstances of the conversion are obscured by legend, but the principal Arab and Hebrew accounts of it have some basic features in common.

Al-Masudi's account of the Jewish rule in Khazaria, quoted earlier on, ends with a reference to a previous work of his, in which he gave a description of those circumstances. That previous work of Masudi's is lost; but there exist two accounts which are based on tile lost book. The first, by Dimaski (written in 1327), reiterates that at the time of Harun al Rashid, the Byzantine Emperor forced the Jews to emigrate; these emigrants came to the Khazar country where they found "an intelligent but uneducated race to whom they offered their religion. The natives found it better than their own and accepted it."

The second, much more detailed account is in al-Bakri's Book of Kingdoms and Roads (eleventh century):

The reason for the conversion to Judaism of the King of the Khazars, who had previously been a pagan, is as follows. He had adopted Christianity. [No other source, as far as I know, mentions this. It may be a substitution more palatable to Muslim readers for the Kagan's short-lived adoption of Islam prior to Judaism.] Then he recognized its falsehood and discussed this matter, which greatly worried him, with one of his high officials. The latter said to him: O king, those in possession of sacred scriptures fall into three groups. Summon them and ask them to state their case, then follow the one who is in possession of the truth..So he sent to the Christians for a bishop. Now there was with the King a Jew, skilled in argument, who engaged him in disputation. He asked the Bishop: "What do you say of Moses, the son of Amran, and the Torah which was revealed to him?"The Bishop replied: "Moses is a prophet and the Torah speaks the truth."Then the Jew said to the King: "He has already admitted the truth of my creed. Ask him now what he believes in.".So the King asked him and he replied: "I say that Jesus the Messiah is the son of Mary, he is the Word, and he has revealed the mysteries in the name of God."Then said the Jew to the King of the Khazars: "He preaches a doctrine which I know not, while he accepts my propositions." But the Bishop was not strong in producing evidence. Then the King asked for a Muslim, and they sent him a scholarly, clever man who was good at arguments. But the Jew hired someone who poisoned him on the journey, and he died. And the Jew succeeded in winning the King for his faith, so that he embraced Judaism.

The Arab historians certainly had a gift for sugaring the pill. Had the Muslim scholar been able to participate in the debate he would have fallen into the same trap as the Bishop, for both accepted the truth of the Old Testament, whereas the upholders of the New Testament and of the Koran were each outvoted two to one. The King's approval of this reasoning is symbolic: he is only willing to accept doctrines which are shared by all three – their common denominator – and refuses to commit himself to any of the rival claims which go beyond that. It is once more the principle of the uncommitted world, applied to theology. The story also implies, as Bury has pointed out, that Jewish influence at the Khazar court must already have been strong before the formal conversion, for the Bishop and the Muslim scholar have to be 'sent for", whereas the Jew is alreadv "with him"(the King).

We now turn from the principal Arab source on the conversion – Masudi and his compilers – to the principal Jewish source. This is the so-called "Khazar Correspondence": an exchange of letters, in Hebrew, between Hasdai Ibn Shaprut, the Jewish chief minister of the Caliph of Cordoba, and Joseph, King of the Khazars or, rather, between their respective scribes. The authenticity of the correspondence has been the subject of controversy but is now generally accepted with due allowance made for the vagaries of later copyists. [A summary of the controversy will be found in Appendix III.] The exchange of letters apparently took place after 954 and before 961, that is roughly at the time when Masudi wrote. To appreciate its significance a word must be said about the personality of Hasdai Ibn Shaprut – perhaps the most brilliant figure in the "Golden Age"(900-1200) of the Jews in Spain.

In 929, Abd-al-Rahman III, a member of the Omayad dynasty, succeeded in unifying the Moorish possessions in the southern and central parts of the Iberian peninsula under his rule, and founded the Western Caliphate. His capital, Cordoba, became the glory of Arab Spain, and a focal centre of European culture with a library of 400000 catalogued volumes. Hasdai, born 910 in Cordoba into a distinguished Jewish family, first attracted the Caliph's attention as a medical practitioner with some remarkable cures to his credit. Abd-al-Rahman appointed him his court physician, and trusted his judgment so completely that Hasdai was called upon, first, to put the state finances in order, then to act as Foreign Minister and diplomatic trouble-shooter in the new Caliphate's complex dealings with Byzantium, the German Emperor Otto, with Castile, Navarra, Arragon and other Christian kingdoms in the north of Spain. Hasdai was a true *uomo universale* centuries before the Renaissance who, in between affairs of state, still found the time to translate medical books into Arabic, to correspond with the learned rabbis of Baghdad and to act as a Maecenas for Hebrew grammarians and poets.

He obviously was an enlightened, yet a devoted Jew, who used his diplomatic contacts to gather information about the Jewish communities dispersed in various parts of the world, and to intervene on their behalf whenever possible. He was particularly concerned about the persecution of Jews in the Byzantine Empire under Romanus. Fortunately, he wielded considerable influence at the Byzantine court, which was vitally interested in procuring the benevolent neutrality of Cordoba during the Byzantine campaigns against the Muslims of the East. Hasdai, who was conducting the negotiations, used this opportunity to intercede on behalf of Byzantine Jewry, apparently with success. According to his own account, Hasdai first heard of the existence of an independent Jewish kingdom from some merchant traders from Khurasan in Persia; but he doubted the truth of their story. Later he questioned the members of a Byzantine diplomatic mission to Cordoba, and they confirmed the merchants' account, contributing a considerable amount of factual detail about the Khazar kingdom, including the name – Joseph – of its present King. Thereupon Hasdai decided to send couriers with a letter to King Joseph.

The letter (which will be discussed in more detail later on) contains a list of questions about the Khazar state, its people, method of government, armed forces, and so on – including an inquiry to which of the twelve tribes Joseph belonged. This seems to indicate that Hasdai thought the Jewish Khazars to hail from Palestine – as the Spanish Jews did – and perhaps even to represent one of the Lost Tribes. Joseph, not being of Jewish descent, belonged, of course, to none of the tribes; in his Reply to Hasdai, he provides, as we shall see, a genealogy of a different kind, but his main concern is to give Hasdai a detailed – if legendary – account of the conversion – which took place two centuries earlier – and the circumstances that led to it.

Joseph's narrative starts with a eulogy of his ancestor, King Bulan, a great conqueror and a wise man who "drove out the sorcerers and idolators from his land". Subsequently an angel appeared to King Bulan in his dreams, exhorting him to worship the only true God, and promising that in exchange He would "bless and multiply Bulan's offspring, and deliver his enemies into his hands, and make his kingdom last to the end of the world".

This, of course, is inspired by the story of the Covenant in Genesis; and it implies that the Khazars too claimed the status of a Chosen Race, who made their own Covenant with the Lord, even though they were not descended from Abraham's seed. But at this point Joseph's story takes an unexpected turn. King Bulan is quite willing to serve the Almighty, but he raises a difficulty:

Thou knowest, my Lord, the secret thoughts of my heart and thou hast searched my kidneys to confirm that my trust is in thee; but the people over which I rule have a pagan mind and I do not know whether they will believe me. If I have found favour and mercy in thine eyes, then I beseech thee to appear also to their Great Prince, to make him support me..The Eternal One granted Bulan's request, he appeared to this Prince in a dream, and when he arose in the morning he came to the King and made it known to him...

There is nothing in Genesis, nor in the Arab accounts of the conversion, about a great prince whose consent has to be obtained. It is an unmistakable reference to the Khazar double kingship. The "Great Prince", apparently, is the Bek; but it is not impossible that the "King"was the Bek, and the "Prince"the Kagan. Moreover according to Arab and Armenian sources, the leader of the Khazar army which invaded Transcaucasia in 731 (i.e., a few years before the presumed date of the conversion) was called "Bulkhan".

Joseph's letter continues by relating how the angel appeared once more to the dreaming King and bade him to build a place of worship in which the Lord may dwell, for: "the sky and the skies above the sky are not large enough to hold me". King Bulan replies bashfully that he does not possess the gold and silver required for such an enterprise, "although it is my duty and desire to carry it out". The angel reassures him: all Bulan has to do is to lead his armies into Dariela and Ardabil in Armenia, where a treasure of silver and a treasure of gold are awaiting him. This fits in with Bulan's or Bulkhan's raid preceding the conversion; and also with Arab sources according to which the Khazars at one time controlled silver and gold mines in the Caucasus.16 Bulan does as the angel told him, returns victoriously with the loot, and builds "a Holy Tabernacle equipped with a sacred coffer [the "Ark of the Covenant"], a candelabrum, an altar and holy implements which have been preserved to this day and are still in my [King Joseph's] possession".

Joseph's letter, written in the second half of the tenth century, more than two hundred years after the events it purports to describe, is obviously a mixture of fact and legend. His description of the scant furnishings of the place of worship, and the paucity of the preserved relics, is in marked contrast to the account he gives in other parts of the letter of the present prosperity of his country. The days of his ancestor Bulan appear to him as remote antiquity, when the poor but virtuous King did not even have the money to construct the Holy Tabernacle – which was, after all, only a tent.

However,Joseph's letter up to this point is merely the prelude to the real drama of the conversion, which he now proceeds to relate. Apparently Bulan's renunciation of idolatry in favour of the "only true God"was only the first step, which still left the choice open between the three monotheistic creeds. At least, this is what the continuation of Joseph's letter seems to imply:

After these feats of arms [the invasion of Armenia], King Bulan's fame spread to all countries. The King of Edom [Byzantium] and the King of the Ishmaelim [the Muslims] heard the news and sent to him envoys with precious gifts and money and learned men to convert him to their beliefs; but the king was wise and sent for a Jew with much knowledge and acumen and put all three together to discuss their doctrines.

So we have another Brains Trust, or round-table conference, just as in Masudi, with the difference that the Muslim has not been poisoned beforehand. But the pattern of the argument is much the same. After long and futile discussions, the King adjourns the meeting for three days, during which the discutants are left to cool their heels in their respective tents; then he reverts to a stratagem. He convokes the discutants separately. He asks the Christian which of the other two religions is nearer the truth, and the Christian answers, "the Jews". He confronts the Muslim with the same question and gets the same reply. Neutralism has once more carried the day.

So much for the conversion. What else do we learn from the celebrated "Khazar Correspondence"? To take Hasdai's letter first: it starts with a Hebrew poem, in the then fashionable manner of the *piyut*, a rhapsodic verse form which contains hidden allusions or riddles, and frequently acrostics. The poem exalts the military victories of the addressee, King Joseph; at the same time, the initial letters of the lines form an acrostic which spells out the full name of Hasdai bar Isaac bar Ezra bar Shaprut, followed by the name of Menahem ben Sharuk. Now this Menahem was a celebrated

Hebrew poet, lexicographer and grammarian, a secretary and protg of Hasdai's. He was obviously given the task of drafting the epistle to King Joseph in his most ornate style, and he took the opportunity to immortalize himself by inserting his own name into the acrostic after that of his patron. Several other works of Menahem ben-Sharuk are preserved, and there can be no doubt that Hasdai's letter is his handiwork.

After the poem, the compliments and diplomatic flourishes, the letter gives a glowing account of the prosperity of Moorish Spain, and the happy condition of the Jews under its Caliph Abd al Rahman, "the like of which has never been known... And thus the derelict sheep were taken into care, the arms of their persecutors were paralysed, and the yoke was discarded. The country we live in is called in Hebrew Sepharad, but the Ishmaelites who inhabit it call it al-Andalus."

Hasdai then proceeds to explain how he first heard about the existence of the Jewish kingdom from the merchants of Khurasan, then in more detail from the Byzantine envoys, and he reports what these envoys told him:

I questioned them [the Byzantines] about it and they replied that it was true, and that the name of the kingdom is al-Khazar. Between Constantinople and this country there is a journey of fifteen days by sea, [This probably refers to the so-Called "Khazarian route": from Constantinople across the Black Sea and up the Don, then across the Don-Volga portage and down the Volga to Itil. (An alternative, shorter route was from Constantinople to the east coast of the Black Sea.)] but they said, by land there are many other people between us and them. The name of the ruling king is Joseph. Ships come to us from their land, bringing fish, furs and all sorts of merchandise. They are in alliance with us, and honoured by us. We exchange embassies and gifts. They are powerful and have a fortress for their outposts and troops which go out on forays from time to time. [The fortress is evidently Sarkel on the Don. "They are honoured by us"fits in with the passage in Constantine Born-in-the-Purple about the special gold seal used in letters to the Kagan. Constantine was the Byzantine Emperor at the time of the Embassy to Spain.]

This bit of information offered by Hasdai to the Khazar King about the King's own country is obviously intended to draw a detailed reply from Joseph. It was good psychology: Hasdai must have known that criticism of erroneous statements flows easier from the pen than an original exposition.

Next, Hasdai relates his earlier efforts to get in touch with Joseph. First he had sent a messenger, a certain Isaac bar Nathan, with instructions to proceed to the Khazar court. But Isaac got only as far as Constantinople, where he was courteously treated, but prevented from continuing the journey. (Understandably so: given the Empire's ambivalent attitude towards the Jewish kingdom, it was certainly not in Constantine's interest to facilitate an alliance between Khazaria and the Cordoba Caliphate with its Jewish Chief Minister.) So Hasdai's messenger returned to Spain, mission unaccomplished. But soon another opportunity offered itself: the arrival at Cordoba of an embassy from Eastern Europe. Among its members were two Jews, Mar Saul and Mar Joseph, who offered to deliver Hasdai's letter to King Joseph. (According to Joseph's reply to Hasdai, it was actually delivered by a third person, one Isaac ben-Eliezer.) Having thus described in detail how his letter came to be written, and his efforts to have it delivered, Hasdai proceeds to ask a series of direct questions which reflect his avidity for more information about every aspect of the Khazar land, from its geography to its rites in observing the Sabbath. The concluding passage in Hasdai's letter strikes a note quite different from that of its opening paragraphs:

I feel the urge to know the truth, whether there is really a place on this earth where harassed Israel can rule itself, where it is subject to nobody. If I were to know that this is indeed the case, I would not hesitate to forsake all honours, to resign my high office, to abandon my family, and to travel over mountains and plains, over land and water, until I arrived at the place where my Lord, the [Jewish] King rules... And I also have one more request: to be informed whether you have any knowledge of [the possible date] of the Final Miracle [the coming of the Messiah] which, wandering from country to country, we are awaiting. Dishonoured and humiliated in our dispersion, we have to listen in silence to those who say: "every nation has its own land and you alone possess not even a shadow of a country on this earth". The beginning of the letter praises the happy lot of the Jews in Spain; the end breathes the bitterness of the exile, Zionist fervour and Messianic hope. But these opposite attitudes have always co-existed in the divided heart of Jews throughout their history. The contradiction in Hasdai's letter gives it an added touch of authenticity. How far his implied offer to enter into the service of the Khazar King is to be taken seriously is another question, which we cannot answer. Perhaps he could not either.

King Joseph's reply is less accomplished and moving than Hasdai's letter. No wonder – as Cassel remarks: 'scholarship and culture reigned not among the Jews of the Volga, but on the rivers of Spain". The highlight of the Reply is the story of the conversion, already quoted. No doubt Joseph too employed a scribe for penning it, probably a scholarly refugee from Byzantium. Nevertheless, the Reply sounds like a voice out of the Old Testament compared to the polished cadences of the tenth-century modern statesman. It starts with a fanfare of greetings, then reiterates the main contents of Hasdai's letter, proudly emphasizing that the Khazar kingdom gives the lie to those who say that "the Sceptre of Judah has forever fallen from the Jews' hands"and "that there is no place on earth for a kingdom of their own". This is followed by a rather cryptic remark to the effect that "already our fathers have exchanged friendly letters which are preserved in our archives and are known to our elders". [This may refer to a ninth-century Jewish traveller, Eldad ha-Dani, whose fantastic tales, much read in the Middle Ages, include mentions of Khazaria which, he says, is inhabited by three of the lost tribes of Israel, and collects tributes from twenty-eight neighbouring kingdoms. Eldad visited Spain around 880 and may or may not have visited the Khazar country. Hasdai briefly mentions him in his letter to Joseph – as if to ask what to make of him.]

Joseph then proceeds to provide a genealogy of his people. Though a fierce Jewish nationalist, proud of wielding the 'sceptre of Judah", he cannot, and does not, claim for them Semitic descent; he traces their ancestry not to Shem, but to Noah's third son, Japheth; or more precisely to Japheth's grandson, Togarma, the ancestor of all Turkish tribes. "We have found in the family registers of our fathers,"Joseph asserts boldly, "that Togarma had ten sons, and the names of their offspring are as follows: Uigur, Dursu, Avars, Huns, Basilii, Tarniakh, Khazars, Zagora, Bulgars, Sabir. We are the sons of Khazar, the seventh..." The identity of some of these tribes, with names spelt in the Hebrew script is rather dubious, but that hardly matters; the characteristic feature in this genealogical exercise is the amalgamation of Genesis with Turkish tribal tradition. [It also throws a sidelight on the frequent description of the Khazars as the people of Magog. Magog, according to Genesis X, 2-3 was the much maligned uncle of Togarma.]

After the genealogy, Joseph mentions briefly some military conquests by his ancestors which carried them as far as the Danube; then follows at great length the story of Bulan's conversion. "From this day onwards,"Joseph continues, "the Lord gave him strength and aided him; he had himself and his followers circumcized and sent for Jewish sages who taught him the Law and explained the Commandments."There follow more boasts about military victories, conquered nations, etc., and then a significant passage:

After these events, one of his [Bulan's] grandsons became King; his name was Obadiab, he was a brave and venerated man who reformed the Rule, fortified the Law according to tradition and usage, built synagogues and schools, assembled a multitude of Israel's sages, gave them lavish gifts of gold and silver, and made them interpret the twenty-four [sacred] books, the Mishna [Precepts] and the Talmud, and the order in which the liturgies are to be said.

This indicates that, about a couple of generations after Bulan, a religious revival or reformation took place (possibly accompanied by a *coup d'état* on the lines envisaged by Artamonov). It seems indeed that the Judaization of the Khazars proceeded in several steps. We remember that King Bulan drove out "the sorcerers and idolators" *before* the angel appeared to him; and that he made his Covenant with the "true God" *before* deciding whether He was the Jewish, Christian or Muslim God. It seems highly probable that the conversion of King Bulan and his followers was another intermediary step, that they embraced a primitive or rudimentary form of Judaism, based on the Bible alone, excluding the Talmud, all rabbinical literature, and the observances derived from it. In this respect they resembled the Karaites, a fundamentalist sect which originated in the eighth century in Persia and spread among Jews all over the world particularly in "Little Khazaria", i.e., the Crimea. Dunlop and some other authorities surmised that between Bulan and Obadiah (i.e., roughly between 740 and 800) some form of Karaism prevailed in the country, and that orthodox "Rabbinic"Judaism was only introduced in the course of Obadiah's religious reform. The point is of some importance because Karaism apparently survived in Khazaria to the end, and villages of Turkish-speaking Karaite Jews, obviously of Khazar origin, still existed in modern times.

Thus the Judaization of the Khazars was a gradual process which, triggered off by political expediency, slowly penetrated into the deeper strata of their minds and eventually produced the Messianism of their period of decline. Their religious commitment survived the collapse of their state, and persisted, as we shall see, in the Khazar-Jewish settlements of Russia and Poland.

After mentioning Obadiah's religious reforms, Joseph gives a list of his successors:

Hiskia his son, and his son Manasseh, and Chanukah the brother of Obadiah, and Isaac his son, Manasseh his son, Nissi his son, Menahem his son, Benjamin his son, Aaron his son, and I am Joseph, son of Aaron the Blessed, and we were all sons of Kings, and no stranger was allowed to occupy the throne of our fathers.

Next, Joseph attempts to answer Hasdai's questions about the size and topography of his country. But he does not seem to have a competent person at his court who could match the skill of the Arab geographers, and his obscure references to other countries and nations add little to what we know from Ibn Hawkal, Masudi and the other Persian and Arabic sources. He claims to collect tribute from thirty-seven nations – which seems a rather tall proposition; yet Dunlop points out that nine of these appear to be tribes living in the Khazar heartland, and the remaining twenty-eight agree quite well with Ibn Fadlan's mention of twenty-five wives, each the daughter of a vassal king (and also with Eldad ha-Dani's dubious tales). We must further bear in mind the multitude of Slavonic tribes along the upper reaches of the Dnieper and as far as Moscow, which, as we shall see, paid tribute to the Khazars.

However that may be, there is no reference in Joseph's letter to a royal harem – only a mention of a single queen and her maids and eunuchs'. These are said to live in one of the three boroughs of Joseph's capital, Itil: "in the second live Israelites, Ishmaelis, Christians and other nations who speak other languages; the third, which is an island, I inhabit myself, with the princes, bondsmen and all the servants that belong to me.... [This division of Itil into three parts is also mentioned, as we have seen, in some of the Arab sources.]We live in the town through the whole of winter, but in the month of Nisan [March-April] we set out and everyone goes to labour in his field and his garden; every clan has his hereditary estate, for which they head with joy and jubilation; no voice of an intruder can be heard there, no enemy is to be seen. The country does not have much rain, but there are many rivers with a multitude of big fish, and many sources, and it is generally fertile and fat in its fields and vineyards, gardens and orchards which are irrigated by the rivers and bear rich fruit... and with God's help I live in peace."

The next passage is devoted to the date of the coming of the Messiah:

We have our eyes on the sages of Jerusalem and Babylon, and although we live far away from Zion, we have nevertheless heard that the calculations are erroneous owing to the great profusion of sins, and we know nothing, only the Eternal knows how to keep the count. We have nothing to hold on only the prophecies of Daniel, and may the Eternal speed up our Deliverance...

The concluding paragraph of Joseph's letter is a reply to Hasdai's apparent offer to enter into the service of the Khazar king:

Thou hast mentioned in thy letter a desire to see my face. I too wish and long to behold thy gracious face and the splendour of thy magnificence, wisdom and greatness; I wish that thy words will come true, that I should know the happiness to hold thee in my embrace and to see thy dear, friendly and agreeable face; thou wouldst be to me as a father, and I to thee as a son; all my people would kiss thy lips; we would come and go according to thy wishes and thy wise counsel.

There is a passage in Joseph's letter which deals with topical politics, and is rather obscure:

With the help of the Almighty I guard the mouth of the river [the Volga] and do not permit the Rus who come in their ships to invade the land of the Arabs... I fight heavy wars with them [the Rus] for if I allowed it they would devastate the lands of Ishmael even to Baghdad.

Joseph here appears to pose as the defender of the Baghdad Caliphate against the Norman-Rus raiders (see Chapter III). This might seem a little tactless in view of the bitter hostility between the Omayad Caliphate of Cordoba (which Hasdai is serving) and the Abassid Caliphs of Baghdad. On the other hand, the vagaries of Byzantine policy towards the Khazars made it expedient for Joseph to appear in the role of a defender of Islam, regardless of the schism between the two Caliphates. At least he could hope that Hasdai, the experienced diplomat, would take the hint.

The meeting between the two correspondents – if ever seriously intended – never took place. No further letters – if any were exchanged – have been preserved. The factual content of the "Khazar Correspondence"is meagre, and adds little to what was already known from other sources. Its fascination lies in the bizarre, fragmentary vistas that it conveys, like an erratic searchlight focussing on disjointed regions in the dense fog that covers the period.

Among other Hebrew sources, there is the "Cambridge Document"(so called after its present location in the Cambridge University Library). It was discovered at the end of the last century, together with other priceless documents in the "Cairo Geniza", the storeroom of an ancient synagogue, by the Cambridge scholar, Solomon Schechter. The document is in a bad state; it is a letter (or copy of a letter) consisting of about a hundred lines in Hebrew; the beginning and the end are missing, so that it is impossible to know who wrote it and to whom it was addressed. King Joseph is mentioned in it as a contemporary and referred to as "my Lord", Khazaria is called "our land"; so the most plausible inference is that the letter was written by a Khazar Jew of King Joseph's court in Joseph's lifetime, i.e., that it is roughly contemporaneous with the "Khazar Correspondence". Some authorities have further suggested that it was addressed to Hasdai ibn Shaprut, and handed in Constantinople to Hasdai's unsuccessful envoy, Isaac bar Nathan, who brought it back to Cordoba (whence it found its way to Cairo when the Jews were expelled from Spain). At any rate, internal evidence indicates that the document originated not later than in the eleventh century, and more likely in Joseph's lifetime, in the tenth.

It contains another legendary account of the conversion, but its main significance is political. The writer speaks of an attack on Khazaria by the Alans, acting under Byzantine instigation, under Joseph's father, Aaron the Blessed. No other Greek or Arab source seems to mention this campaign. But there is a significant passage in Constantine Porphyrogenitus's De Adminisdrando Imperio, written in 947-50, which lends some credibility to the unknown letter-writer's statements:

Concerning Khazaria, how war is to be made upon them and by whom. As the Ghuzz are able to make war on the Khazars, being near them, so likewise the ruler of Alania, because the Nine Climates of Khazaria [the fertile region north of the Caucasus] are close to Alania, and the Alan can, if he wishes, raid them and cause great damage and distress to the Khazars from that quarter.

Now, according to Joseph's Letter, the ruler of the Alans paid tribute to him, and whether in fact he did or not, his feelings toward the Kagan were probably much the same as the Bulgar King's. The passage in Constantine, revealing his efforts to incite the Alans to war against the Khazars, ironically reminds one of Ibn Fadlan's mission with a parallel purpose. Evidently, the days of the Byzantine-Khazar rapprochement were long past in Joseph's time.

About a century after the Khazar Correspondence and the presumed date of the Cambridge Document, Jehuda Halevi wrote his once celebrated book, Kuzari, the Khazars. Halevi (1085-1141) is generally considered the greatest Hebrew poet of Spain; the book, however, was written in Arabic and translated later into Hebrew; its sub-title is "The Book of Proof and Argument in Defence of the Despised Faith". Halevi was a Zionist who died on a pilgrimage to Jerusalem; the Kuzari, written a year before his death, is a philosophical tract propounding the view that the Jewish nation is the sole mediator between God and the rest of mankind. At the end of history, all other nations will be converted to Judaism; and the conversion of the Khazars appears as a symbol or token of that ultimate event..In spite of its title, the tract has little to say about the Khazar country itself, which serves mainly as a backdrop for yet another legendary account of the conversion – the King, the angel, the Jewish scholar, etc. – and for the philosophical and theological dialogues between the King and the protagonists of the three religions.

However, there are a few factual references, which indicate that Halevi had either read the correspondence between Hasdai and Joseph or had other sources of information about the Khazar country. Thus we are informed that after the appearance of the angel the King of the Khazars "revealed the secret of his dream to the General of his army", and "the General"also looms large later on – another obvious reference to the dual rule of Kagan and Bek. Halevi also mentions the "histories"and "books of the Khazars"-which reminds one of Joseph speaking of "our archives", where documents of state are kept. Lastly, Halevi twice, in different places of the book, gives the date of the conversion as having taken place "400 years ago"and "in the year 4500"(according to the Jewish calendar). This points to AD 740, which is the most likely date. All in all, it is a poor harvest as far as factual statements are concerned, from a book that enjoyed immense popularity among the Jews of the Middle Ages. But the mediaeval mind was less attracted by fact than by fable, and the Jews were more interested in the date of the coming of the Messiah than in geographical data. The Arab geographers and chroniclers had a similarly cavalier attitude to distances, dates and the frontiers between fact and fancy.

This also applies to the famed German-Jewish traveller, Rabbi Petachia of Ratisbon, who visited Eastern Europe and western Asia between 1170 and 1185. His travelogue, Sibub Ha'olam, "Journey around the World", was apparently written by a pupil, based on his notes or on dictation. It relates how shocked the good Rabbi was by the primitive observances of the Khazar Jews north of the Crimea, which he attributed to their adherence to the Karaite heresy:

And the Rabbi Petachia asked them: "Why do you not believe in the words of the sages [i.e., the Talmudists]?"They replied:

"Because our fathers did not teach them to us." On the eve of the Sabbath they cut all the bread which they eat on the Sabbath. They eat it in the dark, and sit the whole day on one spot. Their prayers consist only of the psalms. [Spending the Sabbath in the dark was a well-known Karaite custom.]

So incensed was the Rabbi that, when he subsequently crossed the Khazar heartland, all he had to say was that it took him eight days, during which "he heard the wailing of women and the barking of dogs".

He does mention, however, that while he was in Baghdad, he had seen envoys from the Khazar kingdom looking for needy Jewish scholars from Mesopotamia and even from Egypt, "to teach their children Torah and Talmud".

While few Jewish travellers from the West undertook the hazardous journey to the Volga, they recorded encounters with Khazar Jews at all principal centres of the civilized world. Rabbi Petachia met them in Baghdad; Benjamin of Tudela, another famous traveller of the twelfth century, visited Khazar notables in Constantinople and Alexandria; Ibraham ben Daud, a contemporary of Judah Halevi's, reports that he had seen in Toledo "some of their descendants, pupils of the wise". Tradition has it that these were Khazar princes – one is tempted to think of Indian princelings sent to Cambridge to study..Yet there is a curious ambivalence in the attitude toward the Khazars of the leaders of orthodox Jewry in the East, centred on the Talmudic Academy in Baghdad.

The Gaon (Hebrew for "excellency") who stood at the head of the Academy was the spiritual leader of the Jewish settlements dispersed all over the Near and Middle East, while the Exilarch, or "Prince of Captivity", represented the secular power over these more or less autonomous communities. Saadiah Gaon (882-942), most famous among the spiritual excellencies, who left voluminous writings, repeatedly refers in them to the Khazars. He mentions a Mesopotamian Jew who went to Khazaria to settle there, as if this were an every-day occurrence. He speaks obscurely of the Khazar court; elsewhere he explains that in the biblical expression "Hiram of Tyre", Hiram is not a proper name but a royal title, "like Caliph for the Ruler of the Arabs, and Kagan for the King of the

Khazars." Thus Khazaria was very much "on the map", in the literal and metaphorical sense, for the leaders of the ecclesiastical hierarchy of oriental Jewry; but at the same time the Khazars were regarded with certain misgivings, both on racial grounds and because of their suspected leanings toward the Karaite heresy. One eleventh-century Hebrew author, Japheth ibn-Ali, himself a Karaite, explains the word mamzer, "bastard", by the example of the Khazars who became Jews without belonging to the Race. His contemporary, Jacob ben-Reuben, reflects the opposite side of this ambivalent attitude by speaking of the Khazars as "a single nation who do not bear the yoke of the exile, but are great warriors paying no tribute to the Gentiles".

In summing up the Hebrew sources on the Khazars that have come down to us, one senses a mixed reaction of enthusiasm, scepticism and, above all, bewilderment. A warriornation of Turkish Jews must have seemed to the rabbis as strange as a circumcized unicorn. During a thousand years of Dispersion, the Jews had forgotten what it was like to have a king and a country. The Messiah was more real to them than the Kagan..As a postscript to the Arab and Hebrew sources relating to the conversion, it should be mentioned that the apparently earliest Christian source antedates them both. At some date earlier than 864, the Westphalian monk, Christian Druthmar of Aquitania, wrote a Latin treatise *Expositio in Evangelium Mattei,* in which he reports that "there exist people under the sky in regions where no Christians can be found, whose name is Gog and Magog, and who are Huns; among them is one, called the Gazari, who are circumcized and observe Judaism in its entirety". This remark occurs àpropos of Matthew. ["And this Gospel of the Kingdom shall be preached in all the world for a witness unto all nations; and then shall the end come."] which has no apparent bearing on it, and no more is heard of the subject.

At about the same time when Druthmar wrote down what he knew from hearsay about the Jewish Khazars, a famed Christian missionary, sent by the Byzantine Emperor, attempted to convert them to Christianity. He was no less a figure than St Cyril, "Apostle of the Slavs", alleged designer of the Cyrillic alphabet. He and his elder brother, St Methodius, were entrusted with this and other proselytizing missions by the Emperor Michael III, on the advice of the Patriarch Photius (himself apparently of Khazar descent, for it is reported that the Emperor once called him in anger "Khazar face"). Cyril's proselytizing efforts seem to have been successful among the Slavonic people in Eastern Europe, but not among the Khazars. He travelled to their country via Cherson in the Crimea; in Cherson he is said to have spent six months learning Hebrew in preparation for his mission; he then took the "Khazarian Way"- the Don-Volga portage – to Itil, and from there travelled along the Caspian to meet the Kagan (it is not said where). The usual theological disputations followed, but they had little impact on the Khazar Jews Even the adulatory Vita Constantine (Cyril's original name) says only that Cyril made a good impression on the Kagan, that a few people were baptized and two hundred Christian prisoners were released by the Kagan as a gesture of goodwill. It was the least he could do for the Emperor's envoy who had gone to so much trouble.

There is a curious sidelight thrown on the story by students of Slavonic philology. Cyril is credited by tradition not only with having devised the Cyrillic but also the Glagolytic alphabet. The latter, according to Baron, was "used in Croatia to the seventeenth century. Its indebtedness to the Hebrew alphabet in at least eleven characters, representing in part the Slavonic sounds, has long been recognized". (The eleven characters are A, B, V, G, E, K, P, R, S, Sch, T.) This seems to confirm what has been said earlier on about the influence of the Hebrew alphabet in spreading literacy among the neighbours of the Khazars.

IT was", wrote D. Sinor,1 "in the second half of the eighth century that the Khazar empire reached the acme of its glory" that is, between the conversion of Bulan and the religious reform under Obadiah. This is not meant to imply that the Khazars owed their good fortune to their Jewish religion. It is rather the other way round: they could afford to be Jews because they were economically and militarily strong.

A living symbol of their power was the Emperor Leo the Khazar, who ruled Byzantium in 775-80 – so named after his mother, the Khazar Princess "Flower" – the one who created a new fashion at the court. We remember that her marriage took place shortly after the great Khazar victory over the Muslims in the battle of Ardabil, which is mentioned in the letter of Joseph and other sources. The two events, Dunlop remarks, "are hardly unrelated". However, amidst the cloak-and-dagger intrigues of the period, dynastic marriages and betrothals could be dangerous. They repeatedly gave cause – or at least provided a pretext – for starting a war. The pattern was apparently set by Attila, the erstwhile overlord of the Khazars. In 450 Attila is said to have received a message, accompanied by an engagement ring, from Honoria, sister to the West Roman Emperor Valentinian III.

This romantic and ambitious lady begged the Hun chieftain to rescue her from a fate worse than death – a forced marriage to an old Senator – and sent him her ring. Attila promptly claimed her as his bride, together with half the Empire as her dowry; and when Valentinian refused, Attila invaded Gaul. Several variations on this quasi-archetypal theme crop up throughout Khazar history. We remember the fury of the Bulgar King about the abduction of his daughter, and how he gave this incident as the main reason for his demand that the Caliph should build him a fortress against the Khazars. If we are to believe the Arab sources, similar incidents (though with a different twist) led to the last flare-up of the Khazar-Muslim wars at the end of the eighth century, after a protracted period of peace.

According to al-Tabari, in AD 798, [The date, however, is uncertain. the Caliph ordered the Governor of Armenia to make the Khazar frontier even more secure by marrying a daughter of the Kagan. This governor was a member of the powerful family of the Barmecides (which, incidentally, reminds one of the prince of that eponymous family in the Arabian Nights who invited the beggar to a feast consisting of rich dish-covers with nothing beneath).

The Barmecide agreed, and the Khazar Princess with her suite and dowry was duly dispatched to him in a luxurious cavalcade (see I, 10). But she died in childbed; the newborn died too; and her courtiers, on their return to Khazaria, insinuated to the Kagan that she had been poisoned. The Kagan promptly invaded Armenia and took (according to two Arab sources)3 50 000 prisoners. The Caliph was forced to release thousands of criminals from his gaols and arm them to stem the Khazar advance.

The Arab sources relate at least one more eighth-century incident of a misfired dynastic marriage followed by a Khazar invasion; and for good measure the Georgian Chronicle has a particularly gruesome one to add to the list (in which the royal Princess, instead of being poisoned, kills herself to escape the Kagan's bed). The details and exact dates are, as usual, doubtful,4 and so is the real motivation behind these campaigns. But the recurrent mention in the chronicles of bartered brides and poisoned queens leaves little doubt that this theme had a powerful impact on people's imagination, and possibly also on political events.

No more is heard about Khazar-Arab fighting after the end of the eighth century. As we enter the ninth, the Khazars seemed to enjoy several decades of peace at least, there is little mention of them in the chronicles, and no news is good news in history. The southern frontiers of their country had been pacified; relations with the Caliphate had settled down to a tacit non-aggression pact; relations with Byzantium continued to be definitely friendly.

Yet in the middle of this comparatively idyllic period there is an ominous episode which fore-shadowed new dangers. In 833, or thereabouts, the Khazar Kagan and Bek sent an embassy to the East Roman Emperor Theophilus, asking for skilled architects and craftsmen to build them a fortress on the lower reaches of the Don. The Emperor responded with alacrity. He sent a fleet across the Black Sea and the Sea of Azov up the mouth of the Don to the strategic spot where the fortress was to be built. Thus came Sarkel into being, the famous fortress and priceless archaeological site, virtually the only one that yielded clues to Khazar history – until it was submerged in the Tsimlyansk reservoir, adjoining the Volga-Don canal. Constantine Porphyrogenitus, who related the episode in some detail, says that since no stones were available in the region, Sarkel was built of bricks, burnt in specially constructed kilns. He does not mention the curious fact (discovered by Soviet archaeologists while the site was still accessible) that the builders also used marble columns of Byzantine origin, dating from the sixth century, and probably salvaged from some Byzantine ruin; a nice example of Imperial thrift.5

The potential enemy against whom this impressive fortress was built by joint Roman-Khazar effort, were those formidable and menacing newcomers on the world scene, whom the West called Vikings or Norsemen, and the East called Rhous or Rhos or Rus.

Two centuries earlier, the conquering Arabs had advanced on the civilized world in a gigantic pincer movement, its left prong reaching across the Pyrenees, its right prong across the Caucasus. Now, during the Viking Age, history seemed to create a kind of mirror image of that earlier phase. The initial explosion which had triggered off the Muslim wars of conquest took place in the southernmost region of the known world, the Arabian desert. The Viking raids and conquests originated in its northernmost region, Scandinavia. The Arabs advanced northward by land, the Norsemen southward by sea and waterways. The Arabs were, at least in theory, conducting a Holy War, the Vikings waged unholy wars of piracy and plunder; but the results, as far as the victims were concerned, were much the same. In neither case have historians been able to provide convincing explanations of the economical, ecological or ideological reasons which transformed these apparently quiescent regions of Arabia and Scandinavia quasi overnight into volcanoes of exuberant vitality and reckless enterprise. Both eruptions spent their force within a couple of centuries but left a permanent mark on the world. Both evolved in this time-span from savagery and destructiveness to splendid cultural achievement. About the time when Sarkel was built by joint Byzantine-Khazar efforts in anticipation of attack by the eastern Vikings, their western branch had already penetrated all the major waterways of Europe and conquered half of Ireland. Within the next few decades they colonized Iceland, conquered Normandy, repeatedly sacked Paris, raided Germany, the Rhne delta, the gulf of Genoa, circumnavigated the Iberian peninsula and attacked Constantinople through the Mediterranean and the Dardanelles-simultaneously with a Rus attack down the Dnieper and across the Black Sea. As Toynbee wrote: "In the ninth century, which was the century in which the Rhos impinged on the Khazars and on the East Romans, the Scandinavians were raiding and conquering and colonizing in an immense arc that eventually extended south-westward... to North America and southeastward to... the Caspian Sea." No wonder that a special prayer was inserted in the litanies of the West: *A furore Normannorum libera nos Domine*.

No wonder that Constantinople needed its Khazar allies as a protective shield against the carved dragons on the bows of the Viking ships, as it had needed them a couple of centuries earlier against the green banners of the Prophet. And, as on that earlier occasion, the Khazars were again to bear the brunt of the attack, and eventually to see their capital laid in ruins.

Not only Byzantium had reason to be grateful to the Khazars for blocking the advance of the Viking fleets down the great waterways from the north. We have now gained a better understanding of the cryptic passage in Joseph's letter to Hasdai, written a century later:

"With the help of the Almighty I guard the mouth of the river and do not permit the Rus who come in their ships to invade the land of the Arabs... I fight heavy wars [with the Rus]."

The particular brand of Vikings which the Byzantines called "Rhos" were called "Varangians" by the Arab chroniclers. The most probable derivation of "Rhos", according to Toynbee, is "from the Swedish word 'rodher', meaning rowers". As for "Varangian", it was used by the Arabs and also in the Russian Primary Chronicle to designate Norsemen or Scandinavians; the Baltic was actually called by them "the Varangian Sea". Although this branch of Vikings originated from eastern Sweden, as distinct from the Norwegians and Danes who raided Western Europe, their advance followed the same pattern. It was seasonal; it was based on strategically placed islands which served as strongholds, armouries and supply bases for attacks on the mainland; and its nature evolved, where conditions were favourable, from predatory raids and forced commerce to more or less permanent settlements and ultimately, amalgamation with the conquered native populations. Thus the Viking penetration of Ireland started with the seizure of the island of Rechru (Lambay) in Dublin Bay; England was invaded from the isle of Thanet; penetration of the Continent started with the conquest of the islands of Walcheren (off Holland) and Noirmoutier (in the estuary of the Loire).

At the eastern extreme of Europe the Northmen were following the same blueprint for conquest. After crossing the Baltic and the Gulf of Finland they sailed up the river Volkhov into Lake Ilmen (south of Leningrad), where they found a convenient island – the

Holmgard of the Icelandic Sagas. On this they built a settlement which eventually grew into the city of Novgorod.*[Not to be confused with Nizhny Novgorod (now re-named Gorky).] From here they forayed on southward on the great waterways: on the Volga into the Caspian, and on the Dnieper into the Black Sea.

The former route led through the countries of the militant Bulgars and Khazars; the latter across the territories of various Slavonic tribes who inhabited the north-western outskirts of the Khazar Empire and paid tribute to the Kagan: the Polyane in the region of Kiev; the Viatichi, south of Moscow; the Radimishchy east of the Dnieper; the Severyane on the river Derna, etc.*[Constantine Porphyrogenitus and the Russian Chronicle are in fair agreement concering the names and locations of these tribes and their subjection to the Khazars.] These Slavs seemed to have developed advanced methods of agriculture, and were apparently of a more timid disposition than their "Turkish" neighbours on the Volga, for, as Bury put it, they became the "natural prey" of the Scandinavian raiders. These eventually came to prefer the Dnieper, in spite of its dangerous cataracts, to the Volga and the Don. It was the Dnieper which became the "Great Waterway" – the *Austrvegr* of the Nordic Sagas – from the Baltic to the Black Sea, and thus to Constantinople. They even gave Scandinavian names to the seven major cataracts, duplicating their Slavonic names; Constantine conscientiously enumerates both versions (e.g., *Baru-fors* in Norse, *Volnyi* in Slavonic, for "the billowy waterfall"). These Varangian-Rus seem to have been a unique blend unique even among their brother Vikings – combining the traits of pirates, robbers and meretricious merchants, who traded on their own terms, imposed by sword and battle-axe. They bartered furs, swords and amber in exchange for gold, but their principal merchandise were slaves. A contemporary Arab chronicler wrote:

In this island [Novgorod] there are men to the number of 100000, and these men constantly go out to raid the Slavs in boats, and they seize the Slavs and take them prisoner and they go to the Khazars and Bulgars and sell them there. [We remember the slave market in Itil, mentioned by Masudi]. They have no cultivated lands, nor seed, and [live by] plunder from the Slavs. When a child is born to them, they place a drawn sword in front of him and his father says: "I have neither gold nor silver, nor wealth which I can bequeath to thee, this is thine inheritance, with it secure prosperity for thyself."

A modern historian, McEvedy, has summed it up nicely:

Viking-Varangian activity, ranging from Iceland to the borders of Turkestan, from Constantinople to the Arctic circle, was of incredible vitality and daring, and it is sad that so much effort was wasted in plundering. The Northern heroes did not deign to trade until they failed to vanquish; they preferred bloodstained, glorious gold to a steady mercantile profit.

Thus the Rus convoys sailing southward in the summer season were at the same time both commercial fleets and military armadas; the two roles went together, and with each fleet it was impossible to foretell at what moment the merchants would turn into warriors. The size of these fleets was formidable. Masudi speaks of a Rus force entering the Caspian from the Volga (in 912-13) as comprising "about 500 ships, each manned by 100 persons". Of these 50000 men, he says, 35000 were killed in battle. [See below, Chapter IV, 1.] Masudi may have been exaggerating, but apparently not much. Even at an early stage of their exploits (*circa* 860) the Rus crossed the Black Sea and laid siege on Constantinople with a fleet variously estimated as numbering between 200 and 230 ships.

In view of the unpredictability and proverbial treacherousness of these formidable invaders, the Byzantines and Khazars had to "play it by ear" as the saying goes. For a century and a half after the fortress of Sarkel was built, trade agreements and the exchange of embassies with the Rus alternated with savage wars. Only slowly and gradually did the Northmen change their character by building permanent settlements, becoming Slavonized by intermingling with their subjects and vassals, and finally, adopting the faith of the Byzantine Church. By that time, the closing years of the tenth century, the "Rus" had become transformed into "Russians". The early Rus princes and nobles still bore Scandinavian names which had been Slavonized: Rurik from Hröekr, Oleg from Helgi, Igor from Ingvar, Olga from Helga, and so on. The commercial treaty which Prince Igor-Ingvar concluded with the Byzantines in 945 contains a list of his companions, only three of which have Slavonic names among fifty Scandinavian names.11

But the son of Ingvar and Helga assumed the Slavonic name Svyatoslav, and from there onward the process of assimilation got into its stride, the Varangians gradually lost their identity as a separate people, and the Norse tradition faded out of Russian history.

It is difficult to form a mental picture of these bizarre people whose savagery sticks out even in that savage age. The chronicles are biased, written by members of nations who had suffered from the northern invaders; their own side of the story remains untold, for the rise of Scandinavian literature came long after the Age of the Vikings, when their exploits had blossomed into legend. Even so, early Norse literature seems to confirm their unbridled lust for battle, and the peculiar kind of frenzy which seized them on these occasions; they even had a special word for it: *berserksgangr* – the berserk way.

The Arab chroniclers were so baffled by them that they contradict not only each other, but also themselves, across a distance of a few lines. Our old friend Ibn Fadlan is utterly disgusted by the filthy and obscene habits of the Rus whom he met at the Volga in the land of the Bulgars. The following passage on the Rus occurs just before his account of the Khazars, quoted earlier on:

They are the filthiest creatures of the Lord. In the morning a servant girl brings a basin full of water to the master of the household; he rinses his face and hair in it, spits and blows his nose into the basin, which the girl then hands on to the next person, who does likewise, until all who are in the house have used that basin to blow their noses, spit and wash their face and hair in it.

In contrast to this, Ibn Rusta writes about the same time: "They are cleanly in regard to their clothing" – and leaves it at that.

Again, Ibn Fadlan is indignant about the Rus copulating and defecating in public, including their King, whereas Ibn Rusta and Gardezi know nothing of such revolting habits. But their own accounts are equally dubious and inconsistent. Thus Ibn Rusta: "They honour their guests and are kind to strangers who seek shelter with them, and everyone who is in misfortune among them.14 They do not allow anyone among them to tyrannize them, and whoever among them does wrong or is oppressive, they find out such a one and expel him from among them."

But a few paragraphs further down he paints a quite different picture -- or rather vignette, of conditions in Rus society:

Not one of them goes to satisfy a natural need alone, but he is accompanied by three of his companions who guard him between them, and each one of them has his sword because of the lack of security and treachery among them, for if a man has even a little wealth, his own brother and his friend who is with him covet it and seek to kill and despoil him.

Regarding their martial virtues, however, the sources are Unanimous: These people are vigorous and courageous and when they descend on open ground, none can escape from them without being destroyed and their women taken possession of, and themselves taken into slavery.

Such were the prospects which now faced the Khazars. Sarkel was built just in time; it enabled them to control the movements of the Rus flotillas along the lower reaches of the Don and the Don-Volga portage (the "Khazarian Way"). By and large it seems that during the first century of their presence on the scene [Very roughly, 830 1.-930.] the plundering raids of the Rus were mainly directed against Byzantium (where, obviously, richer plunder was to be had), whereas their relations with the Khazars were essentially on a trading basis, though not without friction and intermittent clashes. At any rate, the Khazars were able to control the Rus trade routes and to levy their 10 per cent tax on all cargoes passing through their country to Byzantium and to the Muslim lands.

They also exerted some cultural influence on the Northmen, who, for all their violent ways, had a naive willingness to learn from the people with whom they came into contact. The extent of this influence is indicated by the adoption of the title "Kagan" by the early Rus rulers of Novgorod. This is confirmed by both Byzantine and Arab sources; for instance, Ibn Rusta, after describing the island on which Novgorod was built, states "They have a king who is called Kagan Rus." Moreover, Ibn Fadlan reports that the Kagan Rus has a general who leads the army and represents him to the people. Zeki Validi has pointed out that such delegation of the army command was unknown among the Germanic people of the North, where the king must be the foremost warrior; Validi concludes that the Rus obviously imitated the Khazar system of twin rule. This is not unlikely in view of the fact that the Khazars were the most prosperous and culturally advanced people with whom the Rus in the early stages of their conquests made territorial contact. And that contact must have been fairly intense, since there was a colony of Rus merchants in Itil – and also a community of Khazar Jews in Kiev.

It is sad to report in this context that more than a thousand years after the events under discussion, the Soviet regime has done its best to expunge the memory of the Khazars' historic role and cultural achievements. On January 12, 1952, The Times carried the following news item:

EARLY RUSSIAN CULTURE BELITTLED SOVIET HISTORIAN REBUKED

Another Soviet historian has been criticized by Pravda *for belittling the early cul*38 ture and development of the Russian people. He is Professor Artamonov, who, at a recent session of the Department of History and Philosophy at the USSR Academy of Sciences, repeated a theory which he had put forward in a book in 1937 that the ancient city of Kiev owed a great deal to the Khazar peoples. He pictures them in the role of an advanced people who fell victim to the aggressive aspirations of the Russians.

"All these things," says Pravda, *"have nothing in common with historical facts.* The Khazar kingdom which represented the primitive amalgamation of different tribes, played no positive role whatever in creating the statehood of the eastern Slavs. Ancient sources testify that state formations arose among the eastern Slavs long before any record of the Khazars.

The Khazar kingdom, far from promoting the development of the ancient Russian State, retarded the progress of the eastern Slav tribes. The materials obtained by our archaeologists indicate the high level of culture in ancient Russia. Only by flouting the historical truth and neglecting the facts can one speak of the superiority of the Khazar culture. The idealization of the Khazar kingdom reflects a manifest survival of the defective views of the bourgeois historians who belittled the indigenous development of the Russian people.

The erroneousness of this concept is evident. Such a conception cannot be accepted by Soviet historiography."

Artamonov, whom I have frequently quoted, published (besides numerous articles in learned journals) his first book, which dealt with the early history of the Khazars, in 1937. His magnum opus, *History of the Khazars,* was apparently in preparation when *Pravda* struck. As a result, the book was published only ten years later – 1962-carrying a recantation in its final section which amounted to a denial of all that went before – and, indeed, of the author's lifework. The relevant passages in it read:

The Khazar kingdom disintegrated and fell into pieces, from which thc majority merged with other related peoples, and the minority, settling in Itil, lost its nationality and turned into a parasitic class with a Jewish coloration. The Russians never shunned the cultural achievements of the East... But from the Itil Khazars the Russians took nothing. Thus also by the way, the militant Khazar Judaism was treated by other peoples connected with it: the Magyars, Bulgars, Pechenegs, Alans and Polovtsians... The need to struggle with the exploiters from Itil stimulated the unification of the Ghuzz and the Slavs around the golden throne of Kiev, and this unity in its turn created the possibility and prospect for a violent growth not only of the Russian state system, but also of ancient Russian culture. This culture had always been original and never depended on Khazar influence. Those insignificant eastern elements in Rus culture which were passed down by the Khazars and which one usually bears in mind when dealing with the problems of culture ties between the Rus and the Khazars, did not penetrate into the heart of Russian culture, but remained on the surface and were of short duration and small significance. They offer no ground at all for pointing out a "Khazar" period in the history of Russian culture.

The dictates of the Party line completed the process of obliteration which started with the flooding of the remains of Sarkel.

Intensive trading and cultural interchanges did not prevent the Rus from gradually eating their way into the Khazar Empire by appropriating their Slavonic subjects and vassals. According to the Primary Russian Chronicle, by 859-that is, some twenty-five years after Sarkel was built – the tribute from the Slavonic peoples was "divided between the Khazars and the Varangians from beyond the Baltic Sea". The Varangians levied tribute on "Chuds", "Krivichians", etc. – i.e., the more northerly Slavonic people – while the Khazars continued to levy tribute on the Viatichi, the Seviane, and, most important of all, the Polyane in the central region of Kiev. But not for long. Three years later if we can trust the dating (in the Russian Chronicle), the key town of Kiev on the Dnieper, previously under Khazar suzerainty, passed into Rus hands.

This was to prove a decisive event in Russian history, though it apparently happened without an armed struggle. According to the Chronicle, Novgorod was at the time ruled by the (semilegendary) Prince Rurik (Hröekr), who held under his sway all the Viking settlements, the northern Slavonic, and some Finnish people. Two of Rurik's men, Oskold and Dir, on travelling down the Dnieper, saw a fortified place on a mountain, the sight of which they liked; and were told that this was the town of Kiev, and that it "paid tribute to the Khazars". The two settled in the town with their families, "gathered many Northmen to them, and ruled over the neighbouring Slavs, even as Rurik ruled at Novgorod. Some twenty years later Rurik's son Oleg [Helgi] came down and put Oskold and Dir to death, and annexed Kiev to his sway." Kiev soon outshone Novgorod in importance: it became the capital of the Varangians and "the mother of Russian towns"; while the principality which took its name became the cradle of the first Russian state.

Joseph's letter, written about a century after the Rus occupation of Kiev, no longer mentions it in his list of Khazar possessions. But influential Khazar-Jewish communities survived both in the town and province of Kiev, and after the final destruction of their country they were reinforced by large numbers of Khazar emigrants. The Russian Chronicle keeps referring to heroes coming from *Zemlya Zhidovskaya*, "the country of the Jews"; and the "Gate of the Khazars" in Kiev kept the memory of its erstwhile rulers alive till modern times.

We have now progressed into the second half of the ninth century and, before continuing with the tale of the Russian expansion, must turn our attention to some vital developments among the people of the steppes, particularly the Magyars. These events ran parallel with the rise of Rus power and had a direct impact on the Khazars – and on the map of Europe.

The Magyars had been the Khazars' allies, and apparently willing vassals, since the dawn of the Khazar Empire. "The problem of their origin and early wanderings have long perplexed scholars", Macartney wrote; elsewhere he calls it "one of the darkest of historical riddles". About their origin all we know with certainty is that the Magyars were related to the Finns, and that their language belongs to the so-called Finno-Ugrian language family, together with that of the Vogul and Ostyak people living in the forest regions of the northern Urals. Thus they were originally unrelated to the Slavonic and Turkish nations of the steppes in whose midst they came to live – an ethnic curiosity, which they still are to this day. Modern Hungary, unlike other small nations, has no linguistic ties with its neighbours; the Magyars have remained an ethnic enclave in Europe, with the distant Finns as their only cousins. At an unknown date during the early centuries of the Christian era this nomadic tribe was driven out of its erstwhile habitat in the Urals and migrated southward through the steppes, eventually settling in the region between the Don and the Kuban rivers. They thus became neighbours of the Khazars, even before the latter's rise to prominence. For a while they were part of a federation of semi-nomadic people, the Onogurs ("The Ten Arrows" or ten tribes); it is believed that the name "Hungarian" is a Slavonic version of that word;19 while "Magyar" is the name by which they have called themselves from time immemorial.

From about the middle of the seventh to the end of the ninth centuries they were, as already said, subjects of the Khazar Empire. It is a remarkable fact that during this whole period, while other tribes were engaged in a murderous game of musical chairs, we have no record of a single armed conflict between Khazars and Magyars, whereas each of the two was involved at one time or another in wars with their immediate or distant neighbours: Volga Bulgars, Danube Bulgars, Ghuzz, Pechenegs, and so on – in addition to the Arabs and the Rus. Paraphrasing the Russian Chronicle and Arab sources, Toynbee writes that throughout this period the

Magyars "took tribute", on the Khazars' behalf, from the Slav and Finn peoples in the Black Earth Zone to the north of the Magyars' own domain of the Steppe, and in the forest zone to the north of that. The evidence for the use of the name Magyar by this date is its survival in a number of place-names in this region of northerly Russia. These place-names presumably mark the sites of former Magyar garrisons and outposts." Thus the Magyars dominated their Slavonic neighbours, and Toynbee concludes that in levying tribute, "the Khazars were using the Magyars as their agents, though no doubt the Magyars made this agency profitable for themselves as well".

The arrival of the Rus radically changed this profitable state of affairs. At about the time when Sarkel was built, there was a conspicuous movement of the Magyars across the Don to its west bank. From about 830 onward, the bulk of the nation was re-settled in the region between the Don and the Dnieper, later to be named Lebedia. The reason for this move has been much debated among historians; Toynbee's explanation is both the most recent and the most plausible:

We may... infer that the Magyars were in occupation of the Steppe to the west of the Don by permission of their Khazar suzerains... Since the Steppecountry had previously belonged to the Khazars, and since the Magyars were the Khazars' subordinate allies, we may conclude that the Magyars had not established themselves in this Khazar territory against the Khazars' will... Indeed we may conclude that the Khazars had not merely permitted the Magyars to establish themselves to the west of the Don, but had actually planted them there to serve the Khazars' own purposes. The re-location of subject peoples for strategic reasons was a device that had been practised by previous nomad empire builders... In this new location, the Magyars could help the Khazars to check the south-eastward and southward advance of tile Rhos. The planting of the Magyars to the west of the Don will have been all of a piece with the building of the fortress Sarkel on tile Don's eastern bank.

This arrangement worked well enough for nearly half a century. During this period the relation between Magyars and Khazars became even closer, culminating in two events which left lasting marks on the Hungarian nation. First, the Khazars gave them a king, who founded the first Magyar dynasty; and, second, several Khazar tribes joined the Magyars and profoundly transformed their ethnic character.

The first episode is described by Constantine in *De Administrando* (*circa* 950), and is confirmed by the fact that the names he mentions appear independently in the first Hungarian Chronicle (eleventh century). Constantine tells us that before the Khazars intervened in the internal affairs of the Magyar tribes, these had no paramount king, only tribal chieftains; the most prominent of these was called Lebedias (after whom Lebedia was later named): And the Magyars consisted of seven hordes, but at that time they had no ruler, either native or foreign, but there were certain chieftains among them, of which the principal chieftain was the aforementioned Lebedias... And the Kagan, the ruler of Khazaria, on account of their [the Magyars'] valour and military assistance, gave their first chieftain, the man called Lebedias, a noble Khazar lady as wife, that he might beget children of her; but Lebedias, by some chance, had no family by that Khazar woman.

Another dynastic alliance which had misfired. But the Kagan was determined to strengthen the ties which bound Lebedias and his tribes to the Khazar kingdom:

After a little time had passed, the Kagan, the ruler of Khazaria, told the Magyars... to send to him their first chieftain. So Lebedias, coming before the Kagan of Khazaria, asked him for the reason why he had sent for him. And the Kagan said to him: We have sent for you for this reason: that, since you are well-born and wise and brave and the first of the Magyars, we may promote you to be the ruler of your race, and that you may be subject to our Laws and Orders.

But Lebedias appears to have been a proud man; he declined, with appropriate expressions of gratitude, the offer to become a puppet king, and proposed instead that the honour should be bestowed on a fellow chieftain called Almus, or on Almus's son, Arpad. So the Kagan, "pleased at this speech", sent Lebedias with a suitable escort back to his people; and they chose Arpad to be their king. The ceremony of Arpad's installation took place "after the custom and usage of the Khazars, raising him on their shields. But before this Arpad the Magyars never had any other ruler; wherefore the ruler of Hungary is drawn from his race up to this day."

"This day" in which Constantine wrote was *circa* 950, that is, a century after the event. Arpad in fact led his Magyars in the conquest of Hungary; his dynasty reigned till 1301, and his name is one of the first that Hungarian schoolboys learn. The Khazars had their fingers in many historic pies.

The second episode seems to have had an even more profound influence on the Hungarian national character. At some unspecified date, Constantine tells us, there was a rebellion (apostasia) of part of the Khazar nation against their rulers. The insurgents consisted of three tribes, "which were called Kavars [or Kabars], and which were of the Khazars' own race. The Government prevailed; some of the rebels were slaughtered and some fled the country and settled with the Magyars, and they made friends with one another. They also taught the tongue of the Khazars to the Magyars, and up to this day they speak the same dialect, but they also speak the other language of the Magyars. And because they proved themselves more efficient in wars and the most manly of the eight tribes [i.e., the seven original Magyar tribes plus the Kabars], and leaders in war, they were elected to be the first horde, and there is one leader among them, that is in the [originally] three hordes of the Kavars, who exists to this day."

To dot his i's, Constantine starts his next chapter with a list "of the hordes of Kavars and Magyars. First is that which broke off from the Khazars, this above-mentioned horde of the Kavars.", etc. The horde or tribe which actually calls itself "Magyar" comes only third. It looks as if the Magyars had received – metaphorically and perhaps literally – a blood transfusion from the Khazars. It affected them in several ways. First of all we learn, to our surprise, that at least till the middle of the tenth century both the Magyar and Khazar languages were spoken in Hungary. Several modern authorities have commented on this singular fact. Thus Bury wrote: "The result of this double tongue is the mixed character of the modern Hungarian language, which has supplied specious argument for the two opposite opinions as to the ethnical affinities of the Magyars." Toynbee remarks that though the Hungarians have ceased to be bilingual long ago, they were so at the beginnings of their state, as testified by some two hundred loan-words from the old Chuvash dialect of Turkish which the Khazars spoke.

The Magyars, like the Rus, also adopted a modified form of the Khazar double-kingship. Thus Gardezi: "... Their leader rides out with 20000 horsemen; they call him Kanda [Hungarian: Kende] and this is the title of their greater king, but the title of the person who effectively rules them is Jula. And the Magyars do whatever their Jula commands." There is reason to believe that the first Julas of Hungary were Kabars. There is also some evidence to indicate that among the dissident Kabar tribes, who *de facto* took over the leadership of the Magyar tribes, there were Jews, or adherents of "a judaizing religion". It seems quite possible – as Artamonov and Bartha have suggested – that the Kabar *apostasia* was somehow connected with, or a reaction against, the religious reforms initiated by King Obadiah. Rabbinical law, strict dietary rules, Talmudic casuistry might have gone very much against the grain of these steppe-warriors in shining armour. If they professed "a judaizing religion", it must have been closer to the faith of the ancient desert-Hebrews than to rabbinical orthodoxy. They may even have been followers of the fundamentalist sect of Karaites, and hence considered heretics. But this is pure speculation.

The close cooperation between Khazars and Magyars came to an end when the latter, AD 896, said farewell to the Eurasian steppes, crossed the Carpathian mountain range, and conquered the territory which was to become their lasting habitat. The circumstances of this migration are again controversial, but one can at least grasp its broad outlines. During the closing decades of the ninth century yet another uncouth player joined the nomad game of musical chairs: the pechenegs. [Or "Paccinaks", or in Hungarian, "Bescnyk".] What little we know about this Turkish tribe is summed up in Constantine's description of them as an insatiably greedy lot of Barbarians who for good money can be bought to fight other Barbarians and the Rus. They lived between the Volga and the Ural rivers under Khazar suzerainty; according to Ibn Rusta, the Khazars "raided them every year" to collect the tribute due to them.

Toward the end of the ninth century a catastrophe (of a nature by no means unusual) befell the Pechenegs: they were evicted from their country by their eastern neighbours. These neighbours were none other than the Ghuzz (or Oguz) whom Ibn Fadlan so much disliked – one of the inexhaustible number of Turkish tribes which from time to time cut loose from their Central-Asiatic moorings and drifted west. The displaced Pechenegs tried to settle in Khazaria, but the Khazars beat them off. [This seems to be the plausible interpretation of Constantine's statement that "the Ghuzz and the Khazars made war on the Pecheisegs". [Cf. Bury, p. 424.]] The Pechenegs continued their westward trek, crossed the Don and invaded the territory of the Magyars. The Magyars in turn were forced to fall back further west into the region between the Dnieper and the Sereth rivers. They called this region *Etel-Kz*, "the land between the rivers". They seem to have settled there in 889; but in 896 the Pechenegs struck again, allied to the Danube Bulgars, whereupon the Magyars withdrew into present-day Hungary.

This, in rough outline, is the story of the Magyars' exit from the eastern steppes, and the end of the Magyar-Khazar connection. The details are contested; some historians maintain, with a certain passion, that the Magyars suffered only one defeat, not two, at the hands of the Pechenegs, and that *Etel-Kz* was just another name for Lebedia, but we can leave these quibbles to the specialists. More intriguing is the apparent contradiction between the image of the Magyars as mighty warriors, and their inglorious retreat from successive habitats. Thus we learn from the Chronicle of Hinkmar of Rheims that in 862 they raided the Fast Frankish Empire – the first of the savage incursions which were to terrorize Europe during the next century. We also hear of a fearful encounter which St Cyril, the Apostle of the Slavs, had with a Magyar horde in 860, on his way to Khazaria. He was saying his prayers when they rushed at him *luporum more ululantes*-"howling in the manner of wolves". His sanctity, however, protected him from harm. Another chronicle mentions that the Magyars, and the Kabars, came into conflict with the Franks in 881; and Constantine tells us that, some ten years later, the Magyars "made war upon Simeon (ruler of the Danube Bulgars) and trounced him soundly, and came as far as Preslav, and shut him up in the fortress called Mundraga, and returned home."

How is one to reconcile all these valiant deeds with the series of retreats from the Don into Hungary, which took place in the same period? It seems that the answer is indicated in the passage in Constantine immediately following the one just quoted:

"... But after Symeon the Bulgar again made peace with the Emperor of the Greeks, and got security, he sent to the Patzinaks, and made an agreement with them to make war on and annihilate the Magyars. And when the Magyars went away on a campaign, the Patzinaks with Symeon came against the Magyars, and completely annihilated their families, and chased away miserably the Magyars left to guard their land. But the Magyars returning, and finding their country thus desolate and ruined, moved into the country occupied by them today [i.e. Hungary].

Thus the bulk of the army was "away on a campaign" when their land and families were attacked; and to judge by the chronicles mentioned above, they were "away" raiding distant countries quite frequently, leaving their homes with little protection. They could afford to indulge in this risky habit as long as they had only their Khazar overlords and the peaceful Slavonic tribes as their immediate neighbours. But with the advent of the land-hungry Pechenegs the situation changed. The disaster described by Constantine may have been only the last of a series of similar incidents. But it may have decided them to seek a new and safer home beyond the mountains, in a country which they already knew from at least two previous forays.

There is another consideration which speaks in favour of this hypothesis. The Magyars seem to have acquired the raiding habit only in the second half of the ninth century – about the time when they received that critical blood-transfusion from the Khazars. It may have proved a mixed blessing. The Kabars, who were "more efficient in war and more manly", became, as we saw, the leading tribe, and infused their hosts with the spirit of adventure, which was soon to turn them into the scourge of Europe, as the Huns had earlier been. They also taught the Magyars "those very peculiar and characteristic tactics employed since time immemorial by every Turkish nation – Huns, Avars, Turks, Pechenegs, Kumans – and by no other... light cavalry using the old devices of simulated flight, of shooting while fleeing, of sudden charges with fearful, wolf-like howling." These methods proved murderously effective during the ninth and tenth centuries when Hungarian raiders invaded Germany, the Balkans, Italy and even France – but they did not cut much ice against the Pechenegs, who used the same tactics, and could howl just as spinechillingly. Thus indirectly, by the devious logic of history, the Khazars were instrumental in the establishment of the Hungarian state, whereas the Khazars themselves vanished into the mist. Macartney, pursuing a similar line of thought, went even further in emphasizing the decisive role played by the Kabar transfusion:

The bulk of the Magyar nation, the true Finno-Ugrians, comparatively (although not very) pacific and sedentary agriculturalists, made their homes in the undulating country... west of the Danube. The plain of the Alfld was occupied by the nomadic race of Kabars, true Turks, herdsmen, horsemen and fighters, the driving force and the army of the nation. This was the race which in Constantine's day still occupied pride of place as the "first of the hordes of the Magyars". It was, I believe, chiefly this race of Kabars which raided the Slavs and Russians from the steppe; led the campaign against the Bulgars in 895; in large part and for more than half a century afterwards, was the terror of half Europe.

And yet the Hungarians managed to preserve their ethnic identity. "The brunt of sixty years of restless and remorseless warfare fell on the Kabars, whose ranks must have been thinned by it to an extraordinary extent. Meanwhile the true Magyars, living in comparative peace, increased their numbers." They also succeeded, after the bilingual period, in preserving their original Finno-Ugric language in the midst of their German and Slav neighbours – in contrast to the Danube Bulgars, who lost their Original Turkish language, and now speak a Slavonic dialect.

However, the Kabar influence continued to make itself felt in Hungary, and even after they became separated by the Carpathian Mountains, the Khazar-Magyar connection was not completely severed. According to Vasiliev, in the tenth century the Hungarian Duke Taksony invited an unknown number of Khazars to settle in his domains. It is not unlikely that these immigrants contained a fair proportion of Khazarian Jews. We may also assume that both the Kabars and the later immigrants brought with them some of their famed craftsmen, who taught the Hungarians their arts.

In the process of taking possession of their new and permanent home, the Magyars had to evict its former occupants, Moravians and Danube Bulgars, who moved into the regions where they still live. Their other Slavonic neighbours too – the Serbs and Croats – were already more or less *in situ*. Thus, as a result of the chain-reaction which started in the distant Urals – Ghuzz chasing Pechenegs, chasing Magyars, chasing Bulgars and Moravians, the map of modern Central Europe was beginning to take shape. The shifting kaleidoscope was settling into a more or less stable jigsaw.

We can now resume the story of the Rus ascent to power where we left it – the bloodless annexation of Kiev by Rurik's men around AD 862. This is also the approximate date when the Magyars were pushed westward by the Pechenegs, thus depriving the Khazars of protection on their western flank. It may explain why the Rus could gain control of Kiev so easily.

But the weakening of Khazar military power exposed the Byzantines, too, to attack by the Rus. Close to the date when the Rus settled in Kiev, their ships, sailing down the Dnieper, crossed the Black Sea and attacked Constantinople. Bury has described the event with much gusto:

> In the month of June, AD 860, the Emperor [Michael III], with all his forces, was marching against the Saracens. He had probably gone far when he received the amazing tidings, which recalled him with all speed to Constantinople. A Russian host had sailed across the Euxine [Black Sea] in two hundred boats, entered the Bosphorus, plundered the monasteries and suburbs on its banks, and overrun the Island of the Princes. The inhabitants of the city were utterly demoralized by the sudden horror of the danger and their own impotence. The troops (Tagmata) which were usually stationed in the neighbourhood of the city were far away with the Emperor... and the fleet was absent. Having wrought wreck and ruin in the suburbs, the barbarians prepared to attack the city. At this crisis... the learned Patriarch, Photius, rose to the occasion; he undertook the task of restoring the moral courage of his fellow-citizens... He expressed the general feeling when he dwelt on the incongruity that the Imperial city, "queen of almost all the world",

should be mocked by a band of slaves [sic] a mean and barbarous crowd. But the populace was perhaps more impressed and consoled when he resorted to the ecclesiastical magic which had been used efficaciously at previous sieges. The precious garment of the Virgin Mother was borne in procession round the walls of the city; and it was believed that it was dipped in the waters of the sea for the purpose of raising a storm of wind. No storm arose, but soon afterwards the Russians began to retreat, and perhaps there were not many among the joyful citizens who did not impute their relief to the direct intervention of the queen of heaven.

We may add, for the sake of piquantry, that the "learned Patriarch", Photius, whose eloquence saved the Imperial city, was none other than "Khazar face" who had sent St Cyril on his proselytizing mission. As for the Rus retreat, it was caused by the hurried return of the Greek army and fleet; but "Khazar face" had saved morale among the populace during the agonizing period of waiting.

Toynbee too has interesting comments to make on this episode. In 860, he writes, the Russians "perhaps came nearer to capturing Constantinople than so far they have ever come since then".41 And he also shares the view expressed by several Russian historians, that the attack by the eastern Northmen's Dnieper flotilla across the Black Sea was coordinated with the simultaneous attack of a western Viking fleet, approaching Constantinople across the Mediterranean and the Dardanelles:

Vasiliev and Paszkievicz and Vernadsky are inclined to believe that the two naval expeditions that thus converged on the Sea of Marmara were not only simultaneous but were concerted, and they even make a guess at the identity of the master mind that, in their view, worked out this strategic plan on the grand scale. They suggest that Rurik of Novgorod was the same person as Rorik of Jutland.

This makes one appreciate the stature of the adversary with whom the Khazars had to contend. Nor was Byzantine diplomacy slow in appreciating it – and to play the double game which the situation seemed to demand, alternating between war, when it could not be avoided, and appeasement in the pious hope that the Russians would eventually be converted to Christianity and brought into the flock of the Eastern Patriarchate. As for the Khazars, they were an important asset for the time being, and would be sold out on the first decent – or indecent – opportunity that offered itself

For the next two hundred years Byzantine-Russian relations alternated between armed conflict and treaties of friendship. Wars were waged in 860 (siege of Constantinople), 907, 941, 944, 969-71; and treaties concluded in 838-9, 861,911,945, 957, 971. About the contents of these more or less secret agreements we know little, but even what we know shows the bewildering complexity of the game. A few years after the siege of Constantinople the Patriarch Photius (still the same) reports that the Rus sent ambassadors to Constantinople and – according to the Byzantine formula for pressurized proselytizing – "besought the Emperor for Christian baptism". As Bury comments:

"We cannot say which, or how many, of the Russian settlements were represented by this embassy, but the object must have been to offer amends for the recent raid, perhaps to procure the deliverance of prisoners. It is certain that some of the Russians agreed to adopt Christianity... but the seed did not fall on very fertile ground. For upwards of a hundred years we hear no more of the Christianity of the Russians. The treaty, however, which was concluded between AD 860 and 866, led probably to other consequences."

Among these consequences was the recruiting of Scandinavian sailors into the Byzantine fleet – by 902 there were seven hundred of them. Another development was the famous "Varangian Guard", an lite corps of Rus and other nordic mercenaries, including even Englishmen. In the treaties of 945 and 971 the Russian rulers of the Principality of Kiev undertook to supply the Byzantine Emperor with troops on request. In Constantine potphyrogenitus' day, i.e., the middle of the tenth century, Rus fleets on the Bosphorus were a customary sight; they no longer caine to lay siege on Constantinople but to sell their wares. Trade was meticulously well regulated (except when armed clashes intervened): according to the Russian Chronicle, it was agreed in the treaties of 907 and 911 that the Rus visitors should enter Constantinople through one city gate only, and not more thin fifty at a time, escorted by officials; that they were to receive during their stay in the city as much grain as they required and also up to Six months' supply of other provisions, in monthly deliveries, including bread, wine, meat, fish, fruit and bathing facilities (if required). To make sure that all transactions should be nice and proper, black-market dealings in currency were punished by amputation of one hand. Nor were proselytizing efforts neglected, as the ultimate means to achieve peaceful coexistence with the increasingly powerful Russians.

But it was hard going. According to the Russian Chronicle, when Oleg, Regent of Kiev, concluded the treaty of 911 with the Byzantines, "the Emperors Leo and Alexander [joint rulers], after agreeing upon the tribute and mutually binding themselves by oath, kissed the cross and invited Oleg and his men to swear an oath likewise. According to the religion of the Rus, the latter swore by their weapons and by their god Perun, as well as by Volos, the god of cattle, and thus confirmed the treaty."

Nearly half a century and several battles and treaties later, victory for the Holy Church seemed in sight: in 957 Princess Olga of Kiev (widow of Prince Igor) was baptized on the occasion of her state visit to Constantinople (unless she had already been baptized once before her departure – which again is controversial).

The various banquets and festivities in Olga's honour are described in detail in *De Caerimonus*, though we are not told how the lady reacted to the Disneyland of mechanical toys displayed in the Imperial throne-room – for instance, to the stuffed lions which emitted a fearful mechanical roar. (Another distinguished guest, Bishop Liutprand, recorded that he was able to keep his sang-froid only because he was forewarned of the surprises in store for visitors.)

The occasion must have been a major headache for the master of ceremonies (which was Constantine himself), because not only was Olga a female sovereign, but her retinue, too, was female; the male diplomats and advisers, eighty-two of them, "marched self-effacingly in the rear of the Russian delegation".46 [Nine kinsmen of Olga's, twenty diplomats, forty-three commercial advisers, one priest, two interpreters, six servants of the diplomats and Olga's special interpreter.]

Just before the banquet there was a small incident, symbolic of the delicate nature of Russian-Byzantine relations. When the ladies of the Byzantine court entered, they fell on their faces before the Imperial family, as protocol required. Olga remained standing "but it was noticed, with satisfaction, that she slightly if perceptibly inclined her head. She was put in her place by being seated, as the Muslim state guests had been, at a separate table." The Russian Chronicle has a different, richly embroidered version of this state visit. When the delicate subject of baptism was brought up, Olga told Constantine "that if he desired to baptize her, he should perform this function himself; otherwise she was unwilling to accept baptism". The Emperor concurred, and asked the Patriarch to instruct her in the faith.

The Patriarch instructed her in prayer and fasting, in almsgiving and in the maintenance of chastity. She bowed her head, and like a sponge absorbing water, she eagerly drank in his teachings...

After her baptism, the Emperor summoned Olga and made known to her that he wished her to become his wife. But she replied, "How can you marry me, after yourself baptizing me and calling me your daughter? For among Christians that is unlawful, as you yourself must know." Then the Emperor said, "Olga, you have outwitted me."

When she got back to Kiev, Constantine "sent a message to her, saying, 'Inasmuch as I bestowed many gifts upon you, you promised me that on your return to Ros you would send me many presents of slaves, wax and furs, and despatch soldiery to aid me.' Olga made answer to the envoys that if the Emperor would spend as long a time with her in the Pochayna as she had remained on the Bosphorus, she would grant his request. With these words, she dismissed the envoys."

This Olga-Helga must have been a formidable Scandinavian Amazon. She was, as already mentioned, the widow of Prince Igor, supposedly the son of Rurik, whom the Russian Chronicle describes as a greedy, foolish and sadistic ruler. In 941 he had attacked the Byzantines with a large fleet, and "of the people they captured, some they butchered, others they set up as targets and shot at, some they seized upon, and after binding their hands behind their backs, they drove iron nails through their heads.

Many sacred churches they gave to the flames." In the end they were defeated by the Byzantine fleet, spouting Greek fire through tubes mounted in the prows of their ships. "Upon seeing the flames, the Russians cast themselves into the sea-water, but the survivors returned home [where] they related that the Greeks had in their possession the lightning from heaven, and had set them on fire by pouring it forth, so that the Russes could not conquer them." [Toynbee does not hesitate to call this famous secret weapon of the Greeks "napalm". It was a chemical of unknown composition, perhaps a distilled petroleum fraction, which ignited spontaneously on contact with water, and could not be put out by water.] This episode was followed by another treaty of friendship four years later. As a predominantly maritime nation, the Rus were even more impressed by the Greek fire than others who had attacked Byzantium, and the "lightning from heaven" was a strong argument in favour of the Greek Church. Yet they were still not ready for conversion.

When Igor was killed in 945 by the Derevlians, a Slavonic people upon which he had imposed an exorbitant tribute, the widowed Olga became Regent of Kiev. She started her rule by taking fourfold revenge on the Derevlians: first, a Derevlian peace mission was buried alive; then a delegation of notables was locked in a bath-house and burned alive; this was followed by another massacre, and lastly the main town of the Derevlians was burnt down. Olga's bloodlust seemed truly insatiable until her baptism. From that day onward, the Chronicle informs us, she became "the precursor of Christian Russia, even as daybreak precedes the sun, and as the dawn precedes the day. For she shone like the moon by night, and she was radiant among the infidels like a pearl in the mire." In due course she was canonized as the first Russian saint of the Orthodox Church.

Yet in spite of the great to-do about Olga's baptism and her state visit to Constantine, this was not the last word in the stormy dialogue between the Greek Church and the Russians. For Olga's son, Svyatoslav, reverted to paganism, refused to listen to his mother's entreaties, "collected a numerous and valiant army and, stepping light like a leopard, undertook many campaigns"51 among them a war against the Khazars and another against the

Byzantines. It was only in 988, in the reign of his son, St Vladimir, that the ruling dynasty of the Russians definitely adopted the faith of the Greek Orthodox Church – about the same time as Hungarians, Poles, and Scandinavians, including the distant Icelanders, became converted to the Latin Church of Rome. The broad outlines of the lasting religious divisions of the world were beginning to take shape; and in this process the Jewish Khazars were becoming an anachronism. The growing *rapprochement* between Constantinople and Kiev, in spite of its ups and downs, made the importance of Itil gradually dwindle; and the presence of the Khazars athwart Rus-Byzantine trade-routes, levying their 10 per cent tax on the increasing flow of goods, became an irritant both to the Byzantine treasury and the Russian warrior merchants.

Symptomatic of the changing Byzantine attitude to their former allies was the surrender of Cherson to the Russians. For several centuries Byzantines and Khazars had been bickering and occasionally skirmishing, for possession of that important Crimean port; but when Vladimir occupied Cherson in 987, the Byzantines did not even protest; for, as Bury put it, "the sacrifice was not too dear a price for perpetual peace and friendship with the Russian state, then becoming a great power".

The sacrifice of Cherson may have been justified; but the sacrifice of the Khazar alliance turned out to be, in the long run, a short-sighted policy.

FALL

IN discussing Russian-Byzantine relations in the ninth and tenth centuries, I have been able to quote at length from two detailed sources; Constantine's *De Administrando* and the Primary Russian Chronicle. But on the Russian-Khazar confrontation during the same period-to which we now turn-we have no comparable source material; the archives of Itil, if they ever existed, have gone with the wind, and for the history of the last hundred years of the Khazar Empire we must again fall back on the disjointed, casual hints found in various Arab chronicles and geographies.

The period in question extends from *circa* 862-the Russian occupation of Kiev-to *circa* 965-the destruction of Itil by Svyatoslav. After the loss of Kiev and the retreat of the Magyars into Hungary, the former western dependencies of the Khazar Empire (except for parts of the Crimea) were no longer under the Kagan's control; and the Prince of Kiev could without hindrance address the Slavonic tribes in the Dnieper basin with the cry, "Pay nothing to the Khazars!"

The Khazars may have been willing to acquiesce in the loss of their hegemony in the west, but at the same time there was also a growing encroachment by the Rus on the east, down the Volga and into the regions around the Caspian. These Muslim lands bordering on the southern half of the "Khazar Sea"-Azerbaijan, Jilan, Shirwan, Tabaristan, Jurjan-were tempting targets for the Viking fleets, both as objects of plunder and as trading posts for commerce with the Muslim Caliphate. But the approaches to the Caspian, past Itil through the Volga delta, were controlled by the Khazars-as the approaches to the Black Sea had been while they were still holding Kiev. And "control" meant that the Rus had to solicit permission for each flotilla to pass, and pay the 10 per cent customs due-a double insult to pride and pocket.

For some time there was a precarious *modus vivendi*. The Rus flotillas paid their due, sailed into the Khazar Sea and traded with the people around it. But trade, as we saw, frequently became a synonym for plunder. Some time between 864 and 8842 a Rus expedition attacked the port of Abaskun in Tabaristan. They were defeated, but in 910 they returned, plundered the city and countryside and carried off a number of Muslim prisoners to be sold as slaves. To the Khazars this must have been a grave embarrassment, because of their friendly relations with the Caliphate, and also because of the crack regiment of Muslim mercenaries in their standing army. Three years later-AD 913-matters came to a head in an armed confrontation which ended in a bloodbath.

This major incident-already mentioned briefly has been described in detail by Masudi, while the Russian Chronicle passes it over in silence. Masudi tells us that "some time after the year of the Hegira 300 [AD 912-913] a Rus fleet of 500 ships, each manned by 100 persons" was approaching Khazar territory:

When the ships of the Rus came to the Khazars posted at the mouth of the strait... they sent a letter to the Khazar king, requesting to be allowed to pass through his country and descend his river, and so enter the sea of the Khazars... on condition that they should give him half of what they might take in booty from the peoples of the sea-coast. He granted them permission and they... descended the river to the city of Itil and passing through, came out on the estuary of the river, where it joins the Khazar Sea. From the estuary to the city of Itil the river is very large and its waters abundant. The ships of the Rus spread throughout the sea. Their raiding parties were directed against Jilan, Jurjan, Tabaristan, Abaskun on the coast of Jurjan, the naphtha country [Baku] and the region of Azerbaijan.... The Rus shed blood, destroyed the women and children, took booty and raided and burned in all directions...

They even sacked the city of Ardabil-at three days' journey inland. When the people recovered from the shock and took to arms, the Rus, according to their classic strategy, withdrew from the coast to the islands near Baku. The natives, using small boats and merchant vessels, tried to dislodge them.

But the Rus turned on them and thousands of the Muslims were killed or drowned. The Rus continued many months in this sea... When they had collected enough booty and were tired of what they were about, they started for the mouth of the Khazar river, informing the king of the Khazars, and conveying to him rich booty, according to the conditions which he had fixed with them... The Arsiyah [the Muslim mercenaries in the Khazar army] and other Muslims who lived in Khazaria learned of the situation of the Rus, and said to the king of the Khazars: leave us to deal with these people. They have raided the lands of the Muslims, our brothers, and have shed blood and enslaved women and children. And he could not gainsay them. So he sent for the Rus, informing them of the determination of the Muslims to fight them.

The Muslims [of Khazaria] assembled and went forth to find the Rus, proceeding downstream [on land, from Itil to the Volga estuary]. When the two armies came within sight of each other, the Rus disembarked and drew up in order of battle against the Muslims, with whom were a number of Christians living in Itil, so that they were about 15000 men, with horses and equipment. The fighting continued for three days. God helped the Muslims against them. The Rus were put to the sword. Some were killed and others were drowned. of those slain by the Muslims on the banks of the Khazar river there were counted about 30000...

Five thousand of the Rus escaped, but these too were killed, by the Burtas and the Bulgars. This is Masudi's account of this disastrous Rus incursion into the Caspian in 912-13. It is, of course, biased. The Khazar ruler comes out of it as a double-crossing rascal who acts, first as a passive accomplice of the Rus marauders, then authorizes the attack on them, but simultaneously informs them of the ambush prepared by "the Muslims" under his own command. Even of the Bulgars, Masudi says "they are Muslims"-although Ibn Fadlan, visiting the Bulgars ten years later, describes them as still far from being converted. But though coloured by religious prejudice, Masudi's account provides a glimpse of the dilemma or several dilemmas-confronting the Khazar leadership. They may not have been unduly worried about the misfortunes suffered by the people on the Caspian shores; it was not a sentimental age. But what if the predatory Rus, after gaining control of Kiev and the Dnieper, were to establish a foothold on the Volga? Moreover, another Rus raid into the Caspian might bring down the wrath of the Caliphate-not on the Rus themselves, who were beyond its reach, but on the innocent-well, nearly innocent-Khazars.

Relations with the Caliphate were peaceful, yet nevertheless precarious, as an incident reported by Ibn Fadlan indicates. The Rus raid described by Masudi took place in 912-13; Ibn Fadlan's mission to Bulgar in 921-2. His account of the incident in question is as follows:3

The Muslims in this city [Itil] have a cathedral mosque where they pray and attend on Fridays. It has a high minaret and several muezzins [criers who call for prayer from the minaret]. When the king of the Khazars was informed in a.H. 310 [AD 922] that the Muslims had destroyed the synagogue which was in Dar al-Babunaj [unidentified place in Muslim territory], he gave orders to destroy the minaret, and he killed the muezzins. And he said: "If I had not feared that not a synagogue would be left standing in the lands of Islam, but would be destroyed, I would have destroyed the mosque too."

The episode testifies to a nice feeling for the strategy of mutual deterrence and the dangers of escalation. It also shows once more that the Khazar rulers felt emotionally committed to the fate of Jews in other parts of the world.

Masudi's account of the 912-13 Rus incursion into the Caspian ends with the words: "There has been no repetition on the part of the Rus of what we have described since that year." As coincidences go, Masudi wrote this in the same year-943-in which the Rus repeated their incursion into the Caspian with an even greater fleet; but Masudi could not have known this. For thirty years, after the disaster of 913, they had lain off that part of the world; now they felt evidently strong enough to try again; and it is perhaps significant that their attempt coincided, within a year or two, with their expedition against the Byzantines, under the swashbuckling Igor, which perished under the Greek fire. In the course of this new invasion, the Rus gained a foothold in the Caspian region in the city of Bardha, and were able to hold it for a whole year. In the end pestilence broke out among the Rus, and the Azerbaijanis were able to put the survivors to flight. This time the Arab sources do not mention any Khazar share in the plunder-nor in the fighting. But Joseph does in his letter to Hasdai, written some years later:

"I guard the mouth of the river and do not permit the Rus who come in their ships to invade the land of the Arabs... I fight heavy wars with them." [In the so called "long version" of the same letter (see Appendix III), there is another sentence which may or may not have been added by a copyist: "If I allowed them for one hour, they would destroy all the country of the Arabs as far as Baghdad... " Since the Rus sat on the Caspian not for an hour, but for a year, the boast sounds rather hollow-though a little less so if we take it to refer not to the past but to the future.]

Whether or not on this particular occasion the Khazar army participated in the fighting, the fact remains that a few years later they decided to deny the Russians access to the "Khazar Sea" and that from 943 onward we hear no more of Rus incursions into the Caspian. This momentous decision, in all likelihood motivated by internal pressures of the Muslim community in their midst, involved the Khazars in "heavy wars" with the Rus. Of these, however, we have no records beyond the statement in Joseph's letter. They may have been more in the nature of skirmishes except for the one major campaign of AD 965, mentioned in the Old Russian Chronicle, which led to the breaking up of the Khazar Empire.

The leader of the campaign was Prince Svyatoslav of Kiev, son of Igor and Olga. We have already heard that he was "stepping light as a leopard" and that he "undertook many campaigns"-in fact he spent most of his reign campaigning. In spite of the constant entreaties of his mother, he refused to be baptized, "because it would make him the laughing stock of his subjects". The Russian Chronicle also tells us that "on his expeditions he carried neither waggons nor cooking utensils, and boiled no meat, but cut off small strips of horseflesh, game or beef, and ate it after roasting it on the coals. Nor did he have a tent, but he spread out a horse-blanket under him, and set his saddle under his head; and all his retinue did likewise." When he attacked the enemy, he scorned doing it by stealth, but instead sent messengers ahead announcing: "I am coming upon you."

To the campaign against the Khazars, the Chronicler devotes only a few lines, in the laconic tone which he usually adopts in reporting on armed conflicts:

Svyatoslav went to the Oka and the Volga, and on coming in contact with the Vyatichians [a Slavonic tribe inhabiting the region south of modern Moscow], he inquired of them to whom they paid tribute. They made answer that they paid a silver piece per ploughshare to the Khazars. When they [the Khazars] heard of his approach, they went out to meet him with their Prince, the Kagan, and the armies came to blows. When the battle thus took place, Svyatoslav defeated the Khazars and took their city of Biela Viezha.

Now Biela Viezha-the White Castle-was the Slavonic name for Sarkel, the famed Khazar fortress on the Don; but it should be noted that the destruction of Itil, the capital, is nowhere mentioned in the Russian Chronicle-a point to which we shall return..The Chronicle goes on to relate that Svyatoslav "also conquered the Yasians and the Karugians" [Ossetians and Chirkassians], defeated the Danube Bulgars, was defeated by the Byzantincs, and on his way back to Kiev was murdered by a horde of Pechenegs. "They cut off his head, and made a cup out of his skull, overlayed it with gold, and drank from it."

Several historians have regarded the victory of Svyatoslav as the end of Khazaria-which, as will be seen, is demonstrably wrong. The destruction of Sarkel in 965 signalled the end of the Khazar Empire, not of the Khazar state-as 1918 signalled the end of the Austro-Hungarian Empire, but not of Austria as a nation. Khazar control of the far-flung Slavonic tribes-which, as we have seen, stretched to the vicinity of Moscow-had now come to a definite end; but the Khazar heartland between Caucasus, Don and Volga remained intact. The approaches to the Caspian Sea remained closed to the Rus, and we hear of no further attempt on their part to force their way to it. As Toynbee pointedly remarks:

"The Rhus succeeded in destroying the Khazar Steppe-empire, but the only Khazar territory that they acquired was Tmutorakan on the Tanian peninsula [facing the Crimea], and this gain was ephemeral... It was not till half-way through the sixteenth century that the Muscovites made a permanent conquest, for Russia, of the river Volga... to the river's dbouchure into the Caspian Sea."

After the death of Svyatoslav, civil war broke out between his sons, out of which the youngest, Vladimir, emerged victorious. He too started life as a pagan, like his father, and he too, like his grandmother Olga, ended up as a repentant sinner, accepted baptism and was eventually canonized. Yet in his youth St Vladimir seemed to have followed St Augustine's motto: Lord give me chastity, but not yet. The Russian Chronicle is rather severe about this:

Now Vladimir was overcome by lust for women. He had three hundred concubines at Vyshgorod, three hundred at Belgorod, and two hundred at Berestovo. He was insatiable in vice. He even seduced married women and violated young girls, for he was a libertine like Solomon. For it is said that Solomon had seven hundred wives and three hundred concubines. He was wise, yet in the end he came to ruin. But Vladimir, though at first deluded, eventually found salvation. Great is the Lord, and great his power and of his wisdom there is no end.

Olga's baptism, around 957 did not cut much ice, even with her own son. Vladimir's baptism, AD 989, was a momentous event which had a lasting influence on the history of the world..It was preceded by a series of diplomatic manoeuvrings and theological discussions with representatives of the four major religions-which provide a kind of mirror image to the debates before the Khazar conversion to Judaism. Indeed, the Old Russian Chronicle's account of these theological disputes constantly remind one of the Hebrew and Arab accounts of King Bulan's erstwhile Brains Trust-only the outcome is different..This time there were four instead of three contestants-as the schism between the Greek and the Latin churches was already an accomplished fact in the tenth century (though it became official only in the eleventh)..The Russian Chronicle's account of Vladimir's conversion first mentions a victory he achieved against the Volga Bulgars, followed by a treaty of friendship. "The Bulgars declared: 'May peace prevail between us till stone floats and straw sinks.'" Vladimir returned to Kiev, and the Bulgars sent a Muslim religious mission to convert him. They described to him the joys of Paradise where each man will be given seventy fair women. Vladimir listened to them "with approval", but when it came to abstinence from pork and wine, he drew the line.

"'Drinking,' said he, 'is the joy of the Russes. We cannot exist without that pleasure.'"8.Next came a German delegation of Roman Catholics, adherents of the Latin rite. They fared no better when they brought up, as one of the main requirements of their faith, fasting according to one's strength. "... Then Vladimir answered: 'Depart hence; our fathers accepted no such principle.'"9.The third mission consisted of Khazar Jews. They came off worst. Vladimir asked them why they no longer ruled Jerusalem. "They made answer: 'God was angry at our forefathers, and scattered us among the Gentiles on account of our sins.' The Prince then demanded: 'How can you hope to teach others while you yourselves are cast out and scattered abroad by the hand of God? Do you expect us to accept that fate also?'".The fourth and last missionary is a scholar sent by the Greeks of Byzantium. He starts with a blast against the Muslims, who are "accursed above all men, like Sodom and Gomorrah, upon which the Lord let fall burning stones, and which he buried and submerged.... For they moisten their excrement, and pour the water into their mouths, and annoint their beards with it, remembering Mahomet.... Vladimir, upon hearing these statements, spat upon the earth, saying: 'This is a vile thing.'"10.The Byzantine scholar then accuses the Jews of having crucified God, and the Roman Catholics-in much milder terms-of having "modified the Rites". After these preliminaries, he launches into a long exposition of the Old and New Testaments, starting with the creation of the world. At the end of it, however, Vladimir appears only half convinced, for when pressed to be baptized he replies, "I shall wait yet a little longer." He then sends his own envoys, "ten good and wise men", to various countries to observe their religious practices. In due time this commission of inquiry reports to him that the Byzantine Service is "fairer than the ceremonies of other nations, and we knew not whether we were in heaven or on earth".

But Vladimir still hesitates, and the Chronicle continues with a non-sequitur:."After a year had passed, in 988, Vladimir proceeded with an armed force against Cherson, a Greek city...." (We remember that control of this important Crimean port had been for a long time contested between Byzantines and Khazars.) The valiant Chersonese refused to surrender. Vladimir's troops constructed earthworks directed at the city walls, but the Chersonese "dug a tunnel under the city wall, stole the heaped-up earth and carried it into the city, where they piled it up". Then a traitor shot an arrow into the Rus camp with a message: "There are springs behind you to the east, from which water flows in pipes. Dig down and cut them off" When Vladimir received this information, he raised his eyes to heaven and vowed that if this hope was realized, he would be baptized.

He succeeded in cutting off the city's water supply, and Cherson surrendered. Thereupon Vladimir, apparently forgetting his vow, "sent messages to the Emperors Basil and Constantine [joint rulers at the time], saying: 'Behold, I have captured your glorious city. I have also heard that you have an unwedded sister. Unless you give her to me to wife, I shall deal with your own city as I have with Cherson.'".The Emperors replied: "If you are baptized you shall have her to wife, inherit the Kingdom of God, and be our companion in the faith."

And so it came to pass. Vladimir at long last accepted baptism, and married the Byzantine Princess Anna. A few years later Greek

Christianity became the official religion not only of the rulers but of the Russian people, and from 1037 onward the Russian Church was governed by the Patriarch of Constantinople.

It was a momentous triumph of Byzantine diplomacy. Vernadsky calls it "one of those abrupt turns which make the study of history so fascinating... and it is interesting to speculate on the possible course of history had the Russian princes... adopted either of these faiths [Judaism or Islam] instead of Christianity.... The acceptance of one or another of these faiths must necessarily have determined the future cultural and political development of Russia. The acceptance of Islam would have drawn Russia into the circle of Arabian culture-that is, an Asiatic-Egyptian culture. The acceptance of Roman Christianity from the Germans would have made Russia a country of Latin or European culture. The acceptance of either Judaism or Orthodox Christianity insured to Russia cultural independence of both Europe and Asia."

But the Russians needed allies more than they needed independence, and the East Roman Empire, however corrupt, was still a more desirable ally in terms of power, culture and trade, than the crumbling empire of the Khazars. Nor should one underestimate the role played by Byzantine statesmanship in bringing about the decision for which it had worked for more than a century. The Russian Chronicle's naive account of Vladimir's game of procrastination gives us no insight into the diplomatic manoeuvrings and hard bargaining that must have gone on before he accepted baptism-and thereby, in fact, Byzantine tutelage for himself and his people. Cherson was obviously part of the price, and so was the dynastic marriage to Princess Anna. But the most important part of the deal was the end of the Byzantine-Khazar alliance against the Rus, and its replacement by a Byzantine-Russian alliance against the Khazars. A few years later, in 1016, a combined Byzantine-Russian army invaded Khazaria, defeated its ruler, and "subdued the country" (see below, IV, 8). Yet the cooling off towards the Khazars had already started, as we have seen, in Constantine Porphyrogenitus's day, fifty years before Vladimir's conversion. We remember Constantine's musings on "how war is to be made on Khazaria and by whom". The passage quoted earlier on (II, 7) continues:

If the ruler of Alania does not keep the peace with the Khazars but considers the friendship of the Emperor of the Romans to be of greater value to him, then, if the Khazars do not choose to maintain friendship and peace with the Emperor, the Alan can do them great harm. He can ambush their roads and attack them when they are off their guard on their route to Sarkel and to "the nine regions" and to Cherson... Black Bulgaria [the Volga Bulgars] is also in a position to make war on the Khazars.

Toynbee, after quoting this passage, makes the following, rather touching comment:

If this passage in Constantine Porphyrogenitus's manual for the conduct of the East Roman Imperial Government's foreign relations had ever fallen into the hands of the Khazar Khaqan and his ministers, they would have been indignant. They would have pointed out that nowadays Khazaria was one of the most pacific states in the world, and that, if she had been more warlike in her earlier days, her arms had never been directed against the East Roman Empire. The two powers had, in fact, never been at war with each other, while, on the other hand, Khazaria had frequently been at war with the East Roman Empire's enemies, and this to the Empire's signal advantage. Indeed, the Empire may have owed it to the Khazars that she had survived the successive onslaughts of the Sasanid Persian Emperor Khusraw II Parviz and the Muslim Arabs.... And thereafter the pressure on the Empire of the Arabs' onslaught had been relieved by the vigour of the Khazars' offensivedefensive resistance to the Arabs' advance towards the Caucasus. The friendship between Khazaria and the Empire had been symbolized and sealed in two marriage-alliances between their respective Imperial families. What, then, had been in Constantine's mind when he had been thinking out ways of tormenting Khazaria by inducing her neighbours to fall upon her?

The answer to Toynbee's rhetorical question is obviously that the Byzantines were inspired by Realpolitik-and that, as already said, theirs was not a sentimental age. Nor is ours.

Nevertheless, it turned out to be a short-sighted policy. To quote Bury once more:

The first principle of Imperial policy in this quarter of the world was the maintenance of peace with the Khazars. This was the immediate consequence of the geographical position of the Khazar Empire, lying as it did between the Dnieper and the Caucasus. From the seventh century, when Heraclius had sought the help of the Khazars against Persia, to the tenth, in which the power of Itil declined, this was the constant policy of the Emperors. It was to the advantage of the Empire that the Chagan should exercise an effective control over his barbarian neighbours.16

This "effective control" was now to be transferred from the Khazar Kagan to the Rus Kagan, the Prince of Kiev. But it did not work. The Khazars were a Turkish tribe of the steppes, who had been able to cope with wave after wave of Turkish and Arab invaders; they had resisted and subdued the Bulgars, Burtas, Pechenegs, Ghuzz, and so on. The Russians and their Slav subjects were no match for the nomad warriors of the steppes, their mobile strategy and guerilla tactics.*[The most outstanding Russian epic poem of the period, "The Lay of Igor's Host", describes one of the disastrous campaigns of the Russians against the Ghuzz.] As a result of constant nomad pressure, the centres of Russian power were gradually transferred from the southern steppes to the wooded north, to the principalities of Galiczia, Novgorod and Moscow. The Byzantines had calculated that Kiev would take over the role of Itil as the guardian of Eastern Europe and centre of trade; instead, Kiev went into rapid decline. It was the end of the first chapter of Russian history, followed by a period of chaos, with a dozen independent principalities waging endless wars against each other..This created a power vacuum, into which poured a new wave of conquering nomads-or rather a new off-shoot of our old friends the Ghuzz, whom Ibn Fadlan had found even more abhorrent than the other Barbarian tribes which he was obliged to visit. These "pagan and godless foes", as the Chronicle describes them, were called Polovtsi by the Russians, Kumans by the Byzantines, Kun by the Hungarians, Kipchaks by their fellow Turks. They ruled the steppes as far as Hungary from the late eleventh to the thirteenth century (when they, in turn, were swamped by the Mongol invasion).*[One substantial branch of the Kumans, fleeing from the Mongols, was granted asylum in Hungary in 1241, and merged with the native population. "Kun" is still a frequent surname in Hungary.] They also fought several wars against the Byzantines. Another branch of the Ghuzz, the Seljuks (named after their ruling dynasty) destroyed a huge Byzantine army in the historic battle of Manzikert (1071) and captured the Emperor Romanus IV Diogenes. Henceforth the Byzantines were unable to prevent the Turks from gaining control of most provinces of Asia Minor-the present-day Turkey-which had previously been the heartland of the East Roman Empire.

One can only speculate whether history would have taken a different course if Byzantium had not abandoned its traditional policy, maintained throughout the three previous centuries, of relying on the Khazar stronghold against the Muslim, Turkish and Viking invaders. Be that as it may, Imperial *Realpolitik* turned out to have been not very realistic.

During the two centuries of Kuman rule, followed by the Mongol invasion, the eastern steppes were once more plunged into the Dark Ages, and the later history of the Khazars is shrouded in even deeper obscurity than their origin. The references to the Khazar state in its final period of decline are found mainly in Muslim sources; but they are, as we shall see, so ambiguous that almost every name, date and geographical indication is open to several interpretations. Historians, famished for facts, have nothing left but a few bleached bones to gnaw at like starving bloodhounds, in the forlorn hope of finding some hidden morsel to sustain them.

In the light of what has been said before, it appears that the decisive event precipitating the decline of Khazar power was not Svyatoslav's victory, but Vladimir's conversion. How important was in fact that victory, which nineteenth-century historians *[Following a tradition set by Fraehn in 1822, in the Memnoirs of the Russian Academy.] habitually equated with the end of the Khazar state? We remember that the Russian Chronicle mentions only the destruction of Sarkel, the fortress, but not the destruction of Itil, the capital.

That Itil was indeed sacked and devastated we know from several Arab sources, which are too insistent to be ignored; but when and by whom it was sacked is by no means clear. Ibn Hawkal, the principal source, says it was done by the Rus who "utterly destroyed Khazaran, Samandar and Itil"-apparently believing that Khazaran and Itil were different towns, whereas we know that they were one twin-town; and his dating of the event differs from the Russian Chronicle's dating of the fall of Sarkel which Ibn Hawkal does not mention at all, just as the Chronicle does not mention the destruction of Itil. Accordingly, Marquart suggested that Itil was sacked not by Svyatoslav's Rus, who only got as far as Sarkel, but by some fresh wave of Vikings. To complicate matters a little more, the second Arab source, ibn Miskawayh, says that it was a body of "Turks" which descended on Khazaria in the critical year 965. By "Turks" he may have meant the Rus, as Barthold maintained. But it could also have been a marauding horde of Pechenegs, for instance. It seems that we shall never know who destroyed Itil, however long we chew the bones.

And how seriously was it destroyed? The principal source, Ibn Hawkal, first speaks of the "utter destruction" of Itil, but then he also says, writing a few years later, that "Khazaran is still the centre on which the Rus trade converges". Thus the phrase "utter destruction" may have been an exaggeration. This is the more likely because he also speaks of the "utter destruction" of the town of Bulghar, capital of the Volga Bulgars. Yet the damage which the Rus caused in Bulghar could not have been too important, as we have coins that were minted there in the year 976-7-only about ten years after Svyatoslav's raid; and in the thirteenth century Buighar was still an important city. As Dunlop put it:

The ultimate source of all statements that the Russians destroyed Khazaria in the tenth century is no doubt IbnHawkal... Ibn Hawkal, however, speaks as positively of the destruction of Bulghar on the middle Volga. It is quite certain that at the time of the Mongol attacks in the thirteenth century Bulghar was a flourishing cornmunity. Was the ruin of Khazaria also temporary?

It obviously was. Khazaran-Itil, and the other towns of the Khazars, consisted mostly of tents, wooden dwellings and "round houses" built of mud, which were easily destroyed and easily rebuilt; only the royal and public buildings were of brick.

The damage done must nevertheless have been serious, for several Arab chroniclers speak of a temporary exodus of the population to the Caspian shore or islands. Thus Ibn Hawkal says the Khazars of Itil fled from the Rus to one of the islands of the "naphta coast" [Baku], but later returned to Itil and Khazaran with the aid of the Muslim Shah of Shirwan. This sounds plausible since the people of Shirwan had no love for the Rus who had plundered their shores earlier on. Other Arab chroniclers, Ibn Miskawayh and Muqaddasi (writing later than Ibn HIawkal), also speak of an exodus of Khazars and their return with Muslim help. According to Ibn Miskawayh, as a price for this help "they all adopted Islam with the exception of their king".

Muquadassi has a different version, which does not refer to the Rus invasion; he only says that the inhabitants of the Khazar town went down to the sea and came back converted to Islam. The degree of his reliability is indicated by the fact that he describes Bulghar as being closer to the Caspian than Itil, which amounts to placing Glasgow south of London.*[Yet one modern authority, Barthold, called him "one of the greatest geographers of all time".[Quoted by Dunlop (1954), p. 245]].In spite of the confused and biased nature of these accounts, which seems all too obvious, there is probably some truth in them. The psychological shock of the invasion, the flight to the sea, and the necessity of buying Muslim help may have led to some deal which gave the Muslim community in Khazaria a greater say in the affairs of state; we remember a similar deal with Marwan two centuries earlier (I, 7), which involved the Kagan himself, but left no mark on Khazar history.

According to yet another Arab source-Biruni, who died in 1048-Itil, in his time, was in ruins-or rather, once more in ruins.18 It was rebuilt again, but henceforth it went under the name of Saksin.*["The probability is that Saksin was identical with, or at least at no great distance from Khazaran-ltil, and the name may be the older Sarisshin revived" (Dunlop, p.248, quoting Minorski).] It figures repeatedly in the chronicles well into the twelfth century as "a large town on the Volga, surpassed by none in Turkestan", and eventually, according to one source, became the victim of inundations. Another century later the Mongol ruler Batu built his capital on its site.

In summing up what the Russian Chronicle and the Arab sources tell us about the catastrophe of 965, we can say that Itil was devastated to an unknown extent by the Rus or some other invaders, but rebuilt more than once; and that the Khazar state emerged from the ordeal considerably weakened. But there can be little doubt that inside its shrunken frontiers it survived for at least another two hundred years, i.e., to the middle of the twelfth century, and perhaps-though more doubtfully-until the middle of the thirteenth.

The first non-Arab mention of Khazaria after the fatal year 965 seems to occur in a travel report by Ibrahim Ibn Jakub, the Spanish-Jewish ambassador to Otto the Great, who, writing probably in 973, describes the Khazars as still flourishing in his time.21 Next in chronological order is the account in the Russian Chronicle of Jews from Khazaria arriving in Kiev AD 986, in their misfired attempt to convert Vladimir to their faith.

As we enter the eleventh century, we read first of the already mentioned joint Byzantine-Rus campaign of 1016 against Khazaria, in which the country was once more defeated. The event is reported by a fairly reliable source, the twelfth-century Byzantine chronicler Cedrenus.22 A considerable force was apparently needed, for Cedrenus speaks of a Byzantine fleet, supported by an army of Russians. The Khazars evidently had the qualities of a Jack-in-the-Box, derived from their Turkish origin, or Mosaic faith, or both. Cedrenus also says that the name of the defeated Khazar leader was Georgius Tzul. Georgius is a Christian name; we know from an earlier report that there were Christians as well as Muslims in the Kagan's army. The next mention of the Khazars is a laconic entry in the Russian Chronicle for the year 1023, according to which "[Prince] Mtislav marched against his brother [Prince] Yaroslav with a force of Khazars and Kasogians". *[The Kasogians or Kashaks were a Caucasian tribe under Khazar rule and may or may not have been the ancestors of the Cossacks.] Now Mtislav was the ruler of the shortlived principality of Tmutorakan, centred on the Khazar town of Tamatarkha (now Taman) on the eastern side of the straights of Kerch. This, as already said, was the only Khazar territory that the Rus occupied after their victory of 965. The Khazars in Mtislav's army were thus probably levied from the local population by the Russian prince. lSeven years later (AD 1030) a Khazar army is reported to have defeated a Kurdish invading force, killed 10000 of its men and captured their equipment. This would be added evidence that the Khazars were still very much alive and kicking, if one could take the report at face value. But it comes from a single twelfthcentury Arab source, ibn-al-Athir, not considered very reliable.

Plodding on in our chronology, anxious to pick up what morsels of evidence are left, we come across a curious tale about an obscure Christian saint, Eustratius. Around AD 1100, he was apparently a prisoner in Cherson, in the Crimea, and was ill-treated by his "Jewish master", who forced ritual Passover food on him.23 One need not put much trust in the authenticity of the story (St Eustratius is said to have survived fifteen days on the cross); the point is that it takes a strong Jewish influence in the town for granted-in Cherson of all places, a town nominally under Christian rule, which the Byzantines tried to deny to the Khazars, which was conquered by Vladimir but reverted later (circa 990) to Byzantium..They were still equally powerful in Tinutorakan. For the year 1079 the Russian Chronicle has an obscure entry: "The Khazars [of Tmutorakan] took Oleg prisoner and shipped him overseas to Tsargrad [Constantinople]." That is all. Obviously the Byzantines were engaged in one of their cloakand-dagger intrigues, favouring one Russian prince against his competitors. But we again find that the Khazars must have wielded considerable power in this Russian town, if they were able to capture and dispatch a Russian prince. Four years later Oleg, having come to terms with the Byzantines, was allowed to return to Tmutorakan where "he slaughtered the Khazars who had counseled the death of his brother and had plotted against himself". Oleg's brother Roman had actually been killed by the Kipchak-Kumans in the same year as the Khazars captured Oleg. Did they also engineer his brother's murder by the Kumans? Or were they victims of the Byzantines' Macchiavellian game of playing off Khazars and Rus against each other? At any rate, we are approaching the end of the eleventh century, and they are still very much on the scene.

A few years later, *sub anno* 1106, the Russian Chronicle has another laconic entry, according to which the Polovtsi, i.e., the Kumans, raided the vicinity of Zaretsk (west of Kiev), and the Russian prince sent a force out to pursue them, under the command of the three generals Yan, Putyata and "Ivan, the Khazar". This is the last mention of the Khazars in the Old Russian Chronicle, which stops ten years later, in 1116.

But in the second half of the twelfth century, two Persian poets, Khakani (*circa* 1106-90) and the better-known Nizami (*circa* 1141-1203) mention in their epics a joint Khazar-Rus invasion of Shirwan during their lifetime. Although they indulged in the writing of poetry, they deserve to be taken seriously as they spent most of their lives as civil servants in the Caucasus, and had an intimate knowledge of Caucasian tribes. Khakani speaks of "Dervent Khazars"-Darband being the defile or "turnstile" between the Caucasus and the Black Sea, through which the Khazars used to raid Georgia in the good old days of the seventh century, before they developed a more sedate style of life. Did they revert, towards the end, to the unsettled nomad-warrior habits of their youth?

After-or possibly before-these Persian testimonies, we have the tantalizingly short and grumpy remarks of that famed Jewish traveller, Rabbi Petachia of Regensburg, quoted earlier on (II, 8). We remember that he was so huffed by the lack of Talmudic learning among the Khazar Jews of the Crimean region that when he crossed Khazaria proper, he only heard "the wailing of women and the barking of dogs". Was this merely a hyperbole to express his displeasure, or was he crossing a region devastated by a recent Kuman raid? The date is between 1170 and 1185; the twelfth century was drawing to its close, and the Kumans were now the omnipresent rulers of the steppes..As we enter the thirteenth century, the darkness thickens, and even our meagre sources dry up. But there is at least one reference which comes from an excellent witness. It is the last mention of the Khazars as a nation, and is dated between 1245-7. By that time the Mongols had already swept the Kumans out of Eurasia and established the greatest nomad empire the world had as yet seen, extending from Hungary to China.

In 1245, Pope Innocent IVsent a mission to Batu Khan, grandson of Jinghiz Khan, ruler of the western part of the Mongol Empire, to explore the possibilities of an understanding with this new world power-and also no doubt to obtain information about its military strength. Head of this mission was the sixty-year-old Franciscan friar, Joannes de Plano Carpini. He was a contemporary and disciple of St Francis of Assisi, but also an experienced traveller and Church diplomat who had held high offices in the hierarchy.

The mission set out on Easter day 1245 from Cologne, traversed Germany, crossed the Dnieper and the Don, and arrived one year later at the capital of Batu Khan and his Golden Horde in the Volga estuary: the town of Sarai Batu, alias Saksin, alias Itil.

After his return to the west, Carpini wrote his celebrated Historica Mongolorum. It contains, amidst a wealth of historical, ethnographical and military data, also a list of the people living in the regions visited by him. In this list, enumerating the people of the northern Caucasus, he mentions, along with the Alans and Circassians, the "Khazars observing theJewish religion". It is, as already said, the last known mention of them before the curtain falls. But it took a long time until their memory was effaced. Genovese and Venetian merchants kept referring to the Crimea as "Gazaria" and that name occurs in Italian documents as late as the sixteenth century. This was, however, by that time merely a geographical designation, commemorating a vanished nation.

Yet even after their political power was broken, they left marks of Khazar-Jewish influence in unexpected places, and on a variety of people.

.Among them were the Seljuk, who may be regarded as the true founders of Muslim Turkey. Towards the end of the tenth century, this other offshoot of the Ghuzz had moved southwards into the vicinity of Bokhara, from where they were later to erupt into Byzantine Asia Minor and colonize it. They do not enter directly into our story, but they do so through a backdoor, as it were, for the great Seljuk dynasty seems to have been intimately linked with the Khazars. This Khazar connection is reported by Bar Hebracus (1226-86), one of the greatest among Syriac writers and scholars; as the name indicates, he was of Jewish origin, but converted to Christianity, and ordained a bishop at the age of twenty.

Bar Hebraeus relates that Seljuk's father, Tukak, was a commander in the army of the Khazar Kagan, and that after his death, Seljuk himself, founder of the dynasty, was brought up at the Kagan's court. But he was an impetuous youth and took liberties with the Kagan, to which the Katoun-the queen-objected; as a result Seljuk had to leave, or was banned from the court.

Another contemporary source, ibn-al-Adim's *History of Aleppo*, also speaks of Seljuk's father as "one of the notables of the Khazar Turks";25 while a third, Ibn Hassul,26 reports that Seljuk "struck the King of the Khazars with his sword and beat him with a mace which he had in his hand...." We also remember the strong ambivalent attitude of the Ghuzz towards the Khazars, in Ibn Fadlan's travellogue..Thus there seems to have been an intimate relationship between the Khazars and the founders of the Seljuk dynasty, followed by a break. This was probably due to the Seljuks' conversion to Islam (while the other Ghuzz tribes, such as the Kumans, remained pagans). Nevertheless, the Khazar-Judaic influence prevailed for some time even after the break. Among the four sons of Seljuk, one was given the exclusively Jewish name of Israel; and one grandson was called Daud (David). Dunlop, usually a very cautious author, remarks:

In view of what has already been said, the suggestion is that these names are due to the religious influence among the leading families of the Ghuzz of the dominant Khazars. The "house of worship" among the Ghuzz mentioned by Qazwini might well have been a synagogue.

We may add here that-according to Artamonov-specifically Jewish names also occurred among that other Ghuzz branch, the Kumans. The sons of the Kuman Prince Kobiak were called Isaac and Daniel.

Where the historians' resources give out, legend and folklore provide useful hints. The Primary Russian Chronicle was compiled by monks; it is saturated with religious thought and long biblical excursions. But parallel with the ecclesiastical writings on which it is based, the Kiev period also produced a secular literature-the so-called bylina, heroic epics or folk-songs, mostly concerned with the deeds of great warriors and semi-legendary princes. The "Lay of Igor's Host", already mentioned, about that leader's defeat by the Kumans, is the best known among them. The bylina were transmitted by oral tradition and-according to Vernadsky "were still chanted by peasants in remote villages of northern Russia in the beginning of the twentieth century".

In striking contrast to the Russian Chronicle, these epics do not mention by name the Khazars or their country; instead they speak of the "country of the Jews" (*Zemlya Jidovskaya*), and of its inhabitants as "Jewish heroes" (*Jidovin bogatir*) who ruled the steppes and fought the armies of the Russian princes. One such hero, the epics tell us, was a giant Jew, who came "from the Zemlya Jidovskaya to the steppes of Tsetsar under Mount Sorochin, and only the bravery of Vladimir's general, Ilya Murometz, saved Vladimir's army from the Jews". There are several versions of this tale, and the search for the whereabouts of Tsetsar and Mount Sorochin provided historians with another lively game. But, as Poliak has pointed out, "the point to retain is that in the eyes of the Russian people the neighbouring Khazaria in its final period was simply 'the Jewish state', and its army was an army of Jews". This popular Russian view differs considerably from the tendency among Arab chroniclers to emphasize the importance of the Muslim mercenaries in the Khazar forces, and the number of mosques in Itil (forgetting to count the synagogues)..The legends which circulated among Western Jews in the Middle Ages provide a curious parallel to the Russian bylina..To quote Poliak again: "The popular Jewish legend does not remember a 'Khazar' kingdom but a kingdom of the 'Red Jews'." And Baron comments:

> The Jews of other lands were flattered by the existence of an independent Jewish state. Popular imagination found here a particularly fertile field. Just as the biblically minded Slavonic epics speak of "Jews" rather than Khazars, so did western Jews long after spin romantic tales around those "red Jews", so styled perhaps because of the slight Mongolian pigmentation of many Khazars.

Another bit of semi-legendary, semi-historical folklore connected with the Khazars survived into modern times, and so fascinated Benjamin Disraeli that he used it as material for a historical romance: The Wondrous Tale of Alroy.

In the twelfth century there arose in Khazaria a Messianic movement, a rudimentary attempt at a Jewish crusade, aimed at the conquest of Palestine by force of arms. The initiator of the movement was a Khazar Jew, one Solomon ben Duji (or Ruhi or Roy), aided by his son Menahem and a Palestinian scribe. "They wrote letters to all the Jews, near and far, in all the lands around them.... They said that the time had come in which God would gather Israel, His people from all lands to Jerusalem, the holy city, and that Solomon Ben Duji was Elijah, and his son the Messiah."*[The main sources for this movement are a report by the Jewish traveller Benjamin of Tudela (see above, II, 8); a hostile account by the Arab writer Yahya al-Maghribi, and two Hebrew manuscripts found in the Cairo Geniza (see above, II, 7). They add up to a confusing mosaic; I have followed Baron's careful interpretation (Vol. III, p.204; Vol. IV, pp.202-4, and notes).]

These appeals were apparently addressed to the Jewish communities in the Middle East, and seemed to have had little effect, for the next episode takes place only about twenty years later, when young Menahem assumed the name David al-Roy, and the title of Messiah. Though the movement originated in Khazaria, its centre soon shifted to Kurdistan. Here David assembled a substantial armed force-possibly of local Jews, reinforced by Khazars-and succeeded in taking possession of the strategic fortress of Amadie, north-east of Mosul. From here he may have hoped to lead his army to Edessa, and fight his way through Syria into the Holy Land.

The whole enterprise may have been a little less quixotic than it seems now, in view of the constant feuds between the various Muslim armies, and the gradual disintegration of the Crusader strongholds. Besides, some local Muslim commanders might have welcomed the prospect of a Jewish crusade against the Christian Crusaders..Among the Jews of the Middle East, David certainly aroused fervent Messianic hopes. One of his messengers came to Baghdad and-probably with excessive zeal-instructed its Jewish citizens to assemble on a certain night on their flat roofs, whence they would be flown on clouds to the Messiah's camp. A goodly number of Jews spent that night on their roofs awaiting the miraculous flight..But the rabbinical hierarchy in Baghdad, fearing reprisals by the authorities, took a hostile attitude to the pseudo-Messiah and threatened him with a ban. Not surprisingly, David al-Roy was assassinated-apparently in his sleep, allegedly by his own father-in-law, whom some interested party had bribed to do the deed..His memory was venerated, and when Benjamin of Tudela travelled through Persia twenty years after the event, "they still spoke lovingly of their leader".

But the cult did not stop there. According to one theory, the six-pointed "shield of David" which adorns the modern Israeli flag, started to become a national symbol with David al-Roy's crusade. "Ever since," writes Baron, "it has been suggested, the six-cornered 'shield of David', theretofore mainly a decorative motif or a magical emblem, began its career toward becoming the chief national-religious symbol of Judaism. Long used interchangeably with the pentagram or the 'seal of Solomon', it was attributed to David in mystic and ethical German writings from the thirteenth century on, and appeared on the Jewish flag in Prague in 1527.".Baron appends a qualifying note to this passage, pointing out that the connection between al-Roy and the six-pointed star "still awaits further elucidation and proof". However that may be, we can certainly agree with Baron's dictum which concludes his chapter on Khazaria:

During the half millenium of its existence and its aftermath in the East European communities, this noteworthy experiment in Jewish statecraft doubtless exerted a greater influence on Jewish history than we are as yet able to envisage.

THE evidence quoted in the previous pages indicates that-contrary to the traditional view held by nineteenth-century historians-the Khazars, after the defeat by the Russians in 965, lost their empire but retained their independence within narrower frontiers, and their Judaic faith, well into the thirteenth century. They even seem to have reverted to some extent to their erstwhile predatory habits. Baron comments:

In general, the reduced Khazar kingdom persevered. It waged a more or less effective defence against all foes until the middle of the thirteenth century, when it fell victim to the great Mongol invasion set in motion by Jenghiz Khan. Even then it resisted stubbornly until the surrender of all its neighbours. Its population was largely absorbed by the Golden Horde which had established the centre of its empire in Khazar territory. But before and after the Mongol upheaval the Khazars sent many offshoots into the unsubdued Slavonic lands, helping ultimately to build up the great Jewish centres of eastern Europe.

Here, then, we have the cradle of the numerically strongest and culturally dominant part of modern Jewry..The "offshoots" to which Baron refers were indeed branching out long before the destruction of the Khazar state by the Mongols-as the ancient Hebrew nation had started branching into the Diaspora long before the destruction of Jerusalem. Ethnically, the Semitic tribes on the waters of the Jordan and the Turko-Khazar tribes on the Volga were of course "miles apart", but they had at least two important formative factors in common. Each lived at a focal junction where the great trade routes connecting east and west, north and south intersect; a circumstance which predisposed them to become nations of traders, of enterprising travellers, or "rootless cosmopolitans"-as hostile propaganda has unaffectionately labelled them. But at the same time their exclusive religion fostered a tendency to keep to themselves and stick together, to establish their own communities with their own places of worship, schools, residential quarters and ghettoes (originally self-imposed) in whatever town or country they settled. This rare combination of wanderlust and ghetto-mentality, reinforced by Messianic hopes and chosen-race pride, both ancient Israelites and mediaeval Khazars shared-even though the latter traced their descent not to Shem but to Japheth.

This development is well illustrated by what one might call the Khazar Diaspora in Hungary..We remember that long before the destruction of their state, several Khazar tribes, known as the Kabars, joined the Magyars and migrated to Hungary. Moreover, in the tenth century, the Hungarian Duke Taksony invited a second wave of Khazar emigrants to settle in his domains. Two centuries later John Cinnamus, the Byzantine chronicler, mentions troops observing the Jewish law, fighting with the Hungarian army in Dalmatia, AD 1154.

There may have been small numbers of "real Jews" living in Hungary from Roman days, but there can be little doubt that the majority of this important portion of modern Jewry originated in the migratory waves of Kabar-Khazars who play such a dominant part in early Hungarian history. Not only was the country, as Constantine tells us, bilingual at its beginning, but it also had a form of double kingship, a variation of the Khazar system: the king sharing power with his general in command, who bore the title of Jula or Gyula (still a popular Hungarian first name). The system lasted to the end of the tenth century, when St Stephen embraced the Roman Catholic faith and defeated a rebellious Gyula-who, as one might expect, was a Khazar, "vain in the faith and refusing to become a Christian".

This episode put an end to the double kingship, but not to the influence of the Khazar-Jewish community in Hungary. A reflection of that influence can be found in the "Golden Bull"-the Hungarian equivalent of Magna Carta-issued AD 1222 by King Endre (Andrew) II, in which Jews were forbidden to act as mintmasters, tax collectors, and controllers of the royal salt monopoly-indicating that before the edict numerous Jews must have held these important posts. But they occupied even more exalted positions. King Endre's custodian of the Revenues of the Royal Chamber was the Chamberlain Count Teka, a Jew of Khazar origin, a rich landowner, and apparently a financial and diplomatic genius. His signature appears on various peace treaties and financial agreements, among them one guaranteeing the payment of 2000 marks by the Austrian ruler Leopold II to the King of Hungary.

One is irresistibly reminded of a similar role played by the Spanish Jew Hasdai ibn Shaprut at the court of the Caliph of Cordoba. Comparing similar episodes from the Palestinian Diaspora in the west and the Khazar Diaspora in the east of Europe, makes the analogy between them appear perhaps less tenuous..It is also worth mentioning that when King Endre was compelled by his rebellious nobles to issue, reluctantly, the Golden Bull, he kept Teka in office against the Bull's express provisions. The Royal Chamberlain held his post happily for another eleven years, until papal pressure on the King made it advisable for Teka to resign and betake himself to Austria, where he was received with open arms. However, King Endre's son Bela IV, obtained papal permission to call him back. Teka duly returned, and perished during the Mongol invasion.*[I am indebted to Mrs St G. Saunders for calling my attention to the Teka episode, which seems to have been overlooked in the literature on the Khazars.]

The Khazar origin of the numerically and socially dominant element in the Jewish population of Hungary during the Middle Ages is thus relatively well documented. It might seem that Hungary constitutes a special case, in view of the early Magyar-

Khazar connection; but in fact the Khazar influx into Hungary was merely a part of the general mass-migration from the Eurasian steppes toward the West, i.e., towards Central and Eastern Europe. The Khazars were not the only nation which sent offshoots into Hungary. Thus large numbers of the self-same Pechenegs who had chased the Magyars from the Don across the Carpathians, were forced to ask for permission to settle in Hungarian territory when they in turn were chased by the Kumans; and the Kumans shared the same fate when, a century later, they fled from the Mongols, and some 40000 of them "with their slaves" were granted asylum by the Hungarian King Bela.

At relatively quiescent times this general westward movement of the Eurasian populations was no more than a drift; at other times it became a stampede; but the consequences of the Mongol invasion must rank on this metaphoric scale as an earthquake followed by a landslide. The warriors of Chief Tejumin, called "Jinghiz Khan", Lord of the Earth, massacred the population of whole cities as a warning to others not to resist; used prisoners as living screens in front of their advancing lines; destroyed the irrigation network of the Volga delta which had provided the Khazar lands with rice and other staple foods; and transformed the fertile steppes into the "wild fields"-dikoyeh pole-as the Russians were later to call them: an unlimited space without farmers or shepherds, through which only mercenary horsemen pass in the service of this or that rival ruler-or people escaping from such rule". The Black Death of 1347-8 accelerated the progressive depopulation of the former Khazar heartland between Caucasus, Don and Volga, where the steppe-culture had reached its highest level-and the relapse into barbarism was, by contrast, more drastic than in adjoining regions. As Baron wrote: "The destruction or departure of industrious Jewish farmers, artisans and merchants left behind a void which in those regions has only recently begun to be filled."7 Not only Khazaria was destroyed, but also the Volga Bulgar country, together with the last Caucasian strongholds of the Alans and Kumans, and the southern Russian principalities, including Kiev. During the period of disintegration of the Golden Horde, from the fourteenth century onward, the anarchy became, if possible, even worse. "In most of the European steppes emigration was the only way left open for populations who wanted to secure their lives and livelihood". The migration toward safer pastures was a protracted, intermittent process which went on for several centuries. The Khazar exodus was part of the general picture.

It had been preceded, as already mentioned, by the founding of Khazar colonies and settlements in various places in the Ukraine and southern Russia. There was a flourishing Jewish community in Kiev long before and after the Rus took the town from the Khazars. Similar colonies existed in Perislavel and Chernigov. A Rabbi Mosheh of Kiev studied in France around 1160, and a Rabbi Abraham of Chernigov studied in 1181 in the Talmud School of London. The "Lay of Igor's Host" mentions a famous contemporary Russian poet called Kogan-possibly a combination of Cohen (priest) and Kagan. Some time after Sarkel, which the Russians called Biela Veza, was destroyed the Khazars built a town of the same name near Chernigov.

There is an abundance of ancient place names in the Ukraine and Poland, which derive from "Khazar" or "Zhid" (Jew): Zydowo, Kozarzewek, Kozara, Kozarzow, Zhydowska Vola, Zydaticze, and so on. They may have once been villages, or just temporary encampments of Khazar-Jewish communities on their long trek to the west. Similar place-names can also be found in the Carpathian and Tatra mountains, and in the eastern provinces of Austria. Even the ancient Jewish cemeteries of Cracow and Sandomierz, both called "Kaviory", are assumed to be of Khazar-Kabar origin.

While the main route of the Khazar exodus led to the west, some groups of people were left behind, mainly in the Crimea and the Caucasus, where they formed Jewish enclaves surviving into modern times. In the ancient Khazar stronghold of Tamatarkha (Taman), facing the Crimea across the straits of Kerch, we hear of a dynasty of Jewish princes who ruled in the fifteenth century under the tutelage of the Genovese Republic, and later of the Crimean Tartars. The last of them, Prince Zakharia, conducted negotiations with the Prince of Muscovi, who invited Zakharia to come to Russia and let himself be baptized in exchange for receiving the privileges of a Russian nobleman. Zakharia refused, but Poliak has suggested that in other cases "the introduction of Khazar-

Jewish elements into exalted positions in the Muscovite state may have been one of the factors which led to the appearance of the 'Jewish heresy' (Zhidovst-buyushtchik) among Russian priests and noblemen in the sixteenth century, and of the sect of Sabbath-observers (Subbotniki) which is still widespread among Cossacks and peasants".

Another vestige of the Khazar nation are the "Mountain Jews" in the north-eastern Caucasus, who apparently stayed behind in their original habitat when the others left. They are supposed to number around eight thousand and live in the vicinity of other tribal remnants of the olden days: Kipchaks and Oghuz. They call themselves Dagh Chufuty (Highland Jews) in the Tat language which they have adopted from another Caucasian tribe; but little else is known about them.*[The above data appear in A. H. Kniper's article Caucasus, People of in the 1973 printing of the Enc. Brit., based on recent Soviet sources. A book by George Sava, Valley of the Forgotten People (London, 1946) contains a description of a purported visit to the mountain Jews, rich in melodrama but sadly devoid of factual information.] Other Khazar enclaves have survived in the Crimea, and no doubt elsewhere too in localities which once belonged to their empire. But these are now no more than historic curios compared to the mainstream of the Khazar migration into the Polish-Lithuanian regions-and the formidable problems it poses to historians and anthropologists.

The regions in eastern Central Europe, in which the Jewish emigrants from Khazaria found a new home and apparent safety, had only begun to assume political importance toward the end of the first millennium.

Around 962, several Slavonic tribes formed an alliance under the leadership of the strongest among them, the Polans, which became the nucleus of the Polish state. Thus the Polish rise to eminence started about the same time as the Khazar decline (Sarkel was destroyed in 965). It is significant that Jews play an important role in one of the earliest Polish legends relating to the foundation of the Polish kingdom. We are told that when the allied tribes decided to elect a king to rule them all, they chose a Jew, named Abraham Prokownik. He may have been a rich and educated Khazar merchant, from whose experience the Slav backwoodsmen hoped to benefit-or just a legendary figure; but, if so, the legend indicates that Jews of his type were held in high esteem. At any rate, so the story goes on, Abraham, with unwonted modesty, resigned the crown in favour of a native peasant named Piast, who thus became the founder of the historic Piast dynasty which ruled Poland from circa 962 to 1370.

Whether Abraham Prochownik existed or not, there are plenty of indications that the Jewish immigrants from Khazaria were welcomed as a valuable asset to the country's economy and government administration. The Poles under the Piast dynasty, and their Baltic neighbours, the Lithuanians,* [The two nations became united in a series of treaties, starting in 1386, into the Kingdom of Poland. For the sake of brevity, I shall use the term "Polish Jews" to refer to both countries-regardless of the fact that at the end of the eighteenth century Poland was partitioned between Russia, Prussia and Austria, and its inhabitants became officially citizens of these three countries.

Actually the so-called Pale of Settlement within Imperial Russia, to which Jews were confined from 1792 onward, coincided with the areas annexed from Poland plus parts of the Ukraine. Only certain privileged categories of Jews were permitted to live outside the Pale; these, at the time of the 1897 census, numbered only 200000, as compared to nearly five million inside the Pale-i.e., within former Polish territory.] had rapidly expanded their frontiers, and were in dire need of immigrants to colonize their territories, and to create an urban civilization. They encouraged, first, the immigration of German peasants, burghers and craftsmen, and later of migrants from the territories occupied by the Golden Horde,*[Poland and Hungary were also briefly invaded by the Mongols in 1241-42, but they were not occupied-which made all the difference to their future history.] including Armenians, southern Slavs and Khazars.

Not all these migrations were voluntary. They included large numbers of prisoners of war, such as Crimean Tartars, who were put to cultivate the estates of Lithuanian and Polish landlords in the conquered southern provinces (at the close of the fourteenth century the Lithuanian principality stretched from the Baltic to the Black Sea). But in the fifteenth century the Ottoman Turks, conquerors of Byzantium, advanced northward, and the landlords transferred the people from their estates in the border areas further inland.

Among the populations thus forcibly transferred was a strong contingent of Karaites-the fundamentalist Jewish sect which rejected rabbinical learning. According to a tradition which has survived among Karaites into modern times, their ancestors were brought to Poland by the great Lithuanian warrior-prince Vytautas (Vitold) at the end of the fourteenth century as prisoners of war from Sulkhat in the Crimea. In favour of this tradition speaks the fact that Vitold in 1388 granted a charter of rights to the Jews of Troki, and the French traveller, de Lanoi, found there "a great number of Jews" speaking a different language from the Germans and natives. That language was-and still is-a Turkish dialect, in fact the nearest among living languages to the lingua cumanica, which was spoken in the former Khazar territories at the time of the Golden Horde. According to Zajaczkowski, this language is still used in speech and prayer in the surviving Karaite communities in Troki, Vilna, Ponyeviez, Lutzk and Halitch. The Karaites also claim that before the Great Plague of 1710 they had some thirtytwo or thirty-seven communities in Poland and Lithuania.

They call their ancient dialect "the language of Kedar"-just as Rabbi Petachia in the twelfth century called their habitat north of the Black Sea "the land of Kedar"; and what he has to say about them-sitting in the dark through the Sabbath, ignorance of rabbinical learning-fits their sectarian attitude.

Accordingly, Zajaczkowski, the eminent contemporary Turcologist, considers the Karaites from the linguistic point of view as the purest present-day representatives of the ancient Khazars.18 About the reasons why this sect preserved its language for about half a millennium, while the main body of Khazar Jews shed it in favour of the Yiddish lingua franca, more will have to be said later.

The Polish kingdom adopted from its very beginnings under the Piast dynasty a resolutely Western orientation, together with Roman Catholicism. But compared with its western neighbours it was culturally and economically an underdeveloped country. Hence the policy of attracting immigrants-Germans from the west,

Armenians and Khazar Jews from the east-and giving them every possible encouragement for their enterprise, including Royal Charters detailing their duties and special privileges.

In the Charter issued by Boleslav the Pious in 1264, and confirmed by Casimir the Great in 1334, Jews were granted the right to maintain their own synagogues, schools and courts; to hold landed property, and engage in any trade or occupation they chose. Under the rule of King Stephen Bthory (1575-86) Jews were granted a Parliament of their own which met twice a year and had the power to levy taxes on their co-religionists. After the destruction of their country, Khazar Jewry had entered on a new chapter in its history.

A striking illustration for their privileged condition is given in a papal breve, issued in the second half of the thirteenth century, probably by Pope Clement IV, and addressed to an unnamed Polish prince. In this document the Pope lets it be known that the Roman authorities are well aware of the existence of a considerable number of synagogues in several Polish cities-indeed no less than five synagogues in one city alone.*[Probably Wroclaw or Cracow.] He deplores the fact that these synagogues are reported to be taller than the churches, more stately and ornamental, and roofed with colourfully painted leaden plates, making the adjacent Catholic churches look poor in comparison. (One is reminded of Masudi's gleeful remark that the minaret of the main mosque was the tallest building in Itil.) The complaints in the breve are further authenticated by a decision of the Papal legate, Cardinal Guido, dated 1267, stipulating that Jews should not be allowed more than one synagogue to a town. We gather from these documents, which are roughly contemporaneous with the Mongol conquest of Khazaria, that already at that time there must have been considerable numbers of Khazars present in Poland if they had in several towns more than one synagogue; and that they must have been fairly prosperous to build them so "stately and ornamental". This leads us to the question of the approximate size and composition of the Khazar immigration into Poland.

Regarding the numbers involved, we have no reliable information to guide us. We remember that the Arab sources speak of Khazar armies numbering three hundred thousand men involved in the Muslim-Khazar wars; and even if allowance is made for quite wild exaggerations, this would indicate a total Khazar population of at least half a million souls. Ibn Fadlan gave the number of tents of the Volga Bulgars as 50000, which would mean a population of 300000-400000, i.e., roughly the same order of magnitude as the Khazars'. On the other hand, the number of Jews in the Polish-Lithuanian kingdorn in the seventeenth century is also estimated by modern historians at 500000 (5 per cent of the total population).

These figures do not fit in too badly with the known facts about a protracted Khazar migration via the Ukraine to Poland-Lithuania, starting with the destruction of Sarkel and the rise of the Piast dynasty toward the end of the first millennium, accelerating during the Mongol conquest, and being more or less completed in the fifteenth-sixteenth centuries-by which time the steppe had been emptied and the Khazars had apparently been wiped off the face of the earth.*[The last of the ancient Khazar villages on the Dnieper were destroyed in the Cossack revolt under Chmelnicky in the seventeenth century, and the survivors gave a further powerful boost to the number of Jews in the already existing settlement areas of Poland-Lithuania.] Altogether this population transfer was spread out over five or six centuries of trickle and flow. If we take into account the considerable influx of Jewish refugees from Byzantium and the Muslim world into Khazaria, and a small population increase among the Khazars themselves, it appears plausible that the tentative figures for the Khazar population at its peak in the eighth century should be comparable to that of the Jews in Poland in the seventeenth century, at least by order of magnitude-give or take a few hundred thousand as a token of our ignorance. There is irony hidden in these numbers.

According to the article "statistics" in the *Jewish Encyclopaedia,* in the sixteenth century the total Jewish population of the world amounted to about one million. This seems to indicate, as Poliak, Kutschera20 and others have pointed out, that during the Middle Ages the majority of those who professed the Judaic faith were Khazars. A substantial part of this majority went to Poland, Lithuania, Hungary and the Balkans, where they founded that Eastern Jewish community which in its turn became the dominant majority of world Jewry. Even if the original core of that community was diluted and augmented by immigrants from other regions (see below), its predominantly Khazar-Turkish derivation appears to be supported by strong evidence, and should at least be regarded as a theory worth serious discussion. Additional reasons for attributing the leading role in the growth and development of the Jewish community in Poland and the rest of Eastern Europe mainly to the Khazar element, and not to immigrants from the West, will be discussed in the chapters that follow. But it may be appropriate at this point to quote the Polish historian, Adam Vetulani (my italics):

Polish scholars agree that these oldest settlements were founded by Jewish emigres from the Khazar state and Russia, while the Jews from Southern and Western Europe began to arrive and settle only later... and that a certain proportion at least of the Jewish population (in earlier times, the main bulk) originated from the east, from the Khazar country, and later from Kievian Russia.

So much for size. But what do we know of the social structure and composition of the Khazar immigrant community? The first impression one gains is a striking similarity between certain privileged positions held by Khazar Jews in Hungary and in Poland in those early days. Both the Hungarian and Polish sources refer to Jews employed as mintmasters, administrators of the royal revenue, controllers of the salt monopoly, taxcollectors and "money-lenders"-i.e., bankers. This parallel suggests a common origin of those two immigrant communities; and as we can trace the origins of the bulk of Hungarian Jewry to the Magyar-Khazar nexus, the conclusion seems self-evident.

The early records reflect the part played by immigrant Jews in the two countries' budding economic life. That it was an important part is not surprising, since foreign trade and the levying of customs duties had been the Khazars' principal source of income in the past. They had the experience which their new hosts were lacking, and it was only logical that they were called in to advise and participate in the management of the finances of court and nobility. The coins minted in the twelfth and thirteenth centuries with Polish inscriptions in Hebrew lettering are somewhat bizarre relics of these activities. The exact purpose they served is still something of a mystery. Some bear the name of a king (e.g., Leszek, Mieszko), others are inscribed "From the House of Abraham ben Joseph the Prince" (possibly the minter-banker himself), or show just a word of benediction: "Luck" or "Blessing". Significantly, contemporary Hungarian sources also speak of the practice of minting coins from silver provided by Jewish owners.

However-in constrast to Western Europe-finance and commerce were far from being the only fields of Jewish activity. Some rich emigrants became landowners in Poland as Count Teka was in Hungary; Jewish land-holdings comprising a whole village of Jewish farmers are recorded, for instance, in the vicinity of Breslau before 1203; and in the early days there must have been Khazar peasants in considerable numbers, as the ancient Khazar placenames seem to indicate.

A tantalizing glimpse of how some of these villages may have come into being is provided by the Karaite records mentioned before; they relate how Prince Vitold settled a group of Karaite prisoners-of-war in "Krasna", providing them with houses, orchards and land to a distance of one and a half miles. ("Krasna" has been tentatively identified with the Jewish small town Krasnoia in Podolia.)

But farming did not hold out a future for the Jewish community. There were several reasons for this. The rise of feudalism in the fourteenth century gradually transformed the peasants of Poland into serfs, forbidden to leave their villages, deprived of freedom of movement. At the same time, under the joint pressure of the ecclesiastic hierarchy and the feudal landlords, the Polish Parliament in 1496 forbade the acquisition of agricultural land by Jews. But the process of alienation from the soil must have started long before that.

Apart from the specific causes just mentioned-religious discrimination, combined with the degradation of the free peasants into serfs-the transformation of the predominantly agricultural nation of Khazars into a predominantly urban community reflected a common phenomenon in the history of migrations. Faced with different climatic conditions and farming methods on the one hand, and on the other with unexpected opportunities for an easier living offered by urban civilization, immigrant populations are apt to change their occupational structure within a few generations. The offspring of Abruzzi peasants in the New World became waiters and restaurateurs, the grandsons of Polish farmers may become engineers or psychoanalysts.*[The opposite process of colonists settling on virgin soil applies to migrants from more highly developed to under-developed regions.]

However, the transformation of Khazar Jewry into Polish Jewry did not entail any brutal break with the past, or loss of identity. It was a gradual, organic process of change, which-as Poliak has convincingly shown-preserved some vital traditions of Khazar communal life in their new country. This was mainly achieved through the emergence of a social structure, or way of life, found nowhere else in the world Diaspora: the Jewish small town, in Hebrew ayarah, in Yiddish shtetl, in Polish miastecko. All three designations are diminutives, which, however, do not necessarily refer to smallness in size (some were quite big small-towns) but to the limited rights of municipal selfgovernment they enjoyed.

The shtetl should not be confused with the ghetto. The latter consisted of a street or quarter in which Jews were compelled to live within the confines of a Gentile town. It was, from the second half of the sixteenth century onward, the universal habitat of Jews everywhere in the Christian, and most of the Muslim, world. The ghetto was surrounded by walls, with gates that were locked at night. It gave rise to claustrophobia and mental inbreeding, but also to a sense of relative security in times of trouble. As it could not expand in size, the houses were tall and narrow-chested, and permanent overcrowding created deplorable sanitary conditions. It took great spiritual strength for people living in such circumstances to keep their self-respect. Not all of them did.

The *shtetl*, on the other hand, was a quite different proposition-a type of settlement which, as already said, existed only in Poland-Lithuania and nowhere else in the world. It was a selfcontained country town with an exclusively or predominantly Jewish population. The shtetl's origins probably date back to the thirteenth century, and may represent the missing link, as it were, between the market towns of Khazaria and the Jewish settlements in Poland. The economic and social function of these semi-rural, semiurban agglomerations seems to have been similar in both countries. In

Khazaria, as later in Poland, they provided a network of trading posts or market towns which mediated between the needs of the big towns and the countryside.

They had regular fairs at which sheep and cattle, alongside the goods manufactured in the towns and the products of the rural cottage industries were sold or bartered; at the same time they were the centres where artisans plied their crafts, from wheelwrights to blacksmiths, silversmiths, tailors, Kosher butchers, millers, bakers and candlestick-makers. There were also letter-writers for the illiterate, synagogues for the faithful, inns for travellers, and a heder-Hebrew for "room", which served as a school. There were itinerant story-tellers and folk bards (some of their names, such as Velvel Zbarzher, have been preserved)25 travelling from shtetl to shtetl in Poland-and no doubt earlier on in Khazaria, if one is to judge by the survival of story-tellers among Oriental people to our day.

Some particular trades became virtually a Jewish monopoly in Poland. One was dealing in timber-which reminds one that timber was the chief building material and an important export in Khazaria; another was transport. "The dense net of shtetls," writes Poliak, "made it possible to distribute manufactured goods over the whole country by means of the superbly built Jewish type of horse cart. The preponderance of this kind of transport, especially in the east of the country, was so marked amounting to a virtual monopoly-that the Hebrew word for carter, ba'al agalah *[Literally "master of the cart".] was incorporated into the Russian language as balagula. Only the development of the railway in the second half of the nineteenth century led to a decline in this trade."

Now this specialization in coach-building and cartering could certainly not have developed in the closed ghettoes of Western Jewry; it unmistakably points to a Khazar origin. The people of the ghettoes were sedentary; while the Khazars, like other semi-nomadic people, used horseor ox-drawn carts to transport their tents, goods and chattel-including royal tents the size of a circus, fit to accommodate several hundred people. They certainly had the know-how to negotiate the roughest tracks in their new country. Other specifically Jewish occupations were inn-keeping, the running of flour mills and trading in furs-none of them found in the ghettoes of Western Europe.

Such, in broad outlines, was the structure of the Jewish shtetl in Poland. Some of its features could be found in old market towns in any country; others show a more specific affinity with what we know-little though it is-about the townships of Khazaria, which were probably the prototypes of the Polish shtetl.

To these specific features should be added the "pagoda-style" of the oldest surviving wooden shtetl synagogues dating from the fifteenth and sixteenth centuries, which is totally different from both the native style of architecture and from the building style adopted by Western Jews and replicated later on in the ghettoes of Poland. The interior decoration of the oldest shtetl synagogues is also quite different from the style of the Western ghetto; the walls of the shtetl synagogue were covered with Moorish arabesques, and with animal figures characteristic of the Persian influence found in Magyar-Khazar artefactsI, and in the decorative style brought to Poland by Armenian immigrants.

The traditional garb of Polish Jewry is also of unmistakably Eastern origin. The typical long silk kaftan may have been an imitation of the coat worn by the Polish nobility, which itself was copied from the outfit of the Mongols in the Golden Horde-fashions travel across political divisions; but we know that kaftans were worn long before that by the nomads of the steppes. The skull-cap (yarmolka) is worn to this day by orthodox Jews-and by the Uzbeks and other Turkish people in the Soviet Union. On top of the skull-cap men wore the streimel, an elaborate round hat rimmed with fox-fur, which the Khazars copied from the Khasaks-or vice versa. As already mentioned, the trade in fox and sable furs, which had been flourishing in Khazaria, became another virtual Jewish monopoly in Poland. As for the women, they wore, until the middle of the nineteenth century, a tall white turban, which was an exact copy of the Jauluk worn by Khasak and Turkmen women. (Nowadays orthodox Jewesses have to wear instead of a turban a wig made of their own hair, which is shaved off when they get married.) One might also mention in this context-though somewhat dubiously-the Polish Jews' odd passion for gefillte (stuffed) fisch, a national dish which the Polish Gentiles adopted. "Without fish", the saying went, "there is no Sabbath." Was it derived from distant memories of life on the Caspian, where fish was the staple diet?

Life in the shtetl is celebrated with much romantic nostalgia in Jewish literature and folklore. Thus we read in a modern survey of its customs about the joyous way its inhabitants celebrated the Sabbath:

Wherever one is, he will try to reach home in time to greet the Sabbath with his own family. The pedlar travelling from village to village, the itinerant tailor, shoemaker, cobbler, the merchant off on a trip, all will plan, push, hurry, trying to reach home before sunset on Friday evening.

As they press homeward the shammes calls through the streets of the shtetl, "Jews to the bathhouse!" A functionary of the synagogue, the shammes is a combination of sexton and beadle. He speaks with an authority more than his own, for when he calls "Jews to the bathhouse" he is summoning them to a commandment.

The most vivid evocation of life in the shtetl is the surrealistic amalgam of fact and fantasy in the paintings and lithographs of Marc Chagall, where biblical symbols appear side by side with the bearded carter wielding his whip and wistful rabbis in kaftan and yarmolka. It was a weird community, reflecting its weird origins. Some of the earliest small-towns were probably founded by prisoners of war-such as the Karaites of Troki-whom Polish and Lithuanian nobles were anxious to settle on their empty lands. But the majority of these settlements were products of the general migration away from the "wild fields" which were turning into deserts. "After the Mongol conquest", wrote Poliak, "when the Slav villages wandered westward, the Khazar shtetls went with them."

The pioneers of the new settlements were probably rich Khazar traders who constantly travelled across Poland on the much frequented trade routes into Hungary. "The Magyar and Kabar migration into Hungary blazed the trail for the growing Khazar settlements in Poland: it turned Poland into a transit area between the two countries with Jewish communities." Thus the travelling merchants were familiar with conditions in the prospective areas of resettlement, and had occasion to make contact with the landowners in search of tenants. "The landlord would enter into an agreement with such rich and respected Jews" (we are reminded of Abraham Prokownik) "as would settle on his estate and bring in other settlers. They would, as a rule, choose people from the place where they had lived." These colonists would be an assorted lot of farmers, artisans and craftsmen, forming a more or less self-supporting community. Thus the Khazar shtetl would be transplanted and become a Polish shtetl. Farming would gradually drop out, but by that time the adaptation to changed conditions would have been completed.

The nucleus of modern Jewry thus followed the old recipe: strike out for new horizons but stick together.

Two basic facts emerge from our survey: the disappearance of the Khazar nation from its historic habitat, and the simultaneous appearance in adjacent regions to the north-west of the greatest concentration of Jews since the beginnings of the Diaspora. Since the two are obviously connected, historians agree that immigration from Khazaria must have contributed to the growth of Polish Jewry-a conclusion supported by the evidence cited in the previous chapters. But they feel less certain about the *extent* of this contribution-the size of the Khazar immigration compared with the influx of Western Jews, and their respective share in the genetic make-up of the modern Jewish community.

In other words, the fact that Khazars emigrated in substantial numbers into Poland is established beyond dispute; the question is whether they provided the bulk of the new settlement, or only its hard core, as it were. To find an answer to this question, we must get some idea of the size of the immigration of "real Jews" from the West.

Towards the end of the first millennium, the most important settlements of Western European Jews were in France and the Rhineland.*[Not counting the Jews of Spain, who formed a category apart and did not participate in the migratory movements with which we are concerned.] Some of these communities had probably been founded in Roman days, for, between the destruction of Jerusalem and the decline of the Roman Empire, Jews had settled in many of the greater cities under its rule, and were later on reinforced by immigrants from Italy and North Africa. Thus we have records from the ninth century onwards of Jewish communities in places all over France, from Normandy down to Provence and the Mediterranean.

One group even crossed the Channel to England in the wake of the Norman invasion, apparently invited by William the Conqueror,1 because he needed their capital and enterprise. Their history has been summed up by Baron:

They were subsequently converted into a class of "royal usurers" whose main function was to provide credits for both political and economic ventures. After accumulating great wealth through the high rate of interest, these moneylenders were forced to disgorge it in one form or another for the benefit of the royal treasury. The prolonged well-being of many Jewish families, the splendour of their residence and attire, and their influence on public affairs blinded even experienced observers to the deep dangers lurking from the growing resentment of debtors of all classes, and the exclusive dependence of Jews on the protection of their royal masters... Rumblings of discontent, culminating in violent outbreaks in 1189-90, presaged the final tragedy: the expulsion of 1290. The meteoric rise, and even more rapid decline of English Jewry in the brief span of two and a quarter centuries (1066-1290) brought into sharp relief the fundamental factors shaping the destinies of all western Jewries in the crucial first half of the second millennium.

The English example is instructive, because it is exceptionally well documented compared to the early history of the Jewish communities on the Continent. The main lesson we derive from it is that the social-economic influence of the Jews was quite out of proportion with their small numbers. There were, apparently, no more than 2500 Jews in England at any time before their expulsion in 1290.*[According to the classic survey of Joseph Jacobs, The Jews of Angevin England, based on recorded Jewish family names and other documents. [Quoted by Baron, Vol. IV, p. 77.]] This tiny Jewish community in mediaeval England played a leading part in the country's economic Establishment-much more so than its opposite number in Poland; yet in contrast to Poland it could not rely on a network of Jewish small-towns to provide it with a mass-basis of humble craftsmen, of lower-middle-class artisans and workmen, carters and innkeepers; it had no roots in the people. On this vital issue, Angevin England epitomized developments on the Western Continent. The Jews of France and Germany faced the same predicament: their occupational stratification was lopsided and top-heavy. This led everywhere to the same, tragic sequence of events.

The dreary tale always starts with a honeymoon, and ends in divorce and bloodshed. In the beginning the Jews are pampered with special charters, privileges, favours. They are personae gratae like the court alchemists, because they alone have the secret of how to keep the wheels of the economy turning. "In the 'dark ages'," wrote Cecil Roth, "the commerce of Western Europe was largely in Jewish hands, not excluding the slave trade, and in the Carolingian cartularies Jew and Merchant are used as almost interchangeable terms." But with the growth of a native mercantile class, they became gradually excluded not only from most productive occupations, but also from the traditional forms of commerce, and virtually the only field left open to them was lending capital on interest. "... The floating wealth of the country was soaked up by the Jews, who were periodically made to disgorge into the exchequer..." The archetype of Shylock was established long before Shakespeare's time.

In the honeymoon days, Charlemagne had sent a historic embassy in 797 to Harun al-Rashid in Baghdad to negotiate a treaty of friendship; the embassy was composed of the Jew Isaac and two Christian nobles. The bitter end came when, in 1306, Philip le Bel expelled the Jews from the kingdom of France. Though later some were allowed to return, they suffered further persecution, and by the end of the century the French community of Jews was virtually extinct.*[The modern community of Jews in France and England was founded by refugees from the Spanish Inquisition in the sixteenth and seventeenth centuries.]

If we turn to the history of German Jewry, the first fact to note is that "remarkably, we do not possess a comprehensive scholarly history of German Jewry... The Germanica Judaica is merely a good reference work to historic sources shedding light on individual communities up to 1238." It is a dim light, but at least it illuminates the territorial distribution of the Western-Jewish communities in Germany during the critical period when Khazar-Jewish immigration into Poland was approaching its peak. lOne of the earliest records of such a community in Germany mentions a certain Kalonymous, who, in 906, emigrated with his kinsfolk from Lucca in Italy to Mavence. About the same time we hear of Jews in Spires and Worms, and somewhat later in other places-Trves, Metz, Strasbourg, Cologne-all of them situated in a narrow strip in Alsace and along the Rhine valley. The Jewish traveller Benjamin of Tudela visited the region in the middle of the twelfth century and wrote: "In these cities there are many Israelites, wise men and rich." But how many are "many"? In fact very few, as will be seen.

Earlier on, there lived in Mayence a certain Rabbi Gershom ben Yehuda (circa 960-1030) whose great learning earned him the title "Light of the Diaspora" and the position of spiritual head of the French and Rhenish-German community. At some date around 1020 Gershom convened a Rabbinical Council in Worms, which issued various edicts, including one that put a legal stop to polygamy (which had anyway been in abeyance for a long time). To these edicts a codicil was added, which provided that in case of urgency any regulation could be revoked "by an assembly of a hundred delegates from the countries Burgundy, Normandy, France, and the towns of Mayence, Spires and Worms". In other rabbinical documents too, dating from the same period, only these three towns are named, and we can only conclude that the other Jewish communities in the Rhineland were at the beginning of the eleventh century still too insignificant to be mentioned.7 By the end of the same century, the Jewish communities of Germany narrowly escaped complete extermination in the outbursts of mob-hysteria accompanying the First Crusade, AD 1096. F. Barker has conveyed the crusader's mentality with a dramatic force rarely encountered in the columns of the Encyclopaedia Britannica:

He might butcher all, till he waded ankle-deep in blood, and then at nightfall kneel, sobbing for very joy, at the altar of the Sepulchre-for was he not red from the winepress of the Lord?

The Jews of the Rhineland were caught in that winepress, which nearly squeezed them to death. Moreover, they themselves became affected by a different type of mass hysteria: a morbid yearning for martyrdom. According to the Hebrew chronicler Solomon bar Simon, considered as generally reliable,9 the Jews of Mayence, faced with the alternative between baptism or death at the hands of the mob, gave the example to other communities by deciding on collective suicide:

Imitating on a grand scale Abraham's readiness to sacrifice Isaac, fathers slaughtered their children and husbands their wives. These acts of unspeakable horror and heroism were performed in the ritualistic form of slaughter with sacrificial knives sharpened in accordance with Jewish law. At times the leading sages of the community, supervising the mass immolation, were the last to part with life at their own hands... In the mass hysteria, sanctified by the glow of religious martyrdom and compensated by the confident expectation of heavenly rewards, nothing seemed to matter but to end life before one fell into the hands of the implacable foes and had to face the inescapable alternative of death at the enemy's hand or conversion to Christianity.

Turning from gore to sober statistics, we get a rough idea of the size of the Jewish communities in Germany. The Hebrew sources agree on 800 victims (by slaughter or suicide) in Worms, and vary between 900 and 1300 for Mayence. Of course there must have been many who preferred baptism to death, and the sources do not indicate the number of survivors; nor can we be sure that they do not exaggerate the number of martyrs. At any rate, Baron concludes from his calculations that "the total Jewish population of either community had hardly exceeded the figures here given for the dead alone".11 So the survivors in Worms or in Mayence could only have numbered a few hundred in each case. Yet these two towns (with Spires as a third) were the only ones important enough to be included in Rabbi Gershom's edict earlier on.

Thus we are made to realize that the Jewish community in the German Rhineland was numerically small, even before the First Crusade, and had shrunk to even smaller proportions after having gone through the winepress of the Lord. Yet cast of the Rhine, in central and northern Germany, there were as yet no Jewish communities at all, and none for a long time to come. The traditional conception of Jewish historians that the Crusade of 1096 swept like a broom a mass-migration of German Jews into Poland is simply a legend-or rather an ad hoc hypothesis invented because, as they knew little of Khazar history, they could see no other way to account for the emergence, out of nowhere, of this unprecedented concentration of Jews in Eastern Europe. Yet there is not a single mention in the contemporary sources of any migration, large or small, from the Rhineland further east into Germany, not to mention distant Poland..Thus Simon Dubnov, one of the historians of the older school: "The first crusade which set the Christian masses in motion towards the Asiatic east, drove at the same time the Jewish masses towards the cast of Europe." However, a few lines further down he has to admit: "About the circumstances of this emigration movement which was so important to Jewish history we possess no close information." Yet we do possess abundant information of what these battered Jewish communities did during the first and subsequent crusades. Some died by their own hands; others tried to offer resistance and were lynched; while those who survived owed their good fortune to the fact that they were given shelter for the duration of the emergency in the fortified castle of the Bishop or Burgrave who, at least theoretically, was responsible for their legal protection. Frequently this measure was not enough to prevent a massacre; but the survivors, once the crusading hordes had passed, invariably returned to their ransacked homes and synagogues to make a fresh start.

We find this pattern repeatedly in chronicles: in Treves, in Metz, and many other places. By the time of the second and later crusades, it had become almost a routine: "At the beginning of the agitation for a new crusade many Jews of Mayence, Worms, Spires, Strasbourg, Wrzburg and other cities, escaped to neighbouring castles, leaving their books and precious possessions in the custody of friendly burghers." One of the main sources is the Book of Remembrance by Ephraim bar Jacob, who himself, at the age of thirteen, had been among the refugees from Cologne in the castle of Wolkenburg. Solomon bar Simon reports that during the second crusade the survivors of the Mayence Jews found protection in Spires, then returned to their native city and built a new synagogue. This is the leitmotif of the Chronicles; to repeat it once more, there is not a word about Jewish communities emigrating toward eastern Germany, which, in the words of Mieses, was still Judenrein-clean of Jews-and was to remain so for several centuries.

The thirteenth century was a period of partial recovery. We hear for the first time of Jews in regions adjacent to the Rhineland: the Palatinate (AD 1225); Freiburg (1230), Ulm (1243), Heidelberg (1255), etc.18 But it was to be only a short respite, for the fourteenth century brought new disasters to Franco-German Jewry.

The first catastrophe was the expulsion of all Jews from the royal domains of Philip le Bel. France had been suffering from an economic crisis, to the usual accompaniments of debased currency and social unrest. Philip tried to remedy it by the habitual method of soaking the Jews. He exacted from them payments of 100000 livres in 1292, 215000 livres in 1295, 1299, 1302 and 1305, then decided on a radical remedy for his ailing finances. On June 21, 1306, he signed a secret order to arrest all Jews in his kingdom on a given day, confiscate their property and expel them from the country. The arrests were carried out on July 22, and the expulsion a few weeks later. The refugees emigrated into regions of France outside the King's domain: Provence, Burgundy, Aquitaine, and a few other frudal fiefs. But, according to Mieses, "there are no historical records whatsoever to indicate that German Jewry increased its numbers through the sufferings of the Jewish community in France in the decisive period of its destruction". And no historian has ever suggested that French Jews trekked across Germany into Poland, either on that occasion or at any other time. lUnder Philip's successors there were some partial recalls of Jews (in 1315 and 1350), but they could not undo the damage, nor prevent renewed outbursts of mob persecution. By the end of the fourteenth century, France, like England, was virtually Judenrein.

The second catastrophe of that disastrous century was the Black Death, which, between 1348 and 1350, killed off a third of Europe's population, and in some regions even twothirds. It came from east Asia via Turkestan, and the way it was let loose on Europe, and what it did there, is symbolic of the lunacy of man. A Tartar leader named Janibeg in 1347 was besieging the town of Kaffa (now Feodosia) in the Crimea, then a Genoese trading port. The plague was rampant in Janibeg's army, so he catapulted the corpses of infected victims into the town, whose population became infected in its turn. Genoese ships carried the rats and their deadly fleas westward into the Mediterranean ports, from where they spread inland. The bacilli of Pasteurella pestis were not supposed to make a distinction between the various denominations, yet Jews were nevertheless singled out for special treatment. After being accused earlier on of the ritual slaughter of Christian children, they were now accused of poisoning the wells to spread the Black Death. The legend travelled faster even than the rats, and the consequence was the burning of Jews en masse all over Europe. Once more suicide by mutual self-immolation became a common expedient, to avoid being burned alive. The decimated population of Western Europe did not reach again its pre-plague level until the sixteenth century. As for its Jews, who had been exposed to the twofold attack of rats and men. only a fraction survived. As Kutschera wrote:

The populace avenged on them the cruel blows of destiny and set upon those whom the plague had spared with fire and sword. When the epidemics receded, Germany, according to contemporary historians, was left virtually without Jews. We are led to conclude that in Germany itself the Jews could not prosper, and were never able to establish large and populous communities. How, then, in these circumstances, should they have been able to lay the foundations in Poland of a mass population so dense that at present [AD 1909] it outnumbers the Jews of Germany at the rate of ten to one? It is indeed difficult to understand how the idea ever gained ground that the eastern Jews represent immigrants from the West, and especially from Germany.

Yet, next to the first crusade, the Black Death is most frequently invoked by historians as the deus ex machina which created Eastern Jewry. And, just as in the case of the crusades, there is not a shred of evidence for this imaginary exodus. On the contrary, the indications are that the Jews' only hope of survival on this, as on that earlier occasions, was to stick together and seek shelter in some fortified place or less hostile surroundings in the vicinity. There is only one case of an emigration in the Black Death period mentioned by Mieses: Jews from Spires took refuge from persecution in Heidelberg-about ten miles away. After the virtual extermination of the old Jewish communities in France and Germany in the wake of the Black Death, Western Europe remained

Judenrein for a couple of centuries, with only a few enclaves vegetating on-except in Spain. It was an entirely different stock of Jews who founded the modern communities of England, France and Holland in the sixteenth and seventeenth centuries-the Sephardim (Spanish Jews), forced to flee from Spain where they had been resident for more than a millennium. Their history-and the history of modern European Jewry-lies outside the scope of this book.

We may safely conclude that the traditional idea of a mass-exodus of Western Jewry from the Rhineland to Poland all across Germany-a hostile, Jewless glacis-is historically untenable. It is incompatible with the small size of the Rhenish Communities, their reluctance to branch out from the Rhine valley towards the east, their stereotyped behaviour in adversity, and the absence of references to migratory movements in contemporary chronicles.

ON the evidence quoted in previous chapters, one can easily understand why Polish historians-who are, after all, closest to the sources-are in agreement that "in earlier times, the main bulk of the Jewish population originated from the Khazar country". One might even be tempted to overstate the case by claiming-as Kutschera does-that Eastern Jewry was a hundred per cent of Khazar origin. Such a claim might be tenable if the ill-fated Franco-Rhenish community were the only rival in the search for paternity. But in the later Middle Ages things become more complicated by the rise and fall of Jewish settlements all over the territories of the former Austro-Hungarian monarchy, and the Balkans. Thus not only Vienna and Prague had a considerable Jewish population, but there are no less than five places called Judendorf, "Jew-village", in the Carinthian Alps, and more Judenburgs and Judenstadts in the mountains of Styria. By the end of the fifteenth century, the Jews were expelled from both provinces, and went to Italy, Poland and Hungary; but where did they originally come from? Certainly not from the West. As Mieses put it in his survey of these scattered communities:

During the high Middle Ages we thus find in the east a chain of settlements stretching from Bavaria to Persia, the Causcasus, Asia Minor and Byzantium. [But] westward from Bavaria there is a gap through the whole length of Germany... Just how this immigration of Jews into the Alpine regions came about we do not know, but without doubt the three great reservoirs of Jews from late antiquity played their part: Italy, Byzantium and Persia.

The missing link in this enumeration is, once again, Khazaria, which, as we have seen earlier on, served as a receptacle and transit-station for Jews emigrating from Byzantium and the Caliphate. Mieses has acquired great merit in refuting the legend of the Rhenish origin of Eastern Jewry, but he, too, knew little of Khazar history, and was unaware of its demographic importance. However, he may have been right in suggesting an Italian component among the immigrants to Austria. Italy was not only quasi-saturated with Jews since Roman times, but, like Khazaria, also received its share of immigrants from Byzantium. So here we might have a trickle of "genuine" Jews of Semitic origin into Eastern Europe; yet it could not have been more than a trickle, for there is no trace in the records of any substantial immigration of Italian Jews into Austria, whereas there is plenty of evidence of a reverse migration of Jews into Italy after their expulsion from the Alpine provinces at the end of the fifteenth century. Details like this tend to blur the picture, and make one wish that the Jews had gone to Poland on board the Mayflower, with all the records neatly kept.

Yet the broad outlines of the migratory process are nevertheless discernible. The Alpine settlements were in all likelihood westerly offshoots of the general Khazar migration toward Poland, which was spread over several centuries and followed several different routes-through the Ukraine, the Slavonic regions north of Hungary, perhaps also through the Balkans. A Rumanian legend tells of an invasion-the date unknown-of armed Jews into that country.

There is another, very curious legend relating to the history of Austrian Jewry. It was launched by Christian chroniclers in the Middle Ages, but was repeated in all seriousness by historians as late as the beginning of the eighteenth century. In pre-Christian days, so the legend goes, the Austrian provinces were ruled by a succession of Jewish princes. The Austrian Chronicle, compiled by a Viennese scribe in the reign of Albert III(1350-95) contains a list of no less than twenty-two such Jewish princes, who are said to have succeeded each other. The list gives not only their alleged names, some of which have a distinctly Ural-Altaian ring, but also the length of their rule and the place where they are buried; thus: "Sennan, ruled 45 years, buried at the Stubentor in Vienna; Zippan, 43 years, buried in Tulln"; and so on, including names like Lapton, Ma'alon, Raptan, Rabon, Effra, Sameck, etc. After these Jews came five pagan princes, followed by Christian rulers. The legend is repeated, with some variations, in the Latin histories of Austria by Henricus Gundelfingus, 1474, and by several others, the last one being Anselmus Schram's Flores Chronicorum Austriae, 1702 (who still seems to have believed in its authenticity).

How could this fantastic tale have originated? Let us listen to Mieses again: "The very fact that such a legend could develop and stubbornly maintain itself through several centuries, indicates that deep in the national consciousness of ancient Austria dim memories persisted of a Jewish presence in the lands on the upper Danube in bygone days. Who knows whether the tidal waves emanating from the Khazar dominions in Eastern Europe once swept into the foothills of the Alps-which would explain the Turanian flavour of the names of those princes. The confabulations of mediaeval chroniclers could evoke a popular echo only if they were supported by collective recollections, however vague."

As already mentioned, Mieses is rather inclined to underestimate the Khazar contribution to Jewish history, but even so he hit on the only plausible hypothesis which could explain the origin of the persistent legend. One may even venture to be a little more specific. For more than half a century-up to AD 955-Austria, as far west as the river Enns, was under Hungarian domination. The Magyars had arrived in their new country in 896, together with the Kabar-Khazar tribes who were influential in the nation. The Hungarians at the time were not yet converted to Christianity (that happened only a century later, AD 1000) and the only monotheistic religion familiar to them was Khazar Judaism. There may have been one or more tribal chieftains among them who practised a Judaism of sorts-we remember the Byzantine chronicler, John Cinnamus, mentioning Jewish troops fighting in the Hungarian army.*[See above, V, 2.] Thus there may have been some substance to the legend-particularly if we remember that the Hungarians were still in their savage raiding period, the scourge of Europe. To be under their dominion was certainly a traumatic experience which the Austrians were unlikely to forget. It all fits rather nicely.

Further evidence against the supposedly Franco-Rhenish origin of Eastern Jewry is provided by the structure of Yiddish, the popular language of the Jewish masses, spoken by millions before the holocaust, and still surviving among traditionalist minorities in the Soviet Union and the United States.

Yiddish is a curious amalgam of Hebrew, mediaeval German, Slavonic and other elements, written in Hebrew characters. Now that it is dying out, it has become a subject of much academic research in the United States and Israel, but until well into the twentieth century it was considered by Western linguists as merely an odd jargon, hardly worth serious study. As H. Smith remarked:

"Little attention has been paid to Yiddish by scholars. Apart from a few articles in periodicals, the first really scientific study of the language was Mieses's Historical Grammar published in 1924. It is significant that the latest edition of the standard historical grammar of German, which treats German from the point of view of its dialects, dismisses Yiddish in twelve lines."

At first glance the prevalence of German loanwords in Yiddish seems to contradict our main thesis on the origins of Eastern Jewry; we shall see presently that the opposite is true, but the argument involves several steps. The first is to inquire what particular kind of regional German dialect went into the Yiddish vocabulary. Nobody before Mieses seems to have paid serious attention to this question; it is to his lasting merit to have done so, and to have come up with a conclusive answer. Based on the study of the vocabulary, phonetics and syntax of Yiddish as compared with the main German dialects in the Middle Ages, he concludes:

No linguistic components derived from the parts of Germany bordering on France are found in the Yiddish language. Not a single word from the entire list of specifically Moselle-Franconian origin compiled by J. A. Ballas (Beitrge zur Kunntnis der Trierischen Volkssprache, 1903, 28ff.) has found its way into the Yiddish vocabulary. Even the more central regions of Western Germany, around Frankfurt, have not contributed to the Yiddish language....

Insofar as the origins of Yiddish are concerned, Western Germany can be written off.... Could it be that the generally accepted view, according to which the German Jews once upon a time immigrated from France across the Rhine, is misconceived? The history of the German Jews, of Ashkenazi*[For "Ashkenazi" see below, VIII, I] Jewry, must be revised. The errors of history are often rectified by linguistic research. The conventional view of the erstwhile immigration of Ashkenazi Jews from France belongs to the category of historic errors which are awaiting correction.

He then quotes, among other examples of historic fallacies, the case of the Gypsies, who were regarded as an offshoot from Egypt, "until linguistics showed that they come from India".

Having disposed of the alleged Western origin of the Germanic element in Yiddish, Mieses went on to show that the dominant influence in it are the so-called "East-Middle German" dialects which were spoken in the Alpine regions of Austria and Bavaria roughly up to the fifteenth century. In other words, the German component which went into the hybrid Jewish language originated in the eastern regions of Germany, adjacent to the Slavonic belt of Eastern Europe.

Thus the evidence from linguistics supports the historical record in refuting the misconception of the Franco-Rhenish origins of Eastern Jewry. But this negative evidence does not answer the question how an East-Middle German dialect combined with Hebrew and Slavonic elements became the common language of that Eastern Jewry, the majority of which we assume to have been of Khazar origin.

In attempting to answer this question, several factors have to be taken into consideration. First, the evolution of Yiddish was a long and complex process, which presumably started in the fifteenth century or even earlier; yet it remained for a long time a spoken language, a kind of lingua franca, and appears in print only in the nineteenth century. Before that, it had no established grammar, and "it was left to the individual to introduce foreign words as he desires. There is no established form of pronunciation or spelling... The chaos in spelling may be illustrated by the rules laid down by the Jüdische Volks-Bibliothek:

(1) Write as you speak;

(2) write so that both Polish and Lithuanian Jews may understand you, and;

(3) spell differently words of the same sound which have a different signification."

Thus Yiddish grew, through the centuries, by a kind of untrammelled proliferation, avidly absorbing from its social environments such words, phrases, idiomatic expressions as best served its purpose as a lingua franca. But the culturally and socially dominant element in the environment of mediaeval Poland were the Germans. They alone, among the immigrant populations, were economically and intellectually more influential than the Jews. We have seen that from the early days of the Piast dynasty, and particularly under Casimir the Great, everything was done to attract immigrants to colonize the land and build "modern" cities. Casimir was said to have "found a country of wood and left a country of stone". But these new cities of stone, such as Krakau (Cracow) or Lemberg (Lwow) were built and ruled by German immigrants, living under the so-called Magdeburg law, i.e., enjoying a high degree of municipal selfgovernment. Altogether not less than four million Germans are said to have immigrated into Poland, providing it with an urban middleclass that it had not possessed before. As Poliak has put it, comparing the German to the Khazar immigration into Poland: "the rulers of the country imported these masses of much-needed enterprising foreigners, and facilitated their settling down according to the way of life they had been used to in their countries of origin: the German town and the Jewish shtetl". (However, this tidy separation became blurred when later Jewish arrivals from the West also settled in the towns and formed urban ghettoes.).Not only the educated bourgeoisie, but the clergy too, was predominantly German-a natural consequence of Poland opting for Roman Catholicism and turning toward Western civilization, just as the Russian clergy after Vladimir's conversion to Greek orthodoxy was predominantly Byzantine. Secular culture followed along the same lines, in the footsteps of the older Western neighbour. The first Polish university was founded in 1364 in Cracow, then a predominantly German city.*[One of its students in the next century was Nicolaus Copernicus or Mikolaj Koppernigk whom both Polish and German patriots later claimed as their national.] As Kutschera, the Austrian, has put it, rather smugly:

The German colonists were at first regarded by the people with suspicion and distrust; yet they succeeded in gaining an increasingly firm foothold, and even in introducing the German educational system. The Poles learnt to appreciate the advantages of the higher culture introduced by the Germans and to imitate their foreign ways. The Polish aristocracy, too, grew fond of German customs and found beauty and pleasure in whatever came from Germany.

Not exactly modest, but essentially true. One remembers the high esteem for German Kultur among nineteenth-century Russian intellectuals.

It is easy to see why Khazar immigrants pouring into mediaeval Poland had to learn German if they wanted to get on. Those who had close dealings with the native populace no doubt also had to learn some pidgin Polish (or Lithuanian, or Ukrainian or Slovene); German, however, was a prime necessity in any contact with the towns. But there was also the synagogue and the study of the Hebrew thorah. One can visualize a shtetl craftsman, a cobbler perhaps, or a timber merchant, speaking broken German to his clients, broken Polish to the serfs on the estate next door; and at home mixing the most expressive bits of both with Hebrew into a kind of intimate private language. How this hotchpotch became communalized and standardized to the extent to which it did, is any linguist's guess; but at least one can discern some further factors which facilitated the process.

Among the later immigrants to Poland there were also, as we have seen, a certain number of "real" Jews from the Alpine countries, Bohemia and eastern Germany. Even if their number was relatively small, these German-speaking Jews were superior in culture and learning to the Khazars, just as the German Gentiles were culturally superior to the Poles. And just as the Catholic clergy was German, so the Jewish rabbis from the West were a powerful factor in the Germanization of the Khazars, whose Judaism was fervent but primitive. To quote Poliak again:

Those German Jews who reached the kingdom of Poland-Lithuania had an enormous influence on their brethren from the east. The reason why the [Khazar] Jews were so strongly attracted to them was that they admired their religious learning and their efficiency in doing business with the predominantly German cities.... The language spoken at the Heder, the school for religious teaching, and at the house of the Ghevir [notable, rich man] would influence the language of the whole community.14

A rabbinical tract from seventeenth-century Poland contains the pious wish:

"May God will that the country be filled with wisdom and that all Jews speak German."

Characteristically, the only sector among the Khazarian Jews in Poland which resisted both the spiritual and worldly temptations offered by the German language were the Karaites, who rejected both rabbinical learning and material enrichment. Thus they never took to Yiddish. According to the first all-Russian census in 1897, there were 12894 Karaite Jews living in the Tsarist Empire (which, of course, included Poland). Of these 9666 gave Turkish as their mother tongue (i.e., presumably their original Khazar dialect), 2632 spoke Russian, and only 383 spoke Yiddish.

The Karaite sect, however, represents the exception rather than the rule. In general, immigrant populations settling in a new country tend to shed their original language within two or three generations and adopt the language of their new country.*[This does not, of course, apply to conquerors and colonizers, who impose their own language on the natives.] The American grandchildren of immigrants from Eastern Europe never learn to speak Polish or Ukrainian, and find the jabber-wocky of their grandparents rather comic. It is difficult to see how historians could ignore the evidence for the Khazar migration into Poland on the grounds that more than half a millennium later they speak a different language.

Incidentally, the descendants of the biblical Tribes are the classic example of linguistic adaptability. First they spoke Hebrew; in the Babylonian exile, Chaldean; at the time of Jesus, Aramaic; in Alexandria, Greek; in Spain, Arabic, but later Ladino-a Spanish-Hebrew mixture, written in Hebrew characters, the Sephardi equivalent of Yiddish; and so it goes on. They preserved their religious identity, but changed languages at their convenience.

The Khazars were not descended from the Tribes, but, as we have seen, they shared a certain cosmopolitanism and other social characteristics with their co-religionists.

Poliak has proposed an additional hypothesis concerning the early origins of Yiddish, which deserves to be mentioned, though it is rather problematical. He thinks that the "shape of early Yiddish emerged in the Gothic regions of the Khazar Crimea. In those regions the conditions of life were bound to bring about a combination of Germanic and Hebrew elements hundreds of years before the foundation of the settlements in the Kingdoms of Poland and Lithuania."

Poliak quotes as indirect evidence a certain Joseph Barbaro of Venice, who lived in Tana (an Italian merchant colony on the Don estuary) from 1436 to 1452, and who wrote that his German servant could converse with a Goth from the Crimea just as a Florentine could understand the language of an Italian from Genoa. As a matter of fact, the Gothic language survived in the Crimea (and apparently nowhere else) at least to the middle of the sixteenth century. At that time the Habsburg ambassador in Constantinople, Ghiselin de Busbeck, met people from the Crimea, and made a list of words from the Gothic that they spoke. (This Busbeck must have been a remarkable man, for it was he who first introduced the lilac and tulip from the Levant to Europe.) Poliak considers this vocabulary to be close to the Middle High German elements found in Yiddish. He thinks the Crimean Goths kept contact with other Germanic tribes and that their language was influenced by them. Whatever one may think of it, it is a hypothesis worth the linguist's attention.

"In a sense," wrote Cecil Roth, "the Jewish dark ages may be said to begin with the Renaissance.".Earlier on, there had been massacres and other forms of persecution during the crusades, the Black Death, and under other pretexts; but these had been lawless outbreaks of massviolence, actively opposed or passively tolerated by the authorities. From the beginnings of the Counter-Reformation, however, the Jews were legally degraded to not-quitehuman status, in many respects comparable to the Untouchables in the Hindu caste system. "The few communities suffered to remain in Western Europe-i.e., in Italy, Germany, and the papal possessions in southern

France-were subjected at last to all the restrictions which earlier ages had usually allowed to remain an ideal"18-i.e., which had existed on ecclesiastical and other decrees, but had remained on paper (as, for instance, in Hungary, see above, V, 2). Now, however, these "ideal" ordinances were ruthlessly enforced: residential segregation, sexual apartheid, exclusion from all respected positions and occupations; wearing of distinctive clothes: yellow badge and conical headgear. In 1555 Pope Paul IV in his bull cum nimis absurdum insisted on the strict and consistent enforcement of earlier edicts, confining Jews to closed ghettoes. A year later the Jews of Rome were forcibly transferred. All Catholic countries, where Jews still enjoyed relative freedom of movement, had to follow the example.

In Poland, the honeymoon period inaugurated by Casimir the Great had lasted longer than elsewhere, but by the end of the sixteenth century it had run its course. The Jewish communities, now confined to shtetl and ghetto, became overcrowded, and the refugees from the Cossack massacres in the Ukrainian villages under Chmelnicky led to a rapid deterioration of the housing situation and economic conditions. The result was a new wave of massive emigration into Hungary, Bohemia, 'Rumania and Germany, where the Jews who had all but vanished with the Black Death were still thinly spread..Thus the great trek to the West was resumed. It was to continue through nearly three centuries until the Second World War, and became the principal source of the existing Jewish communities in Europe, the United States and Israel. When its rate of flow slackened, the pogroms of the nineteenth century provided a new impetus. "The second Western movement," writes Roth (dating the first from the destruction of Jerusalem), "which continued into the twentieth century, may be said to begin with the deadly Chmelnicky massacres of 1648-49 in Poland."

The evidence quoted in previous chapters adds up to a strong case in favour of those modern historians-whether Austrian, Israeli or Polish who, independently from each other, have argued that the bulk of modern Jewry is not of Palestinian, but of Caucasian origin. The mainstream of Jewish migrations did not flow from the Mediterranean across France and Germany to the east and then back again. The stream moved in a consistently westerly direction, from the Caucasus through the Ukraine into Poland and thence into Central Europe.

When that unprecedented mass-settlement in Poland came into beng, there were simply not enough Jews around in the west to account for it; while in the east a whole nation was on the move to new frontiers..It would of course be foolish to deny that Jews of different origin also contributed to the existing Jewish world-community. The numerical ratio of the Khazar to the Semitic and other contributions is impossible to establish. But the cumulative evidence makes one inclined to agree with the concensus of Polish historians that "in earlier times the main bulk originated from the Khazar country"; and that, accordingly, the Khazar contribution to the genetic make-up of the Jews must be substantial, and in all likelihood dominant.

THE Jews of our times fall into two main divisions: Sephardim and Ashkenazim. The Sephardim are descendants of the Jews who since antiquity had lived in Spain (in Hebrew Sepharad) until they were expelled at the end of the fifteenth century and settled in the countries bordering on the Mediterranean, the Balkans, and to a lesser extent in Western Europe. They spoke a Spanish-Hebrew dialect, Ladino (see VII, 3), and preserved their own traditions and religious rites. In the 1960s, the number of Sephardim was estimated at 500000.

The Ashkenazim, at the same period, numbered about eleven million. Thus, in common parlance, Jew is practically synonymous with Ashkenazi Jew. But the term is misleading, for the Hebrew word Ashkenaz was, in mediaeval rabbinical literature, applied to Germany-thus contributing to the legend that modern Jewry originated on the Rhine. There is, however, no other term to refer to the non-Sephardic majority of contemporary Jewry. For the sake of piquantry it should be mentioned that the Ashkenaz of the Bible refers to a people living somewhere in the vicinity of Mount Ararat and Armenia. The name occurs in Genesis 10, 3 and I Chronciles 1, 6, as one of the sons of Gomer, who was a son of Japheth. Ashkenaz is also a brother of Togarmah (and a nephew of Magog) whom the Khazars, according to King Joseph, claimed as their ancestor. But worse was to come. For Ashkenaz is also named in Jeremiah 51, 27, where the prophet calls his people and their allies to rise and destroy Babylon:

"Call thee upon the kingdoms of Ararat, Minni and Ashkenaz."

This passage was interpreted by the famous Saadiah Gaon, spiritual leader of Oriental Jewry in the tenth century, as a prophecy relating to his own times: Babylon symbolized the Caliphate of Baghdad, and the Ashkenaz who were to attack it were either the Khazars themselves or some allied tribe. Accordingly, says Poliak,1 some learned Khazar Jews, who heard of the Gaon's ingenious arguments, called themselves Ashkenazim when they emigrated to Poland. It does not prove anything, but it adds to the confusion.

Summing up a very old and bitter controversy in a laconic paragraph, Raphael Patai wrote: The findings of physical anthropology show that, contrary to popular view, there is no Jewish race. Anthropometric measurements of Jewish groups in many parts of the world indicate that they differ greatly from one another with respect to all the important physical characteristics-stature, weight, skin colour, cephalic index, facial index, blood groups, etc.

This indeed is the accepted view today among anthropologists and historians. Moreover, there is general agreement that comparisons of cranial indices, blood types, etc., show a greater similarity between Jews and their Gentile host-nation than between Jews living in different countries.

Yet, paradoxically, the popular belief that Jews, or at least certain types of Jews, can be instantly recognized as such, must not be dismissed out of hand-for the simple reason that it has a factual basis in every-day existence. The anthropologists' evidence seems to be at loggerheads with common observation.

However, before attempting to tackle the apparent contradiction, it will be useful to look at a few samples of the data on which the anthropologists' denial of a Jewish race is based. To start with, here is a quotation from the excellent series of booklets on The Race Question in Modern Science published by UNESCO. The author, Professor Juan Comas, draws the following conclusion from the statistical material (his italics):

Thus despite the view usually held, the Jewish people is racially heterogeneous; its constant migrations and its relations-voluntary or otherwise-with the widest variety of nations and peoples have brought about such a degree of crossbreeding that the so-called people of Israel can produce examples of traits typical of every people. For proof it will suffice to compare the rubicund, sturdy, heavily-built Rotterdam Jew with his co-religionist, say, in Salonika with gleaming eyes in a sickly face and skinny, high-strung physique. Hence, so far as our knowledge goes, we can assert that Jews as a whole display as great a degree of morphological disparity among themselves as could be found between members of two or more different races.

Next, we must glance at some of the physical characteristics which anthropologists use as criteria, and on which Comas's conclusions are based.

One of the simplest-and as it turned out, most naive-of these criteria was bodily stature. In The Races of Europe, a monumental work published in 1900, William Ripley wrote: "The European Jews are all undersized; not only this, they are more often absolutely stunted."

He was up to a point right at the time, and he produced ample statistics to prove it. But he was shrewd enough to surmise that this deficiency in height might somehow be influenced by environmental factors. Eleven years later, Maurice Fishberg published The Jews-A Study of Race and Environment, the first anthropological survey of its kind in English. It revealed the surprising fact that the children of East European Jewish immigrants to the USA grew to an average height of 167.9 cm. compared to the 164.2 cm. averaged by their parents-a gain of nearly an inch and a half in a single generation. Since then it has become a commonplace that the descendants of immigrant populations-whether Jews, Italians or Japanese-are considerably taller than their parents, no doubt owing to their improved diet and other environmental factors.

Fishberg then collected statistics comparing the average height of Jews and Gentiles in Poland, Austria, Rumania, Hungary, and so on. The result again was a surprise. In general it was found that the stature of the Jews varied with the stature of the non Jewish population among which they lived. They were relatively tall where the indigenous population is tall, and vice versa. Moreover, within the same nation, and even within the same town (Warsaw) the bodily height of Jews and Gentiles was found to vary according to the degree of prosperity of the district.7 All this does not mean that heredity has no influence on height; but it is overlayed and modified by environmental influences, and is unfit as a criterion of race.

We may now turn to cranial measurements-which were once the great fashion among anthropologists, but are now considered rather outdated. Here we meet again with the same type of conclusion derived from the data:

"A comparison of the cephalic indices of Jewish and non-Jewish populations in various countries reveals a marked similarity between the Jewish and non-Jewish indices in many countries, while showing very wide variations when the cephalic indices of Jewish populations inhabiting different countries are compared. Thus one is driven to the conclusion that this feature, its plasticity not withstanding, points to a racial diversity of the Jews."

This diversity, it should be noted, is most pronounced between Sephardi and Ashkenazi Jews. By and large, the Sephardim are dolichocephalic (long-headed), the Ashkenazim brachycephalic (broad-headed). Kutschera saw in this difference a further proof of the separate racial origin of Khazar-Ashkenazi and Semitic-Sephardi Jews. But we have just seen that the indices of short-or long-headedness are co-variant with the host-nations'-which to some extent invalidates the argument.

The statistics relating to other physical features also speak against racial unity. Generally, Jews are dark-haired and darkeyed. But how general is "generally", when, according to Comas, 49 per cent of Polish Jews were light-haired,9 and 54 per cent of Jewish schoolchildren in Austria had blue eyes ?10 It is true that Virchov11 found "only" 32 per cent of blond Jewish schoolchildren in Germany, whereas the proportion of blond Gentiles was larger; but that merely shows that the co-variance is not absolute-as one would expect. The hardest evidence to date comes from classification by blood groups. A great amount of work has recently been done in this field, but it will be sufficient to quote a single example with a particularly sensitive indicator. In Patai's words: With regard to blood type, Jewish groups show considerable differences among themselves and marked similarities to the Gentile environment. The Hirszfeld "biochemical index"

(A+AB)

(B+AB)

can be used most conveniently to express this. A few typical examples are:

German Jews 2.74, German Gentiles 2.63; Rumanian Jews 1.54, Rumanian Gentiles 1.55; Polish Jews 1.94, Polish Gentiles 1.55; Moroccan Jews 1.63, 79

Moroccan Gentiles 1.63; Iraqi Jews 1.22, Iraqi Gentiles 1.37; Turkistan Jews 0.97, Turkistan Gentiles 0.99.12

One might sum up this situation in two mathematical formulae:

Ga-Ja<Ja-Jb

and:

Ga-Gb ~=

Ja-Jb

That is to say that, broadly speaking, the difference in respect of anthropological criteria between Gentiles (Ga) and Jews (Ja) in a given country (a) is smaller than the difference between Jews in different countries (a and b); and the difference between Gentiles in countries a and b is similar to the difference between Jews in a and b.

It seems appropriate to wind up this section with another quotation from Harry Shapiro's contribution to the UNESCO series-The Jewish People: A Biological History:

The wide range of variation between Jewish populations in their physical characteristics and the diversity of the gene frequencies of their blood groups render any unified racial classification for them a contradiction in terms. For although modern racial theory admits some degree of polymorphism or variation within a racial group, it does not permit distinctly different groups, measured by its own criteria of race, to be identified as one. To do so would make the biological purposes of racial classification futile and the whole procedure arbitrary and meaningless. Unfortunately, this subject is rarely wholly divorced from non-biological considerations, and despite the evidence efforts continue to be made to somehow segregate the Jews as a distinct racial entity.

How did this twin-phenomenon-diversity in somatic features and conformity to the hostnation-come about? The geneticists' obvious answer is: through miscegenation combined with selective pressures.

"This", writes Fishberg, "is indeed the crucial point in the anthropology of the Jews: are they of pure race, modified more or less by environmental influences, or are they a religious sect composed of racial elements acquired by proselytism and intermarriage during their migration in various parts of the world?" And he leaves his readers in no doubt about the answer:

Beginning with Biblical evidence and traditions, it appears that even in the beginning of the formation of the tribe of Israel they were already composed of various racial elements.... We find in Asia Minor, Syria and Palestine at that time many races-the Amorites, who were blondes, dolichocephalic, and tall; the Hittites, a dark-complexioned race, probably of Mongoloid type; the Cushites, a negroid race; and many others. With all these the ancient Hebrews intermarried, as can be seen in many passages in the Bible.

The prophets may thunder against "marrying daughters of a strange god", yet the promiscuous Israelites were not deterred, and their leaders were foremost in giving a bad example. Even the first patriarch, Abraham, cohabited with Hagar, an Egyptian; Joseph married Asenath, who was not only Egyptian but the daughter of a priest; Moses married a Midianite, Zipporah; Samson, the Jewish hero, was a Philistine; King David's mother was a Moabite, and he married a princess of Geshur; as for King Solomon (whose mother was a Hittite), "He loved many strange women, including the daughter of Pharaoh, women of the Moabites, Animonites, Edomites, Zidonians, and Hittites... " And so the chronique scandaleuse goes on. The Bible also makes it clear that the royal example was imitated by many, high and low. Besides, the biblical prohibition of marrying Gentiles exempted female captives in times of war-and there was no shortage of them. The Babylonian exile did not improve racial purity; even members of priestly families married Gentile women. In short, at the beginning of the Diaspora, the Israelites were already a thoroughly hybridized race. So, of course, were most historic nations, and the point would not need stressing if it were not for the persistent myth of the Biblical Tribe having preserved its racial purity throughout the ages.

Another important source of interbreeding were the vast numbers of people of the most varied races converted to Judaism. Witness to the proselytizing zeal of the Jews of earlier times are the black-skinned Falasha of Abyssinia, the Chinese Jews of Kai-Feng who look like Chinese, the Yemenite Jews with their dark olive complexion, the Jewish Berber tribes of the Sahara who look like Tuaregs, and so on, down to our prime example, the Khazars. Nearer home, Jewish proselytizing reached its peak in the Roman Empire between the fall of the Jewish state and the rise of Christianity. Many patrician families in Italy were converted, but also the royal family which ruled the province of Adiabene. Philo speaks of numerous converts in Greece; Flavius Josephus relates that a large proportion of the population of Antioch was Judaized; St Paul met with proselytes on his travels more or less everywhere from Athens to Asia Minor. "The fervour of proselytism", the Jewish historian Th. Reinach wrote:

Was indeed one of the most distinctive traits of Judaism during the Greco-Roman epoch-a trait which it never possessed in the same degree either before or since... It cannot be doubted that Judaism in this way made numerous converts during two or three centuries... The enormous growth of the Jewish nation in Egypt, Cyprus, and Cyrene cannot be accounted for without supposing an abundant infusion of Gentile blood. Proselytism swayed alike the upper and the lower classes of society.

The rise of Christianity slowed down the rate of miscegenation, and the ghetto put a temporary end to it; but before the ghetto-rules were strictly enforced in the sixteenth century, the process still went on. This is shown by the ever-repeated ecclesiastic interdictions of mixed marriages-e.g., by the Council of Toledo, 589; the Council of Rome, 743; the first and second Lateran Councils 1123 and 1139; or the edict of King Ladislav II of Hungary in 1092.

That all these prohibitions were only partly effective is shown, for instance, by the report of the Hungarian Archbishop Robert von Grain to the Pope AD 1229, complaining that many Christian women are married to Jews, and that within a few years "many thousands of Christians" were lost in this way to the Church.

The only effective bar were the ghetto walls. When these crumbled, intermarriages started again. Their rate accelerated to such an extent that in Germany, between 1921 and 1925, out of every 100 marriages involving Jews, 42 were mixed.

As for the Sephardi, or "true" Jews, their sojourn in Spain for more than a millennium left its indelible mark both on themselves and on their hosts. As Arnold Toynbee wrote:

There is every reason to believe that in Spain and Portugal today there is a strong tincture of the blood of these Jewish converts in Iberian veins, especially in the upper and middle classes. Yet the most acut psychoanalyst would find it difficult, if samples of living upper-and middle-class Spanish and Portuguese were presented to him, to detect who had Jewish ancestors.

The process worked both ways. After the massacres of 1391 and 1411 which swept the Peninsula, over 100000 Jews at a moderate estimate-accepted baptism. But a considerable proportion of them continued to practice Judaism in secret. These crypto-Jews, the Marranos, prospered, rose to high positions at court and in the ecclesiastical hierarchy, and intermarried with the aristocracy. After the expulsion of all unrepentant Jews from Spain (1492) and Portugal (1497) the Marranos were regarded with increasing suspicion; many were burned by the Inquisition, the majority emigrated in the sixteenth century to the countries around the Mediterranean, to Holland, England and France. Once in safety, they openly reverted to their faith and, together with the 1492-7 expellees, founded the new Sephardic communities in these countries.

Thus Toynbee's remark about the hybrid ancestry of the upper strata of society in Spain also applies, mutatis mutandis, to the Sephardic communities of Western Europe. Spinoza's parents were Portuguese Marranos, who emigrated to Amsterdam. The old Jewish families of England (who arrived here long before the nineteenth-twentieth century influx from the east), the Montefiores,

Lousadas, Montagues, Avigdors, Sutros, Sassoons, etc., all came out of the Iberian mixing bowl, and can claim no purer racial origin than the Ashkenazis-or the Jews named Davis, Harris, Phillips or Hart.

One distressingly recurrent type of event was miscegenation by rape. That too has a long history starting in Palestine. We are told, for example, that a certain Juda ben Ezekial opposed his son marrying a woman who was not of "the seed of Abraham", whereupon his friend Ulla remarked: "How do we know for certain that we ourselves are not descended from the heathens who violated the maidens of Zion at the siege of Jerusalem?"20 Rape and loot (the amount of the latter often fixed in advance) was considered a natural right of a conquering army.

There is an ancient tradition, recorded by Graetz, which attributes the origin of the earliest Jewish settlements in Germany to an episode reminiscent of the rape of the Sabine women. According to this tradition, a German unit, the Vangioni who fought with the Roman legions in Palestine, "had chosen from the vast horde of Jewish prisoners the most beautiful women, had brought them back to their stations on the shores of the Rhine and the Main, and had compelled them to minister to the satisfaction of their desires. The children thus begotten of Jewish and German parents were brought up by their mothers in the Jewish faith, their fathers not troubling themselves about them. It is these children who are said to have been the founders of the first Jewish communities between Worms and Mayence."

In Eastern Europe rape was even more common. To quote Fishberg again: Such violent infusion of Gentile blood into the veins of the flock of Israel has been especially frequent in Slavonic countries. One of the favourite methods of the Cossacks to wring out money from the Jews was to take a large number of prisoners, knowing well that the Jews would ransom them. That the women thus ransomed were violated by these semi-savage tribes goes without saying. In fact, the "Council of the Four Lands", at its session in the winter of 1650, had to take cognizance of the poor women and children born to them from Cossack husbands during captivity, and thus restore order in the family and social life of the Jews. Similar outrages were... again perpetrated on Jewish women in Russia during the massacres in 1903-5. And yet-to return to the paradox-many people, who are neither racialists nor anti-Semites, are convinced that they are able to recognize a Jew at a single glance. How is this possible if Jews are such a hybrid lot as history and anthropology show them to be? Part of the answer, I think, was given by Ernest Renan in 1883: *"Il n'y a pas un type juif il y a des types juifs."* The type of Jew who can be recognized "at a glance" is one particular type among many others. But only a small fraction of fourteen million Jews belong to that particular type, and those who appear to belong to it are by no means always Jews. One of the most prominent features-literally and metaphorically-which is said to characterize that particular type is the nose, variously described as Semitic, aquiline, hooked, or resembling the beak of an eagle (bec d'aigle).

But, surprisingly, among 2836 Jews in New York City, Fishberg found that only 14 per cent-i.e., one person in seven-had a hooked nose; while 57 per cent were straight-nosed, 20 per cent were snub-nosed and 6.5 per cent had "flat and broad noses". Other anthropologists came up with smiilar results regarding Semitic noses in Poland and the Ukraine. Moreover, among true Semites, such as pure-bred Bedoums, this form of nose does not seem to occur at all. On the other hand, it is "very frequently met among the various Caucasian tribes, and also in Asia Minor. Among the indigenous races in this region, such as the Armenians, Georgians, Ossets, Lesghians, Aissors, and also the Syrians, aquiline noses are the rule.

Among the people living in Mediterranean countries of Europe, as the Greeks, Italians, French, Spanish and Portuguese, the aquiline nose is also more frequently encountered than among the Jews of Eastern Europe. The North American Indians also very often have 'Jewish' noses." Thus the nose alone is not a very safe guide to identification. Only a minority-a particular type of Jew-seems to have a convex nose, and lots of other ethnic groups also have it. Yet intuition tells one that the anthropologists' statistics must be somehow wrong. An ingenious way out of this conundrum was suggested by Beddoc and Jacobs, who maintained that the "Jewish nose" need not be really convex in profile, and may yet give the impression of being "hooked", due to a peculiar "tucking up of the wings", an infolding of the nostrils. That it is a Jewish, and not a Red Indian, Armenian, etc., nose we deduce-at a glance-from the context of other features, including expression, comportment, dress. It is not a process of logical analysis, but rather in the nature of the psychologist's Gestalt perception, the grasping of a configuration as a whole.

Similar considerations apply to each of the facial features considered to be typically Jewish-"sensuous lips"; dark, wavy or crinkly hair; melancholy, or cunning, or bulging or slit Mongol eyes, and so forth. Taken separately, they are common property of the most varied nations; put together, like an identikit, they combine into a prototype of-to say it once more-one particular type of Jew, of Eastern European origin, the type with which we are familiar. But our identi-kit would not fit the various other types of Jews, such as the Sephardim (including their very anglicized descendants in Britain); nor the Slavonic type of Central Europe, nor the blond Teutonic, the slit-eyed Mongoloid, or the crinkly-haired Negroid types of Jews. Nor can we be sure to recognize with certainty even this limited prototype. The collection of portraits published by Fishberg, or Ripley, can be used for a "believe it or not" game, if you cover the caption indicating whether the portrayed person is Jew or Gentile. The same game can be played on a caf terrace anywhere near the shores of the Mediterranean. It will, of course, remain inconclusive because you cannot walk up to the experimental subject and inquire after his or her religion; but if you play the game in company, the amount of disagreement between the observers' verdicts will be a surprise. Suggestibility also plays a part. "Did you know that Harold is Jewish?" "No, but now that you mention it of course I can see it.," "Did you know that (this or that) royal family has Jewish blood?" "No, but now that you mention it... " Hutchinson's Races of Mankind has a picture of three Geishas with the caption: Japanese with Jewish physiognomy. Once you have read the caption you feel: "But of course. How could I have missed it?" And when you have played this game for some time, you begin to see Jewish features-or Khazar features-everywhere.

Bibliography

Bial, Raymond: *The Seminole,* New York, Benchmark Books, 2000.

Brown, Robin C.: *Florida's first People,* Sarasota, Pineapple Press, 1994.

Bullard, Robert D.: *Confronting Environmental Racism: Voices from the Grassroots*, Boston, South End Press, 1993.

Covington, James W.: *The Seminoles of Florida,* Gainesville, University Press of Florida, 1993.

Ehle, John. Trail of Tears: *The Rise and Fall of the Cherokee Nation,* New York, Anchor Press, Doubleday Press, 1988.

Gatschet, Albert S.: *A Migration Legend of the Creek Indians,* Philadelphia, D. G. Brinton, 1884.

Hudson, Charles: *The Southeastern Indians*, Knoxville, The University of Tennessee Press, 1992.

Jay, Edward J.: *A Tribal Village of Middle India,* Calcutta, 1970.

Lawson, Edith R. : *Florida Indians : noble redmen of the South,* St. Petersburg, Valkyrie Press, 1977.

Mazumdar, B. C.: *The Aborigines of the Highlands of Central India,* Calcutta, 1927.

Royce, Charles C.: *The Cherokee Nation of Indians*, Chicago, Aldine Publishing Company, 1975.

Thurston, Edgar: *Castes and Tribes of Southern India*, Madras, 1909.

Weisman, Brent R.: *Unconquered people : Florida's Seminole and Miccosukee Indians,* Gainesville, University Press of Florida, 1999.

Wright, J. L. : *Creeks & Seminoles : the Destruction and Regeneration of the Muscogulge People,* Lincoln, University of Nebraska Press, 1986.

Index

□□□